# THE CULTURAL DIMENSION OF INTERNATIONAL BUSINESS

## second edition

Gary P. Ferraro

*The University of North Carolina at Charlotte*

PRENTICE HALL, Englewood Cliffs, New Jersey 07632

**Library of Congress Cataloging–in–Publication Data**

Ferraro, Gary P.
    The cultural dimension of international business / Gary P.
Ferraro.—2nd ed.
      p.    cm.
    Includes bibliographical references and index.
    ISBN 0–13–146069–2
    1. International business enterprises—Social aspects.
2. Intercultural communication.  3. Technical assistance—
Anthropological aspects.  I. Title.
HD2755.5.F48   1994
302.3'5—dc20                   93–7232
                                 CIP

Acquisitions editor: Nancy Roberts
Editorial/production supervision and
   interior design: Serena Hoffman
Prepress buyer: Kelly Behr
Manufacturing buyer: Mary Ann Gloriande
Cover design: Design Source
Cover: Chester Higgins, Jr./Photo Researchers

 © 1994, 1990 by Prentice-Hall, Inc.
A Simon & Schuster Company
Englewood Cliffs, New Jersey 07632

Printed in the United States of America
10  9  8  7  6  5  4

ISBN 0-13-146069-2

Prentice-Hall International (UK) Limited, *London*
Prentice-Hall of Australia Pty. Limited, *Sydney*
Prentice-Hall Canada Inc., *Toronto*
Prentice-Hall Hispanoamericana, S.A., *Mexico*
Prentice-Hall of India Private Limited, *New Delhi*
Prentice-Hall of Japan, Inc., *Tokyo*
Simon & Schuster Asia Pte. Ltd., *Singapore*
Editora Prentice-Hall do Brasil, Ltda., *Rio de Janeiro*

*To my parents,*
*Ida and Charles,*
*for their unequivocal love and support*

# CONTENTS

# PREFACE

This book is aimed at demonstrating how the theory and insights of cultural anthropology can positively influence the conduct of international business. To date, anthropologists have given embarrassingly little attention to this subject, and writers in the field of international management and marketing, although acknowledging the importance of the cultural dimension, have dealt with it in a cursory and anecdotal fashion. This book—which explores the contributions that cultural anthropology can make to the more effective and humane conduct of international business—can serve the interests of both the international business community and the discipline of anthropology, which is continually searching for new, nonacademic environments in which to make practical contributions. Specifically, the book will take a fourfold approach to understanding the cultural dimension of international business.

*I. Culture-general approach: making the connections between anthropological theory (generalizations) and international business.*

Chapter 2 provides an in-depth look at the concept of culture, what generalizations hold true for all cultures of the world, and the implications of those generalizations for international business. This chapter is predicated on the notion that it is impossible for anyone to master all the specific cultural facts about the thousands of cultures found in the world today. Thus, a more conceptual approach is needed. The chapter begins with various definitions of the culture concept, followed by some important generalizations that can be usefully applied to any cross-cultural situation. The importance of these cultural generalizations for the conduct of international business is then discussed.

*II. Understanding communication patterns—verbal and nonverbal.*

Chapters 3 and 4 examine some of the critical dimensions of communication, both verbal and nonverbal, in a cross-cultural business setting. Effective communication between people from the same cultural and linguistic group is often difficult enough, but when one is attempting to communicate with people who speak little or no English—and have different ideas, attitudes, assumptions, perceptions, and ways of doing things—the chances for miscommunication increase enormously. Chapter 3 examines the critical importance of language competence in an international business situation, the inter-relatedness between language and culture, the situational use of language, and some additional factors such as slang and euphemisms that can further complicate verbal communication in an international business context.

Chapter 4 discusses the importance of knowing the nonverbal communication patterns prevalent in the international business arena. As important as language is to sending and receiving messages, nonverbal communication is perhaps even more important. Not only do nonverbal cues help us interpret verbal messages, but also nonverbal communication is responsible in its own right for the majority of the messages that make up human communication. Six major modes of communicating nonverbally—posture, hand gestures, facial expressions, eye contact, proxemics, and touching—are discussed in a cross-cultural perspective. The aim of this chapter is to demonstrate how many ways there are to miscommunicate in a cross-cultural business setting unless one is familiar with the nonverbal patterns of communication in addition to the linguistic patterns.

*III. Cultural self-awareness: their values and ours.*

Chapter 5, dealing with values, is designed with two purposes in mind. First, it aims to show that people from different cultures view the world from different cultural assumptions. And second, it encourages Western businesspeople to increase their cultural self-awareness—that is, their ability to recognize the influences of *their* culture on *their* thinking and behavior. An increase in cultural self-awareness should make it easier to diagnose difficulties when communicating in a foreign business setting. It should enable the overseas businessperson to discover how a cross-cultural misunderstanding may have arisen from his or her own cultural assumptions rather than from some shortcoming of the culturally different person.

*IV. Culture-specific approach: finding relevant cultural information.*

The final segment of this four-pronged approach involves a discussion of how and where to find the specific cultural information needed for any particular international business assignment. For example, how does one procure current and pertinent data describing the cultural patterns that exist in Djakarta, Madras, or La Paz? Chapter 6 explores a number of anthropological and nonanthropological data sources (both documentary and human) that can be useful in developing a profile of any particular culture. This chapter is based on the assumption that if U.S. businesses are to meet the current challenges of a highly competitive world economy, they will need an ever-increasing flow of information about the cultures of those with whom they are conducting business.

New to this second edition is Chapter 7, which deals with negotiating across cultures. While it is recognized that no two international negotiating situations are ever identical, there are negotiating strategies that are generally valid in most situations. Based on the experiences of successful and culturally sensitive international negotiators, this chapter discusses such general guidelines as: (a) concentrating on long-term relationships; (b) focusing on the interests behind the positions; (c) being attuned to timing; and (d) the need for flexibility, careful preparation, and willingness to listen.

The concluding chapter of this book examines *culture shock,* a phenomenon that can sour an otherwise promising international business assignment. Although there are no ways of totally eliminating this psychologically disorienting experience, there are steps to take before, during, and after an international assignment that can reduce some of the more debilitating symptoms. The chapter concludes with suggestions for minimizing culture shock.

As a final note, attention should be given to the Scenarios appearing at the end of Chapters 2 through 7. The reader is encouraged to analyze these mini-case studies in an attempt to determine why a cultural conflict has arisen and how the conflict or misunderstanding portrayed could have been avoided. Although it is impossible to include examples of every possible cross-cultural conflict in a business setting, these end-of-chapter scenarios are designed to help the reader gain a greater sensitivity to the wide range of potential conflicts that could arise. Explanations of these scenarios appear in the Appendix.

I would like to thank the following reviewers for their helpful suggestions: James E. McConnell, the State University of New York at Buffalo; Tagi Sagafi-Nejad, Loyola College in Maryland; John E. Walsh, Jr., Washington University; Sonja Vegdahl Hur of Big Rapids, Michigan; R. R. Baliga, Babcock Graduate School of Management; and Constance S. Bates, Florida International University.

Gary P. Ferraro

# 1

# CULTURAL ANTHROPOLOGY
# AND
# INTERNATIONAL BUSINESS

How often do we hear people say "the whole argument is academic"? By this statement they mean that despite the elegance of the logic, the whole line of reasoning makes little or no difference. In other words, the term *academic* has become synonymous with *irrelevant*. And in all of academia it is hard to think of other disciplines generally perceived by the public to be any more irrelevant to the everyday world than cultural anthropology, the comparative study of cultures. The student of biology, for example, can apply his or her skills to the solution of vital medical problems; the student of creative arts can produce lasting works of art; and the political science student, owing to a basic understanding of political dynamics, can become a local, state, or national leader. But according to popular perception, the study of cultural anthropology, with its apparent emphasis on the non-Western cultures of the world, has little to offer other than a chance to dabble in the exotic.

To counter the long-held popular view that cultural anthropology is of little use in helping to understand the world around us, an increasing number of cultural anthropologists in recent years have applied the theories, findings, and methods of their craft to a wide range of professional areas. Whereas professionals in such areas as education, urban administration, and the various health services have been coming to grips, albeit reluctantly, with the cultural environments within which they work, those in the area of international business, although having perhaps the greatest need, remain among the most skeptical concerning the relevance of cultural anthropology. In fact, one is struck by how little contact there has been between cultural anthropology and the international business sector. According to Chambers, cultural anthropologists have avoided working with the international business community because of "a highly prejudiced ethical stance which associates commercial success and profit taking with a lack of concern for human welfare" (1985:128). Also, Western multinational corporations have not actively sought the services of cultural anthropologists, whom they generally view as serving little useful purpose, other than making university undergraduates somewhat more interesting cocktail party conversationalists by providing them with tidbits of data about the esoteric peoples of the world. In short, both cultural anthropologists and international businesspersons view the concerns of the other as irrelevant, morally questionable, or trivial.

Clearly, this book rests on the fundamental assumption that to operate effectively in the international business arena one must master the cultural environment by means of purposeful preparation ahead of time. Interestingly, a survey of international businesspeople (Kobrin, 1984) concluded that most acquired their international expertise while they were on the job, or as Kobrin put it, "they learned to play with the kids on the street by being there and doing it" (1984:41). And since so many of the international businesspeople surveyed had acquired their international expertise experientially, they also considered such "hands-on" factors as business travel and overseas assignments to be the most important for future generations of international businesspeople. This survey was particularly noteworthy for the nearly total lack of significance attached by the international businesspeople to such factors as training programs or undergraduate and graduate courses. Although in no way attempting to minimize the value of experiential learning, this book argues that in addition to on-the-job learning (and in most cases, before entering the international marketplace), successful international businesspersons must prepare themselves in a very deliberate manner in order to operate within a new, and frequently very different, cultural environment.

## THE ANTHROPOLOGICAL PERSPECTIVE

When the average American hears the word *anthropologist* two images usually come to mind. The first image is that represented by Harrison Ford in his portrayal of anthropologist Indiana Jones in the film *Raiders of the Lost Ark*. In his search for clues to the secrets of lost civilizations, Indiana Jones spends most of his time being chased by irate cannibals, engaging in hand-to-hand combat with sinister Nazis, and being thrown into pits with thousands of snakes. Although this image is exciting theater, it gives us little insight into what anthropology is all about. The second image of an anthropologist is that of the irrelevant academic who spends every moment out of the classroom interviewing exotic peoples whose cultures are about to become extinct. But anthropology is neither hazardous to the health nor irrelevant. Both these views of anthropology are misleading stereotypes, which obscure both the nature of the discipline and its relevance to the world.

The scientific discipline of anthropology is far less life endangering than Hollywood would have us believe and far more relevant than most of us imagine. To be certain, anthropologists do travel to the far corners of the world studying little-known cultures (cultural anthropologists) and languages (anthropological linguists). Moreover, there are also people who call themselves anthropologists who unearth fossil remains (physical anthropologists) and artifacts (archaeologists) of people who lived thousands, in some cases, millions of years ago. Despite the fact that these four subareas of anthropology frequently deal with different types of data, they are all directed toward a single purpose: that is, the scientific study of human cultures in whatever form, time period, or region of the world in which they might be found. According to Ember and Ember,

*Cultural anthropologists no longer work only in exotic parts of the world.*

Anthropology is concerned explicitly and directly with all varieties of people throughout the world, not only those close at hand or within a limited area. It is also interested in people of all periods. Beginning with the immediate ancestors of humans who lived a few million years ago, anthropology traces the development of humans until the present. Every part of the world that has ever contained a human population is of interest to anthropologists. (1993:2)

Anthropology differs from other disciplines that study humans in that it is much broader in scope both geographically and historically. It comprises four distinct, yet closely related, subfields: (1) archaeology, the study of ancient and prehistoric societies; (2) physical anthropology, the study of humans as biological entities; (3) anthropological linguistics, the comparative study of languages; and (4) cultural anthropology, the search for similarities and differences among contemporary peoples of the world. Even though the discipline encourages all anthropologists to constantly integrate these four fields, increasing disciplinary specialization in recent decades has made it virtually impossible for any anthropologist to cover all four fields in a comprehensive way. When we look at the contributions anthropology can make to the more effective conduct of international business, we are looking primarily at *cultural anthropology* as opposed to any of the other three subfields.

Cultural anthropology seeks to understand how and why contemporary peoples of the world differ in their customary ways of behaving, on the one hand, and how and why they share certain similarities, on the other. It is, in short, the comparative study of cultural differences and similarities found throughout the world. Cultural anthropologists may often appear to be documenting inconsequential cultural facts about little-known peoples of the world, but our learning more and more about the wide range of cultural variations will serve as a check on those who might be apt to generalize about "human nature" solely on observations from their own society. It is not at all unusual for people to assume that their own ways of thinking and acting are unquestionably rational, "natural," or "human." Take, for example, the nonverbal gesture of negation (found in the United States and in other parts of the world), shaking the head from side to side. The comparative study of cultures tells us that there are people from certain parts of India that use this very same gesture to communicate not negation but rather the very opposite idea, affirmation. In fact, there are any number of different ways of nonverbally communicating the idea of negation, all of which are no more or no less rational than shaking the head from side to side. The study of cultural anthropology provides a look at the enormous variations in thinking and acting found in the world today and how many different solutions people have been able to generate for solving the same problem.

Anthropology does more than simply document the enormous variations in human cultures. If anthropology deserves being called a "science," it must go beyond the mere cataloging of cultural differences. It must also identify and describe the commonalities of humans amid the great diversity—that is, the regularities found in all cultural contexts regardless of how different those contexts might appear at first glance. For example, for any society to continue to exist over the long run, it must solve the basic problem of how to pass on its total cultural heritage—all the ideas, values, attitudes, behavior patterns, and so on—to succeeding generations. Should that complexity of cultural traditions not be passed on to future generations, it is not very likely that the society will survive.

Saudis have solved this problem by developing Koranic schools, which pass on the cultural traditions to the younger generations; in parts of West Africa, "bush schools" train young adolescents to become adults; in our own society we rely on a formal system of compulsory education, complete with books, desks and teachers. Although the details of these educational systems vary enormously, there are no known societies in the world today or in the past that have not worked out a system for ensuring that new generations will learn their culture. Thus, the science of anthropology attempts to document the great variations in cultural forms while at the same time looking for both the common strands found in all cultures and the general principles that apply to all cultures.

The strong comparative perspective that anthropologists bring to the study of the human condition helps reduce the probability that their theories will be culture bound. Sociologists and psychologists, for example, concentrating as they have on studies of peoples from Western societies, are more likely to construct theories that are based on Western assumptions of reality. The cross-cultural perspective of anthropological studies has frequently served as a corrective to those disciplines that rely more heavily for their theory construction on data from Western societies. According to Clifford Geertz, cultural anthropologists were the first to recognize

> ... that the world does not divide into the pious and the superstitious; that there are sculptures in jungles and paintings in deserts; that political order is possible without centralized power and principled justice without codified rules; that the norms of reason were not fixed in Greece, the evolution of morality not consummated in England. . . . We have, with no little success, sought to keep the world off balance; pulling out rugs, upsetting tea tables, setting off fire crackers. It has been the office of others to reassure; ours to unsettle. (1984:275)

In addition to being comparative, there are other distinctive features of the anthropological perspective. One point that bears mentioning is that, unlike other social or behavioral sciences, anthropologists analyze cultural differences and similarities in a firsthand manner. Anthropologists rely heavily on experiential learning through the data-gathering technique of participant observation. Psychologists, for example, usually study human behavior by using post facto data rather than actually observing the behavior as it is occurring. Sociologists rely to a very large extent on secondary information gleaned from questionnaires, interviews, and census reports. Historians by definition are removed in time from the people and events that constitute their subject matter. Cultural anthropologists, however, use participant observation—participating in, while making systematic observations about, the cultures under study—as a major method for collecting culturally comparative information. When anthropologists use participant observation, they are sharing the everyday activities of the local people while at the same time they are making detailed descriptive observations of people eating, working, playing, conversing, dancing, fighting, or any other activity that might shed light on their cultural patterns.

Given the nature of the anthropological enterprise, it is not surprising that the founders of modern anthropology developed the tradition of firsthand field observations of cultural behavior. If indeed anthropology had set as its task the comparative study of human cultures, it would have to study *all* human cultures, many of which had not been studied before. In the absence of descriptive studies of exotic cultures in the library, the early anthropologists had no other choice but to learn the language and spend at least a year immersed in the culture of the people under study. Today even though libraries are well stocked with descriptive studies of a wide variety of world cultures, participant observation remains a preferred investigative strategy among contemporary anthropologists.

Thus, cultural anthropologists are trained to analyze the social organizations of various types of societies. Earlier in the present century, cultural anthropologists tended to devote their energies exclusively to the analysis of small-scale, technologically simple, and usually non-Western peoples. Within the last several decades, however, cultural anthropologists have become increasingly involved in the study of more complex societies. Yet whether dealing with simple or complex societies, the focus of cultural anthropologists has been the comparative study of sociocultural organizations wherever, or in whatever form, they may be found.

## CULTURAL ANTHROPOLOGY AND BUSINESS

Since the 1930s cultural anthropologists have conducted a modest amount of research in industrial and corporate settings, focusing largely on corporate cultures in the United States. For example, the human relations school of organizational research of the 1930s and 1940s produced a number of ethnographies showing how informal cultural patterns could influence managerial goals (see Mayo, 1933; Roethlisberger & Dickson, 1939; Gardner, 1945; Warner & Low, 1947; and Richardson & Walker, 1948). More recent studies of corporate cultures have attempted to show how specific configurations of values contribute to the relative success or failure of meeting corporate goals (see Davis, 1984; Denison, 1990; Kotter, 1992; and Frost et al., 1991).

This body of research is predicated on the understanding that in many important respects business organizations are not unlike those societies studied by traditional anthropologists. For example, corporate members, like people found in small-scale, preliterate societies, engage in rituals; perpetuate corporate myths and stories; adhere to a set of norms, symbols, and behavioral expectations; and use specialized vocabularies. Since business organizations tend to be both differentiated and socially stratified, specific roles and statuses can be identified. Also, business organizations, through dealings with such groups as unions, governments, environmental groups, and consumers, can be said to have external relations with other social systems. Given these similarities, cultural anthropologists have been able to make modest contributions to the understanding of domestic business organizations, and they have the potential for making many others.

The anthropological perspective can be useful in the study of purely domestic business organizations, which frequently are comprised of many social components that come from different backgrounds, hold contrasting values and attitudes, and have conflicting loyalties. It is not at all likely that the company vice president will have much in common with the assembly-line worker, the union representative, the president of the local Sierra Club, the OSHA inspector, the janitor, or many members of that diverse group called the buying public. And yet, if the organization is to function effectively, that high management official needs to know about the values, attitudes, expectations, concerns, and behavior patterns of all these people, and others as well. This is particularly true today as more and more minorities are brought into domestic work forces under equal opportunity employment laws. In short, domestic business organizations can be viewed as mini-cultures (comprised of different people with different roles, statuses, and value systems) which operate within the wider national cultural context.

It has been estimated (Garza, 1991:74) that approximately 15 percent of all anthropologists in the United States work in the private sector of the economy, up from about 2 percent just two decades ago. With their traditional emphasis on participant observation, cultural anthropologists are in a unique position to gather information on grass-roots corporate culture from the bottom up. To illustrate, the Xerox Corporation used an anthropologist to help the company devise more effective training programs for their service technicians. Julian Orr, the anthropologist assigned to the project, took the training and went on service calls himself in order to study firsthand the process of repairing a copy machine. But this highly experiential approach to data gathering revealed that the main problem was not repairing the machine but rather teaching people how to use it. Orr found that a large percentage of service calls were not to fix disabled hardware but rather to show employees how to run the machine. That single insight—gained through firsthand participant observation—enabled Xerox to restructure its training programs for service technicians by placing more emphasis on teaching and customer relations.

Failure to consider the cultural context in the domestic organization can, and has, led to misunderstandings, miscommunication, lawsuits, and generally an undermining of the goals of the organization. When moving into the area of international business, the need to be aware of cultural environments becomes even more critical. Here the magnitude of the cultural differences is vastly greater, and consequently, breakdowns of communications usually increase geometrically. Although the anthropological perspective is valuable in understanding any business organization, be it domestic or international, this book will focus on the contributions that cultural anthropology can make to the improvement of international business operations, with particular emphasis on the functional areas of international marketing and management.

## CULTURE AND INTERNATIONAL BUSINESS

Whether we are dealing with issues of marketing, managing, or negotiating, the success or failure of a company abroad depends on how effectively its employees can exercise their skills in a new location. That ability will depend on both their job-related expertise *and* the individual's sensitivity and responsiveness to the new cultural environment. One of the most common factors contributing to failure in international business assignments is the erroneous assumption that if a person is successful in the home environment, he or she will be equally successful in applying technical expertise in a different culture.

Research has shown (Hays, 1974; Tung, 1981) that failures in the overseas business setting most frequently result from an inability to understand and adapt to foreign ways of thinking and acting rather than from technical or professional incompetence. At home U.S. businesspeople equip themselves with vast amounts of knowledge of their employees, customers, and business partners. Market research provides detailed information on values, attitudes, and buying preferences of U.S. consumers; middle- and upper-level managers are well versed in the intricacies of their organization's culture; and labor negotiators must be highly sensitive to what motivates those on the other side of the table. Yet when North Americans turn to the international arena, they frequently are willing to deal with customers, employees, and fellow workers with a dearth of information that at home would be unimaginable.

The literature on international business is filled with examples of business miscues when U.S. corporations attempted to operate in an international context. Some are mildly amusing. Others are downright embarrassing. All of them, to one degree or another, have been costly in terms of money, reputation, or both. For example, when American firms try to market their products in other countries, they often assume that if a marketing strategy or slogan is effective in Cleveland, it will be equally effective in other parts of the world. But problems can arise when changing cultural contexts. According to Senator Paul Simon,

> *Body by Fisher,* describing a General Motors product, came out "Corpse by Fisher" in Flemish, and that did not help sales. . . . *Come Alive With Pepsi* almost appeared in the Chinese version of the *Reader's Digest* as "Pepsi brings your ancestors back from the grave." . . . A major ad campaign in green did not sell in Malaysia, where green symbolizes death and disease. An airline operating out of Brazil advertised that it had plush "rendezvous lounges" on its jets, unaware that in Portuguese, "rendezvous" implied a room for making love. (1980:32)

Insensitivity to the cultural realities of foreign work forces can lead to disastrous results. Lawrence Stessin reports on a North Carolina firm that purchased a textile machinery company near Birmingham, England, in hopes of using it to gain entry into the European market. Shortly after the takeover, the U.S. manager attempted to rectify what he considered to be a major production problem, the time-consuming tea break. Stessin recounts,

> In England, tea breaks can take a half-hour per man, as each worker brews his own leaves to his particular taste and sips out of a large, pint size vessel with the indulgence of a wine taster. . . . Management suggested to the union that perhaps it could use its good offices to speed up the "sipping time" to ten minutes a break. . . . The union agreed to try but failed. . . . Then one Monday morning, the workers rioted. Windows were broken, epithets greeted the executives as they entered the plant and police had to be called to restore order. It seems the company went ahead and installed a tea-vending machine—just put a paper cup under the spigot and out pours a standard brew. The pint sized container was replaced by a five-ounce cup imprinted—as they are in America—with morale-building messages imploring greater dedication to the job and loyalty to the company. . . . The plant never did get back into production. Even after the tea-brewing machine was hauled out, workers boycotted the company and it finally closed down. (1979:223)

Just as inattention to the cultural context can result in some costly blunders in marketing and management, it also can affect seriously the success of international business negotiations. Time, effort, reputation, and even contracts can be lost because of cultural ignorance. Alison Lanier tells of one American executive who paid a very high price for failing to do his cultural homework:

> A top level, high priced vice president had been in and out of Bahrain many times, where liquor is permitted. He finally was sent to neighboring Qatar (on the Arabian Gulf) to conclude a monumental negotiation that had taken endless months to work out. Confident of success, he slipped two miniatures of brandy into his briefcase, planning to celebrate quietly with his colleague after the ceremony. Result: not only was he deported immediately on arrival by a zealous customs man in that strictly Moslem country, but the firm was also "disinvited" and ordered never to return. The Qatari attitude was that this man had tried to flout a deeply-held religious conviction; neither he nor his firm, therefore, was considered "suitable" for a major contract. (1979:160–61)

These are only a few of the examples of the price paid for miscalculating—or simply ignoring—the cultural dimension of international business. The most cursory review of the international business literature will reveal many other similarly costly mistakes. In 1974 Ricks and Arpan published a compendium of international business miscues appropriately entitled *International Business Blunders*. Unfortunately, less than a decade later an entirely new collection has been published (Ricks, 1983), describing only those international business blunders that have occurred since 1974. But the purpose here is not to demonstrate beyond any reasonable doubt the folly and insensitivity of the North American businessperson when operating overseas. Rather, the purpose is to show that the world is changing faster than most of us can calculate, and if American businesspersons are to meet the challenges of an increasingly interdependent world, they will need to develop a better understanding of how cultural variables influence international business enterprises. A healthy dialogue between cultural anthropologists and members of the international business community—which this book seeks to initiate—will be an important step in achieving that needed understanding.

## THE NEED FOR GREATER AWARENESS OF THE CULTURAL ENVIRONMENT

In recent decades there has been a growing tendency of business and industry to become increasingly more globally interdependent. In order to remain competitive, most businesses, both here and abroad, know that they must continue to enter into international/cross-cultural alliances. The overall consequences of this trend for the 1990s and beyond is that more and more companies will be engaging in such activities as joint ventures, licensing agreements, turnkey projects, and foreign capital investments. The creation of the European Economic Community—with its removal of trade barriers, deregulation of certain industries, and the privatization of others—is making Western Europe once again an attractive place for foreign investment. The international marketplace is growing increasingly more competitive due to the rapid and successful industrialization of such countries as Korea, Singapore, and Taiwan, as well as many third world countries. And of course, the weakening of the U.S. dollar in recent years has brought about a dramatic increase in foreign investments in the United States.

It has become a cliché to say that the world is shrinking or becoming a "global village." Rapid technological developments in transportation and communications in recent decades have brought the peoples of the world closer together in a physical sense. Unfortunately, there has not been a concomitant revolution in cross-cultural understanding among all the peoples of the world. And of course, no one could argue that we have witnessed any degree of cultural homogenization of world populations. What we can agree on, however, is that the world is becoming increasingly more interdependent. Despite George Washington's warnings against "entangling alliances," there is no way that any of us can isolate ourselves from the rest of the world. We are, whether we like it or not, enmeshed in global concerns far beyond the wildest dreams, or nightmares, of our founding fathers.

---

What follows are just a few illustrations of how extensively the lives of all the world's peoples are interconnected:

- The United States remains highly reliant on other countries for a number of important minerals. For example, the United States imports 100 percent of all its graphite, manganese, mica, columbium, and strontium and more than 90 percent of its bauxite, alumina, and diamonds (*World Almanac and Book of Facts,* 1992:685).

- The United States is the fourth largest Spanish-speaking nation in the world. Approximately 62 percent of the city of Miami, for example, is of Spanish origin (U.S. Department of Commerce, 1991:59).

- During the decade of the 1980s, immigration into the United States doubled from 530,639 in 1980 to 1,090,924 in 1989 (U.S. Department of Commerce, 1991b:9).

- In 1991, foreigners were indebted to banks in the United States to the tune of $633 billion (U.S. Department of Treasury, 1992:110).

- Direct foreign investments in the United States have increased from $13.2 billion in 1970 to $403.7 billion in 1990, more than a thirtyfold increase in two decades (*World Almanac and Book of Facts,* 1992:153).

- United States direct investments abroad have increased from $335 billion in 1988 to more than $421 billion just two years later in 1990 (*World Almanac and Book of Facts,* 1992:142).

---

How well the United States will fare in this increasingly interdependent world in the decades to come is not altogether predictable. If the last several decades are a reliable indicator, the future is not particularly bright for the United States to remain a leader in world economic affairs. During the quarter of a century immediately following World War II, the United States enjoyed unprecedented and unparalleled economic success. Our postwar technologies gave rise to products that the world wanted and we were very willing and able to supply, everything from atomic energy and microelectronics to Levis and Big Macs. The United States, owing to its technology, managerial techniques, and investment capital, was in the enviable position of being the "only game in town." During this period our world market shares were large and we enjoyed a healthy balance of payments. Then, in the early 1970s, the trade surpluses that we had enjoyed for so long disappeared and we began to have trade deficits. Ironically, it was in 1976—our bicentennial year—that our trade accounts moved into a negative imbalance. The substantial trade deficit of over $9 billion in 1976 ballooned to over $100 billion by 1990, with little hope for reducing the imbalance in the immediate future, short of some major efforts on the part of the U.S. government.

Some would argue that this serious negative trade imbalance is largely the result of the enormous costs of importing high-priced oil from the Middle East. Yet despite the dramatic increase in energy costs, the fact remains that the imbalance is also a direct result of not exporting our own goods as well as we have in past decades. For example, according to the President's Export Council (1980:14), the U.S. share of free-world exports fell from 15.4 percent at the start of the 1970s to 12.1 percent at the end. Copeland and Griggs (1985) document the weakening position of the United States in the international marketplace with greater specificity:

> In the Middle East, the United States is losing ground in services ranging from health care to construction. Whittaker Corporation recently lost its exclusive $1.4 billion hospital-management contract in Saudi Arabia. The new American embassy in Riyadh is being built by a Korean company. In France, Motorola lost out to the Japanese when France's Thomson group chose Oki Electric Industry Company to expand the French company's semiconductor business. . . . Western shipping has been lost to Taiwan's Evergreen Marine Corporation, which is likely to become the world's largest container line by 1986. In real estate, Canada's Olympia and York Development Ltd. has become the world's largest developer. Even Hollywood is feeling the pinch of increased competition from abroad: foreign countries are showing a growing preference for films of their own culture and shunning American-made movies. (1985:xvii)

The inescapable conclusion of these data is that we are not selling our goods and services to the world as successfully as we did during our expansionist past.

*Anthropologists can serve as consultants to help people understand their international business partners.*

American businesses must realize by now that—despite what may have occurred in the past—the product will no longer sell itself. Since there are so many good products on the market today, the crucial factor in determining who makes the sale is not so much the intrinsic superiority of the product but rather the skill of the seller in understanding the dynamics of the transaction between himself or herself and the customer. Unfortunately because of our relative success in the past, we are not particularly well equipped to meet the challenges of the international economic arena during the twenty-first century.

One of the most eloquent and personal statements of the need for international businesspersons to become better attuned to other languages and cultures was made by Senator Paul Simon of Illinois:

> The international market is in some respects similar to the domestic market. For several years I was in the newspaper and job printing business, publishing weekly newspapers in small communities and printing everything from business forms to funeral notices. I bought newsprint from Pioneer Paper Company because they had the best price, and envelopes from the Roodhouse Envelope Company for the same reason. But for most supplies, competitive prices were fairly close, and then I bought the salesperson rather than the product. The salesperson who knew about my family and my interests, who had read an article I had written—who "spoke my language"—got me as a customer. If someone had come to my office speaking only Japanese, he might have had the best product in the world but I would probably not have bought from him. The world market is no different. To sell effectively in Italy, speak Italian. (1980:31)

Part of the problem lies in the fact that many U.S. companies, particularly middle-sized ones, have not attempted to sustain sales and production by venturing into the international marketplace. While there has been an increase during the 1980s in the number of U.S. firms exporting, it remains that fewer than 1 percent of all U.S. companies is responsible for 80 percent of all U.S. exporting activities. Even though most U.S. corporations have competed successfully in domestic markets, with a unified language and business practices, they have not been very adept at coping with the wide range of different languages, customs, and cultural assumptions found in the international business arena. For many of the firms that do enter foreign markets, success has been inconsistent at best. Nowhere is this better illustrated than in the area of Americans living and working abroad.

Statistics on the premature return rate of expatriate Americans (that is, those returning from overseas working assignments before the end of their contracts) vary widely throughout the international business literature. Estimates of attrition rates in the late 1970s (Harris, 1979:49; Edwards, 1978:42) ran as high as 65 to 85 percent for certain industries. More recent figures, while not as high, still serve to illustrate how difficult it is for Americans to live and work successfully abroad. For example, Caudron

(1991:27) cites premature returns of Americans living in Saudi Arabia to be as high as 68 percent; 36 percent in Japan; 27 percent in Brussels; and 18 percent in London, a city that one would expect most Americans to adjust to easily. Regardless of whether we are dealing with attrition rates of 68 percent or 18 percent, the costs are enormous. Considering that it costs a firm between three and five times an employee's base salary to keep that employee and his or her family in a foreign assignment, the financial considerations alone can be staggering (Van Pelt & Wolniansky, 1990:40). And of course, these costs refer only to premature returns. There is no way of measuring the additional losses incurred by those firms whose personnel don't become such statistics. Those personnel who stay in their overseas assignments are frequently operating with decreased efficiency, and owing to their less than perfect adjustment to the foreign cultural environment, often cost their firms enormous losses in time, reputation, and successful contracts.

Our nation's leaders from both the public and private sectors have recognized the seriousness of the trade deficit. In its report of December 1980, the President's Export Council, made up of leaders in American business, government, and labor, recommended that the problem of shrinking world markets must be attacked on a number of fronts simultaneously. The council's major recommendations included (1) increasing national export consciousness by establishing a permanent Export Council and providing more export information and assistance through the Department of Commerce; (2) strengthening the federal government's international trade functions; (3) eliminating such export disincentives as taxation of overseas Americans, foreign application of our antitrust laws, and the Foreign Corrupt Practices Act; and (4) improving U.S. export incentives such as financing, export insurance, tax benefits, and the creation of trading companies. Interestingly, none of the recommendations even remotely alluded to the need for more emphasis on foreign language study and cross-cultural education. Despite this glaring oversight the relationship between expanding exports and stimulating language and cultural studies must not go unnoticed. Since we do not take seriously the study of other languages and cultures, we simply are not getting to know our international customers, and not surprisingly, we are not selling abroad as well as we could.

## INTERNATIONAL COMPETENCY—A NATIONAL PROBLEM

The situation that has emerged in the last decade is that as the world grows more interdependent, we Americans can no longer expect to solve all the world's problems by ourselves, nor is it possible to declare ourselves immune from them. If our nation is to continue to be a world leader we must build deep into our national psyche the need for international competency—that is, a specialized knowledge of foreign cultures, including professional proficiency in languages, and an understanding of the major political, economic, and social variables affecting the conduct of international and intercultural affairs.

At the same time that we are faced with an ever-increasing need for international competency, the resources our nation is devoting to its development are declining. This problem is not limited to the area of business. It is, rather, a national problem that affects many aspects of American life, including our national security, diplomacy, scientific advancement, and international political relations, in addition to economics. Future generations of American businesspersons, however, must be drawn from the society at large, and it is this society, through its educational institutions, that has not in the past placed central importance on educating the general populace for international competence.

Several recent national reports on international education (National Governors' Association, 1989; Council on International Educational Exchange, 1988), indicate that there is a significant shortfall in our international competence:

- The United States continues to be the only country in the world where it is possible to earn a college degree without taking any courses in a foreign language.
- Fewer that 1 percent of the U.S. military personnel stationed abroad can use the language of their host country.
- Only 17 percent of U.S. elementary schools offer any form of foreign language instruction.
- More than half (53 percent) of U.S. undergraduates take no foreign language courses whatsoever during their four years of university education.

Our national inability to handle foreign languages is paralleled by our less than adequate understanding of foreign affairs.

- Approximately half of all American adults are not able to locate the Republic of South Africa on a world map.
- A UN study of 30,000 students (age 10–14) in nine countries found that U.S. students ranked next to last in their understanding of foreign cultures.
- In a recent survey only 30% of American adults could locate Holland on a map of Europe.
- A recent survey found that Americans watching television news programs understood the major points of only one third of the international stories.
- One in every four high school seniors in Dallas, Texas, could not identify the country bordering the United States to the south.

Given the relatively low priority that international competency has had in our educational institutions in recent years, it is not surprising that those Americans who are expected to function successfully in a multicultural environment are so poorly prepared for the task. If the international dimension is weak in our general education programs today, it is even weaker in our business school curricula. According to a report of the Task Force on Business and International Education of the American Council on Education, " . . . over 75% of the graduating DBA's (or PhD's in business) have had no international business courses during their graduate studies . . . " (Nehrt, 1977:3).

While graduate schools in business have increased their international offerings since the 1970s, courses on the cultural environment of international business have received relatively little attention. This general neglect of cross-cultural issues in business education is generally reflected in the attitudes of the international business community. To illustrate, in a study of 127 U.S. firms with international operations, respondents showed very little concern for the cultural dimension of international business. When asked what should be included in the education of an international businessperson, respondents mentioned—almost without exception—only technical courses. There was, in other words, almost no interest shown in language, culture, or history of one's foreign business partners (Reynolds & Rice, 1988:56).

> Whenever Westerners believe that other cultures have nothing worthwhile to offer, they are engaging in a type of cultural arrogance that can be self-defeating, as Professor Howard Perlmutter of the Wharton School of Business reminds us:
>
> > If you have a joint venture with a Japanese company, they'll send 24 people here to learn everything you know, and you'll send one person there to tell them everything you know. . . . (Kupfer, 1988:58)

However we choose to measure it, there is substantial evidence to suggest that as a nation our people are poorly equipped to deal with the numerous challenges of our changing world. Whether we are talking about language competence, funding for international education, opportunities for foreign exchange, or simply the awareness of global knowledge, the inadequacies are real and potentially threatening to many areas of our national welfare, including international business in particular. The problem referred to in recent literature as a national crisis has no easy solution. What is required initially is broad public awareness of the problem followed by concerted actions on a number of fronts.

One way of helping to meet the challenge is by creating a dialogue between (1) people whose professions are directly and negatively affected by the problem and (2) cultural anthropologists, whose major objective is the comparative study of cultural systems.

The creation of such a dialogue between cultural anthropologists and international businesspersons is hardly the whole answer. Our recent national decline in the world marketplace is the result of a complex series of factors, which include (in addition to intercultural awareness) international trade barriers; a lack of government incentives for small and middle-sized corporations to become export oriented; and the existence of a number of export disincentives such as our taxation of Americans working overseas, the extraterritorial application of our antitrust laws, and U.S. antiboycott laws, among others. What is surprising, though, is how little recognition has been given to the area of cross-cultural understanding as one of a number of factors contributing to our recent decline in international market shares. As a long overdue corrective, this text focuses on how cultural variations can affect the conduct of international business.

# 2

# CULTURE AND INTERNATIONAL BUSINESS: A CONCEPTUAL APPROACH

As mentioned in the preceding chapter, anthropologists do more than simply accumulate and catalog information on the world's exotic and not so exotic cultures. Like other scientists, they attempt to generate theories about culture that apply to all human populations. Since it is impossible for any individual to master every cultural fact about every culture in the world, a more theoretical approach can be instructive. That is, a number of general concepts about culture can be applied to a wide variety of cross-cultural situations, regardless of whether one is dealing with Nigerians, Peruvians, or Appalachian coal miners.

This chapter will explore what is meant—and what is not meant—by the term *culture*. In addition to defining this central anthropological concept, the chapter will also examine six important generalizations concerning the concept of culture and their significance for the U.S. businessperson operating in the world marketplace. Being equipped with such general concepts can facilitate the adjustment to an unfamiliar cultural environment.

## CULTURE DEFINED

In everyday usage, the term *culture* refers to the finer things in life, such as the fine arts, literature, and philosophy. Under this very narrow definition of the term, the "cultured person" is one who prefers Handel to hard rock; can distinguish between the artistic styles of Monet and Manet; prefers pheasant under glass to grits and red-eye gravy, and 12-year-old Chivas Regal to Budweiser; and spends his or her leisure time reading Kierkegaard rather than watching wrestling on television. For the anthropologist, however, the term *culture* has a much broader meaning that goes far beyond mere personal refinements. The only requirement for being cultured is to be human. Thus, all people have culture. The scantily clad Dani of New Guinea is as much a cultural animal as is Isaac Stern. For the anthropologist, cooking pots, spears, and mud huts are as legitimate items of culture as symphonies, oil paintings, and great works of literature.

The term *culture* has been defined in a variety of ways. Even among anthropologists, who claim culture as their guiding conceptual principle, there is no agreement on a single definition of the term. In fact, Kroeber and Kluckhohn (1952) identified over 160 different definitions of culture. One of the earliest widely cited definitions, offered by E. B. Tylor (1871) over a century ago, defined culture as "that complex whole which includes knowledge, belief, art, morals, law, custom, and any other capabilities and habits acquired by man as a member of society" (1871:1). More recently Kluckholn and Kelly have referred to culture as "all the historically created designs for living, explicit and implicit, rational, irrational, and nonrational, which exist at any given time as potential guides for the behavior of men" (1945:97). Herskovits spoke of culture as being "the man made part of the environment" (1955:305), and Downs defined culture as being "a mental map which guides us in our relations to our surroundings and to other people" (1971:35).

Running the risk of adding to the confusion, we will offer still another definition: *Culture is everything that people have, think, and do as members of their society.* The three verbs in this definition (*have, think,* and *do*) can help us identify the three major structural components of the concept of culture. That is, in order for a person to *have* something, some material object must be present. When people *think,* ideas, values, attitudes, and beliefs are present. When people *do,* they behave in certain socially prescribed ways. Thus culture is made up of (1) material objects; (2) ideas, values, and attitudes; and (3) normative or expected patterns of behavior.

The final phrase of our working definition, "as members of a society." should serve as a reminder that culture is *shared* by at least two or more people, and of course real, live societies are always larger than that. There is, in other words, no such thing as the culture of a hermit. If a solitary individual thinks and behaves in a certain way, that thought or action is idiosyncratic, not cultural. For an idea, a thing, or a behavior to be considered cultural, it must be shared by some type of social group or society.

---

Anthropologist Hendrick Serrie (1986:xvi–xvii) has provided an excellent example of how an anthropological understanding of local cultural patterns in southern Mexico prevented the costly mistake of mass-producing a solar cooker developed for this area. Designed to reduce the use of firewood for cooking by encouraging the use of solar energy, these solar stoves, with the assistance of a 4-foot parabolic reflector, produced levels of heat comparable to a wood fire. Although initial demonstrations of the cooker caught the interest of the local people, there were a number of cultural features that militated against the widespread acceptance of this new technological device. To illustrate, (1) the major part of the cooking in this part of Mexico is done early in the morning and in the early evening, at those times when solar radiation is at its lowest level; and (2) although the solar stove was very effective for boiling beans or soups, it was inadequate for cooking tortillas, a basic staple in the local diet. Thus, for these and other cultural reasons it was decided not to mass-produce and market the solar cookers for this region of the world because even though the cooker worked well *technically,* it made little sense *culturally.*

---

In addition to this working definition, a number of features of the concept of culture should be made explicit. The remainder of this chapter will briefly examine these features that hold true for all cultures and discuss why they are valuable insights into the cultural environment of international business.

## CULTURE IS LEARNED

*Culture is transmitted through the process of learning and interacting with one's environment rather than through the genetic process.* Culture can be thought of as a storehouse of all the knowledge of a society. The child who is born into any society finds that the problems that confront all people have already been solved by those who have lived before. For example, material objects, methods for acquiring food, language, rules of government, forms of marriage, and systems of religion have already been discovered and are functioning within the culture when a child is born. If a male child is born into a small country village in Spain, for example, it is quite likely that during his lifetime he will acquire his food by farming, pay allegiance to the Spanish government, enjoy bullfighting, and be a Catholic. If a male child is born into an East African herding society, in contrast, he will probably acquire his food from his cattle, obey the laws of his elders, spend his leisure time telling tribal folktales, and worship his ancestors as gods. Although both these children will grow up to behave quite differently, one basic principle concerning culture is clear. Both children *were born into* an already existing culture. Each child has only to *learn* the various solutions to these basic human problems that his culture has set down for him. Once these solutions are learned, behavior becomes almost automatic. In other words, culture is passed on from one generation to another within a society; it is not inborn or instinctive.

The learned nature of culture is dramatically illustrated by Amram Scheinfeld (1950:505), who writes of an American-Chinese man:

> . . . Fung Kwok Keung, born Joseph Rhinehart (of German-American stock), who, at the age of 2, was adopted by a Chinese man on Long Island and three years later taken to China, where he was reared in a small town (Nam Hoy, near Canton) with the family of his foster father until he was 20. Returning then to New York (in 1928), he was so completely Chinese in all but appearance that he had to be given "Americanization" as well as English lessons to adapt him to his new life. A few years later, after the outbreak of World War II, he was drafted into the American army and sent to Italy. In many ways he was alien to the other American soldiers and tried continuously to be transferred to service in China, but army red tape held him fast in Italy until the war's end. Back again in New York, Rhinehart-Fung at this writing works as a compositor on a Chinese newspaper (an intricate job which few but Chinese could handle), and stills speaks English very imperfectly, with a Chinese accent.

If the power of cultural learning needs documentation, one only has to cite the cases of extremely isolated children. Today there are a number of tragic, yet well-documented, instances of infants who have been shut away in closets or attics with only the barest minimum of human contact during their formative years. One such case was that of Anna, who at nearly six years of age was found tied to a chair in the attic of her grandfather's house in a condition that was barely human. According to Kingsley Davis, " . . . she had no glimmering of speech, absolutely no ability to walk, no sense of gesture, not the least capacity to feed herself . . . and no comprehension of cleanliness" (1947:434). At age eight and a half, after spending three years in a home for retarded children, Anna had made dramatic progress in developing human characteristics. She could bounce and catch a ball, she had become toilet trained, she could feed and dress herself, and she had developed a speech proficiency of about a normal two-year-old.

Since Anna had received virtually no socialization or meaningful human interaction during the first six years of her life, it appears quite clear that her early motor and mental retardation was the direct result of this human deprivation. She had few, if any, opportunities to learn her culture, and in the absence of such learning, infants cannot hope to develop into functioning humans. The significance of this tragic case demonstrates how little one's biological resources, when taken alone, can contribute to one's humanness.

Despite the enormous variations in the details of cultures throughout the world, all people acquire their culture through the same process—that is, learning. It is sometimes easy to fall into the trap of thinking that since the Australian Bushman and the Central African Pygmy do not know what we know, they must be childlike, ignorant, and generally incapable of learning. These primitives, the argument goes, have not learned

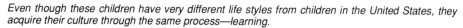

*Even though these children have very different life styles from children in the United States, they acquire their culture through the same process—learning.*

about calculus, Shakespeare, or the Los Angeles Dodgers because they are not as intelligent as we are. Yet there is no evidence whatsoever to suggest even remotely that people in some cultures are less efficient learners than people in other cultures. What the comparative study of culture does tell us, however, is that people in different cultures learn different cultural content—that is, different ideas, values, behavior patterns, and so on—and they learn that content every bit as efficiently as anyone else. For example, despite the inability of the average Kikuyu of East Africa to solve a problem by using differential equations, they would be able to recite exactly how they are related (step by step) to a network of hundreds of kinspeople. The Kikuyu farmers have mastered what to us is a bewildering amount of kinship information because their culture places great emphasis on such knowledge if the rather complex Kikuyu marriage and kinship system is to work. The Bushman hunters in Namibia are at ease in determining which direction the wounded impala traveled when the herd they have been tracking split and went in two different directions. Such a problem for them is certainly no easier to solve than a typical verbal problem found on the S.A.T. exam: "A is to B as B is to ?" And it is more relevant to their everyday survival. Hence, people from different cultures learn those things that contribute to adjusting to their particular environments.

This notion that culture is acquired through the process of learning has several important implications for the conduct of international business. First, such an understanding can lead to greater tolerance for cultural differences, a prerequisite for effective intercultural communication within a business setting. Second, the learned nature of culture serves as a reminder that since we have mastered our own culture through the process of learning, it is possible (albeit more difficult) to *learn* to function in other cultures as well. Thus, cross-cultural expertise for Western businesspersons can be accomplished through effective training programs. And finally, the learned nature of culture leads us to the inescapable conclusion that foreign work forces, although perhaps lacking certain job-related skills at the present time, are perfectly capable of learning those skills in the future, provided they are exposed to culturally relevant training programs.

## CULTURE INFLUENCES BIOLOGICAL PROCESSES

If we stop to consider it, the great majority of our conscious behavior is acquired through learning and interacting with other members of our culture. Even those responses to our purely biological needs (that is, eating, coughing, defecating) are frequently influenced by our cultures. For example, all people share a biological need for food. Unless a minimum number of calories is consumed, starvation will occur. Therefore, all people eat. But *what* we eat, *how often* we eat, *how much* we eat, *with whom* we eat, and *according to what set of rules* are regulated, at least in part, by our culture.

Clyde Kluckhohn, an anthropologist who spent many years in Arizona and New Mexico studying the Navajo, provides us with a telling example of how culture affects biological processes:

> I once knew a trader's wife in Arizona who took a somewhat devilish interest in producing a cultural reaction. Guests who came her way were often served delicious sandwiches filled

with a meat that seemed to be neither chicken nor tuna fish yet was reminiscent of both. To queries she gave no reply until each had eaten his fill. She then explained that what they had eaten was not chicken, not tuna fish, but the rich, white flesh of freshly killed rattlesnakes. The response was instantaneous—vomiting, often violent vomiting. A biological process is caught into a cultural web. (1968:25–26)

This is a dramatic illustration of how culture can influence biological processes. In fact, in this instance, the natural biological process of digestion was not only influenced, it was also reversed. A learned part of our culture (that is, the idea that rattlesnake meat is a repulsive thing to eat) actually triggered the sudden interruption of the normal digestive process. Clearly there is nothing in rattlesnake meat that causes people to vomit, for those who have internalized the opposite idea, that rattlesnake meat should be eaten, have no such digestive tract reversals.

The effects of culturally produced ideas on our bodies and their natural processes take many different forms. For example, instances of the voluntary control of pain reflexes are found in a number of cultures throughout the world. Among the nineteenth-century Cheyenne Indians, as part of the religious ceremony known as the Sun Dance, young men were taught that self-inflicted pain was a way to achieve supernatural visions. One popular method of self-torture was to remain suspended from the top of a high pole, supported only by leather thongs attached to wooden skewers inserted under the skin of the chest or back. The Cheyenne believed that by remaining in what must have been an excruciatingly painful position for long periods of time without showing signs of pain, the young men were able to communicate more directly with the deity. The ritual firewalkers from Fiji are similarly motivated to control pain reflexes voluntarily, for they believe that the capacity to not show pain brings people closer to those supernatural forces that control their lives. The ethnographic examples are too numerous to cite, but whether we are looking at Cheyenne men engaged in the Sun Dance ceremony, Fiji firewalkers, or U.S. women practicing the Lamaze (psychoprophylactic) method of childbirth, the principle is the same: People learn ideas from their cultures that when internalized can actually alter the experience of pain. In other words, a component of culture (that is, ideas) can channel or influence biologically based pain reflexes.

Those nontangible parts of culture, composed of ideas, values, beliefs, and so on, can have powerful effects on the human body. For anyone familiar with the pages of *National Geographic,* the variety of forms of bodily mutilation found throughout human populations is vast. People alter their bodies because their cultures teach them that to do so will make them more attractive, healthier, or more socially acceptable. For instance, women in the Padaung tribe in Burma elongate their necks by wearing large numbers of steel neck rings; Masai men and women in East Africa put increasingly larger pieces of wood through their earlobes, thereby creating loops in their ears; men in New Guinea put bones through their noses; traditional Chinese women had their feet tightly bound as young girls to retard the growth of their feet; Nubians in the Sudan scar their faces and bodies in intricate geometric designs; Pacific Islanders practice elaborate body tattooing; and the Kikuyu of Kenya circumcise both men and women as part of the rite of passage into adulthood. It has even been reported that a group of people living between

*Here are two examples of how cultural ideas concerning beauty affect how women adorn themselves.*

Canada and Mexico engage in the somewhat barbaric practice of putting holes in their earlobes for the purpose of hanging pieces of jewelry from them. And they practice this type of bodily mutilation for the very same reason that people tattoo their bodies, scar their faces, or put bones through their noses—because their cultures teach them that it is the acceptable thing to do.

The effects that cultural ideas have on our bodies and our bodily processes are not always as benign as the piercing of ears. For example, many of the forms of bodily mutilation, such as circumcision, tattooing, and scarification, can have deleterious effects on one's health, such as the spread of infection. It has been reported by Cannon (1942) that individuals whose cultures include witchcraft can be so thoroughly convinced that they are being bewitched that the resulting severe disturbances of bodily functioning end in death. In the United States it has been suggested that a possible explanation for the greater incidence of urinary tract infections among women is that, for purely social purposes, they avoid urinating more than do men, thereby causing greater stress on the bladder and the greater likelihood of infection. Moreover, the cultural idea of associating slimness with feminine attractiveness in the United States, when taken to excess, can lead to the life-threatening condition of anorexia.

The basic anthropological notion that culture channels biological processes can provide some important insights for the international businessperson when confronted with cross-cultural managerial or marketing problems. For example, in Bombay such a concept should be a reminder not to serve beef noodle soup in the company cafeteria, for to do so might cause a mass exodus to the infirmary. Or if we know that strongly held cultural beliefs in, for example, witchcraft can produce physiological maladies that can render the normally efficient worker dysfunctional, it would be reasonable for the company to have in its employ a local ritual specialist capable of counteracting the witchcraft. It is interesting to speculate if there would have been an infant formula controversy had Nestlé and other Western manufacturers of infant formula products understood the connection between the low levels of technology in third world cultures (that is, lack of unpolluted water, fuel supplies, and refrigeration) and the high mortality rates among those infants using the formula.

## CULTURAL UNIVERSALS

*All cultures of the world—despite many differences—face a number of common problems and share a number of common features, which we call cultural universals.* Even the most casual perusal of an introductory textbook in cultural anthropology leads us to the inescapable conclusion that there are many societies on the face of the earth with their own unique cultures. The determination of how many different cultures exist today depends largely on how one defines the problem, a definitional question on which there is hardly consensus among the world's anthropologists. We can get a rough approximation of world cultural variation by realizing that there are approximately 850 separate and distinct cultures (speaking mutually unintelligible languages) on the continent of Africa alone. But rather than being preoccupied with the precise number of cultures in the world at any one time, we should emphasize the significance of the variability. That is, the great number of differences between cultures illustrates how flexible and adaptable humans are in relation to other animals, for each culture has arrived at different solutions to the universal human problems facing all societies.

As we encounter the many different cultural patterns found throughout the world, there is a natural tendency to become overwhelmed by the magnitude of the differences and overlook the commonalities. Even anthropologists, when describing "their people," tend to emphasize the uniqueness of the culture and only infrequently look at the similarities between cultures. But *all* societies if they are to survive are confronted with fundamental universal needs that must be satisfied. When cultures develop ways of meeting these needs, general cultural patterns emerge. At a very concrete level, differences in the details of cultural patterns exist because different societies have developed different ways of meeting these universal societal needs. Yet at a higher level of abstraction, a number of commonalities exist because all cultures have worked out solutions to certain problems facing all human populations. Let us briefly examine the needs that all cultures must satisfy and the universal cultural patterns that emerge to satisfy these needs.

### Economic Systems

One of the most obvious and immediate needs of a society is to meet the basic physiological requirements of its people. To stay alive, all humans need a certain minimal caloric intake; potable water; and to varying degrees, protection from the elements in terms of clothing and shelter. No societies in the world have access to an infinite supply of such basic resources as food, water, clothing, and housing materials. Since these commodities are always in finite supply, each society must develop systematic ways of producing, distributing, and consuming these essential resources. Thus, each society must develop an *economic system*.

To illustrate this principle of cultural universals, we can look at one component of economic systems, namely, forms of distribution. In addition to working out patterned ways of producing basic material goods (or procuring them from the immediate environment), all societies must ensure that these goods are distributed to all those members of the society whose very survival depends on receiving them. In the United States most goods and services are distributed according to the capitalistic mode, based on the principle of "each according to his or her capacity to pay." In such socialistic countries as the People's Republic of China, Albania, and Cuba, goods and services are distributed according to another quite different principle—that is, "each according to his or her need."

These two well-known systems of distribution hardly exhaust the range of possibilities found in the world. The Pygmies of Central Africa distribute goods by a system known as "silent barter," in which the trading partners, in an attempt to attain true reciprocity, avoid face-to-face contact during the exchange. The Bushmen of present-day Namibia distribute the meat of an animal killed in the hunt according to the principle of kinship—that is, each share of meat is determined by how one is related to the hunter. But whatever particular form the system of distribution might take, there are no societies—at least not for long—that have failed to work out and adhere to a well-understood and systematic pattern of distribution.

### Marriage and Family Systems

For a society to continue over time it is imperative that it works out systematic procedures for mating, child rearing, and education. If it fails to do this, it will die in a very short time. No society permits random mating, for all societies have worked out rules for determining who can marry whom, under what conditions, and according to what procedures. All societies, in other words, have patterned systems of *marriage*. And since human infants (as compared to the young of other species) have a particularly long period of dependency on adults, there arises the need for every society to work out systematic ways of meeting the needs of dependent children. If the basic needs of dependent children are not satisfied, they simply will not survive to adulthood, and consequently, the very survival of the society is in jeopardy. Thus we can say that all societies have patterns of *child rearing and family institutions*.

### Educational Systems

In addition to ensuring that the basic physical needs of the child are met, a society must see to it that the children learn the way of life of the society. Rather than expecting each new child to rediscover for himself or herself all the accumulated knowledge of the past, a society must have an organized way of passing on its cultural heritage from one generation to another. This universal societal need for cultural transmission gives rise to some form of *educational system* in every society.

### Social Control Systems

If groups of people are to survive, they must develop some established ways of preserving social order. That is, all societies must develop mechanisms that will ensure that *most* of the people obey *most* of the laws *most* of the time. If this need is not met, people will violate each other's rights to such an extent that anarchy will prevail. Certainly, different societies meet this need for social order in different ways. In the United States, behavior control rests on a number of formal mechanisms, such as a written constitution; local, state, and federal laws; and an elaborate system of courts, penal institutions, and police among other things. Many small-scale, technologically simple societies have less formal means of controlling the behavior of their members. Regardless of the specific methods used, one thing is certain: Every society has a system for coercing people to obey the social rules, and these are called *social control systems*.

### Supernatural Belief Systems

All societies have a certain degree of control over their social and physical environments. There are a number of things that all people in a society can understand and predict. For example, a heavy object when dropped into a lake will sink to the bottom; if I have five dollars and give you two, I will have only three left; the sun always rises in the east and sets in the west. However, there are still many things that we cannot explain or predict with any degree of certainty. Why does a child develop a fatal disease whereas the child's playmate next door does not? Why do tornadoes destroy some houses and leave others unharmed? Why do safe drivers die in auto accidents and careless drivers do not? Such questions have no apparent answers, for they cannot be explained by our conventional systems of justice or rationality. Therefore, societies must develop systems for explaining these unexplainable occurrences. The way people explain the unexplainable is to rely on various types of supernatural explanations such as magic, religion, witchcraft, sorcery, and astrology. Thus all societies, despite variations in form and content, have systems of *supernatural beliefs,* which serve to explain otherwise inexplicable phenomena.

Thus, despite the great variety in the details of cultural features found throughout the world, all cultures, because they must satisfy certain universal needs, have a number of traits in common. This basic anthropological principle, known as *cultural universals,* can be an important tool for helping international businesspersons more fully understand and appreciate culturally different business environments. Greater empathy for cultural differences—a necessary if not sufficient condition for increased knowledge—can be attained if we can avoid concentrating solely on the apparent differences between cultures but appreciate their underlying commonalities as well. According to Robinson,

> . . . the successful international manager is one who sees and feels the similarity of structure of all societies. The same set of variables are seen to operate, although their relative weights may be very different. This capacity is far more important than possession of specific area expertise, which may be gained quite rapidly if one already has an ability to see similarities and ask the right questions—those that will provide the appropriate values or weights for the relevant variables. Such an individual can very quickly orient himself on the sociocultural map. (1983:127)

In other words, we will be less likely to prejudge or be critical of different practices, ideas, or behavior patterns if we can appreciate the notion that they represent different solutions to the same basic human problems facing all cultures of the world, including our own.

## CULTURE CHANGE

*All cultures experience continual change.* Any anthropological account of the culture of any society is a type of snapshot view of one particular time. Should the ethnographer return several years after completing a cultural study, he or she would not find exactly the same situation, for there are no cultures that remain completely static year after year. Early twentieth-century anthropologists—particularly those of the structural/functional orientation—tended to deemphasize cultural dynamics by suggesting that some societies were in a state of equilibrium in which the forces of change were negated by those of cultural conservatism. Although small-scale, technologically simple, preliterate societies tend to be more conservative (and, thus, change less rapidly) than modern, industrialized, highly complex societies, it is now generally accepted that, to some degree, change is a constant feature of all cultures.

Students of culture change recognize that cultural innovation (that is, the introduction of new thoughts, norms, or material items) occurs as a result of both *internal* and *external forces.* Mechanisms of change that operate within a given culture are called *discovery* and *invention.* Despite the importance of discovery and invention, most innovations introduced into a culture are the result of borrowing from other cultures. This process is known as cultural *diffusion,* the spreading of cultural items from one culture to another. The importance of cultural borrowing can be better understood if viewed in terms of economy of effort. That is, it is much easier to borrow someone else's invention or discovery than it is to discover or invent it all over again. In fact, anthropologists generally agree that as much as 90 percent of all things, ideas, and behavioral patterns found in any culture had their origins elsewhere. Individuals in every culture, limited by background and time, can get new ideas with far less effort if they borrow them. This statement holds true for our own culture as well as other cultures, a fact that North Americans frequently tend to overlook.

---

The culture historian Ralph Linton reminds us of the enormous amount of cultural borrowing that has taken place in order to produce the complex culture found in the United States:

> Our solid American citizen awakens in a bed built on a pattern which originated in the Near East but which was modified in Northern Europe before it was transmitted to America. He throws back covers made from cotton, domesticated in India, or linen, domesticated in the Near East, or wool from sheep, also domesticated in the Near East, or silk, the use of which was discovered in China. All of these materials have been spun and woven by processes invented in the Near East. He slips into his moccasins, invented by the Indians of the Eastern woodlands, and goes to the bathroom, whose fixtures are a mixture of European and American inventions, both of recent date. He takes off his pajamas, a garment invented in India, and washes with soap invented by the ancient Gauls. He then shaves, a masochistic rite which seems to have been derived from either Sumer or ancient Egypt.
>
> Returning to the bedroom, he removes his clothes from a chair of southern European type and proceeds to dress. He puts on garments whose form originally derived from the skin clothing of the nomads of the Asiatic steppes, puts on shoes made from skins tanned by a process invented in ancient Egypt and cut to a pattern derived from the classical civilizations of the Mediterranean, and ties around his neck a strip of bright-colored cloth which is a vestigial survival of the shoulder shawls worn by the seventeenth-century Croatians. Before going out for breakfast he glances through the window, made of glass invented in Egypt, and if it is raining puts on overshoes made of rubber discovered by the Central American Indians and takes an umbrella, invented in southeastern Asia. Upon his head he puts a hat made of felt, a material invented in the Asiatic steppes.
>
> On his way to breakfast he stops to buy a paper, paying for it with coins, an ancient Lydian invention. At the restaurant a whole new series of borrowed elements confronts him. His plate is made of a form of pottery invented in China. His knife is of steel, an alloy first made in southern India, his fork a medieval Italian invention, and his spoon a derivative of a Roman original. He begins breakfast with an orange, from the eastern Mediterranean, a canteloupe from Persia, or perhaps a piece of African watermelon. With this he has coffee, an Abyssinian plant, with cream and sugar. Both the domestication of cows and the idea of milking them originated in the Near East, while sugar was first made in India. After his fruit and first coffee he goes on to waffles, cakes made by a Scandinavian technique from wheat domesticated in Asia

> Minor. Over these he pours maple syrup, invented by the Indians of the Eastern woodlands. As a side dish he may have the egg of a species of bird domesticated in Indo-China, or thin strips of the flesh of an animal domesticated in Eastern Asia which have been salted and smoked by a process developed in northern Europe.
>
> When our friend has finished eating he settles back to smoke, an American Indian habit, consuming a plant domesticated in Brazil in either a pipe, derived from the Indians of Virginia, or a cigarette, derived from Mexico. If he is hardy enough he may even attempt a cigar, transmitted to us from the Antilles by way of Spain. While smoking he reads the news of the day, imprinted in characters invented by the ancient Semites upon a material invented in China by a process invented in Germany. As he absorbs the accounts of foreign troubles he will, if he is a good conservative citizen, thank a Hebrew deity in an Indo-European language that he is 100 percent American. (1936:326–27)

Since so much cultural change is the result of diffusion, it deserves a closer examination. Keeping in mind that cultural diffusion varies considerably from situation to situation, we can identify certain regularities that will enable us to make some general statements that hold true for all cultures.

First, cultural diffusion is a *selective* process. Whenever two cultures come into contact, each does not accept everything indiscriminately from the other. If they did, the vast cultural differences that exist today would have long since disappeared. Rather items will be borrowed from another culture only if they prove to be useful and/or compatible. For example, we would not expect to see the diffusion of swine husbandry from the United States to Saudi Arabia, the predominant Muslim population of which holds a strong dietary prohibition on pork. Similarly, polyandry (the practice of a woman having two or more legal husbands at a time) is not likely to be borrowed by the United States because of its obvious lack of fit with other features of mainstream American culture. Successful international marketing requires an intimate knowledge of the cultures found in foreign markets to determine if, how, and to what extent specific products are likely to become accepted by these foreign cultures.

According to a study by Rogers (1971:22–23), the rapidity with which an innovation is adopted—or, indeed, whether it will be adopted at all—is affected by the following five variables:

1. Relative advantage: the extent to which an innovation is thought to be superior to whatever it replaces.
2. Compatibility: the extent to which an innovation is perceived to be congruous with the existing cultural values, attitudes, behavior patterns, and material objects.
3. Complexity: the ease with which an innovation can be understood and utilized.
4. Trialability: the degree to which an innovation can be tested on a limited basis.
5. Observability: the extent to which people in the society can see the positive benefits of the innovation.

Put another way, an innovation is most likely to be diffused into a recipient culture if: (1) it is seen to be superior to what already exists; (2) it is consistent with existing cultural patterns; (3) it is easily understood; (4) it is able to be tested on an experimental basis; and (5) its benefits are clearly visible to a relatively large number of people. These five variables should be considered by international business strategists when considering the introduction of new marketing or managerial concepts into a foreign culture.

Second, cultural borrowing is a two-way process. Early students of change believed that contact between "primitive" societies and "civilized" societies caused the former to accept traits from the latter. This position was based on the assumption that the "inferior" primitive societies had nothing to offer the "superior" civilized societies. Today, however, anthropologists would reject such a position, for it has been found time and again that cultural traits are diffused in both directions.

European contact with the American Indians is a case in point. Native Americans, to be certain, have accepted a great deal from Europeans, but diffusion in the other direction has been significant. For example, it has been estimated (Driver, 1961:584) that those crops that make up nearly half of the world's food supply were originally domesticated by American Indians. These include corn, beans, squash, sweet potatoes, and the so-called "Irish potato." American Indians have given the world such articles of clothing as woolen ponchos, parkas, and moccasins, not to mention American varieties of cotton, a material used widely throughout the world for making clothing. Even the multibillion-dollar pharmaceutical industry in the Western world continues to produce and market commercial drugs first discovered by the American Indians, including such painkillers as cocaine and novacaine, anesthetics, quinine, and laxatives, among others.

Third, very infrequently are borrowed items ever transferred into the recipient culture in exactly their original form. Rather, new ideas, objects, or techniques are usually reinterpreted and reworked so that they can be integrated more effectively into the total configuration of the recipient culture. Lowell Holmes has offered an illuminating example of how the form of a particular innovation from Italy (pizza) has been modified after its incorporation into U.S. culture.

> Originally, this Italian pie was made with mozzarella or scamorza cheese, tomatoes, highly spiced sausage, oregano spice, and a crust made of flour, water, olive oil and yeast. Although this type of pizza is still found in most eastern cities, and in midwestern ones as well, in many cases the dish has been reinterpreted to meet midwestern taste preferences for bland food. Authentic Italian pizza in such states as Kansas, Missouri, Iowa, Nebraska, or the Dakotas is often considered too spicy; therefore, it is possible to purchase in restaurants or in supermarkets pizzas that are topped with American process cheese, have no oregano at all, and in place of spiced sausage, hamburger or even tuna fish rounds out the Americanized version. In many home recipes, the crust is made of biscuit mix. Although the Italians would hardly recognize it, it still carries the name pizza and has become extremely popular. (1971:361–62)

Sometimes the reinterpretation process involves a change in function but not form. While conducting fieldwork in East Africa I observed an example of how the function of an object from one culture can be changed upon adoption into a recipient culture. The Masai, not unlike some other ethnic groups in Kenya and Tanzania, practice the custom of piercing their earlobes and enlarging the hole by inserting increasingly larger pieces of wood until a loop of skin is formed. One group of Masai, rather than

*Most culture change occurs through a process of diffusion, as in the case of this native girl's creative use of light bulbs.*

stretching out their earlobes with pieces of wood, used instead Ever-Ready flashlight batteries obtained from the United States. Although the form of the batteries remained unchanged, the function was definitely reinterpreted.

Fourth, some cultural traits are more easily diffused than others. By and large technological innovations are more likely to be borrowed than are social patterns or belief systems, largely because the usefulness of a particular technological trait can be recognized quickly. For example, a man who walks 5 miles each day to work does not need much convincing to realize that an automobile can get him to work much more quickly and with far less effort. It has proven to be much more difficult, however, to convince a Muslim to become a Hindu or an American middle-class businessperson to become a socialist.

It is important for the international businessperson to understand that to some degree all cultures are constantly experiencing change. The three basic components of culture (things, ideas, and behavior patterns) can undergo additions, deletions, or modifications. Some components die out, new ones are accepted, and existing ones can be changed in some observable way. Although the pace of culture change varies from society to society, when viewing cultures over time, there is nothing as constant as change. This straightforward anthropological insight should remind the international businessperson that (1) any cultural environment today is not exactly the same as it was last year or will be one year hence. The cultural environment, therefore, needs constant monitoring. (2) Despite a considerable lack of fit between the culture of a U.S. corporation operating abroad and its overseas work force, the very fact that cultures can and do change provides some measure of optimism that the cultural gap can eventually be closed.

Moreover, the notion of cultural diffusion has important implications for the conduct of international business. Whether one is attempting to create new markets abroad or instill new attitudes and behaviors in a local work force, it is imperative to understand that cultural diffusion is selective. To know with some degree of predictability which things, ideas, and behaviors are likely to be accepted by a particular culture, those critical variables affecting diffusion such as relative advantage, compatibility, and observability should be understood.

The concept that cultural diffusion is a two-way process should help international managers be more receptive to the idea that the corporate culture, as well as the local culture, may change. In fact, the local culture may have a good deal to offer the corporate culture, provided the corporate culture is open to accepting these new cultural features.

An understanding that cultural diffusion frequently involves some modification of the item is an important idea for those interested in creating new product markets in other cultures. To illustrate, before a laundry detergent—normally packaged in a green box in the United States—would be accepted in certain parts of West Africa, the color of the packaging would need to be changed because the color green is associated with death in certain West African cultures.

Also, the idea that some components of culture are more readily accepted into other cultural environments than others should at least provide some general guidelines for assessing what types of changes in the local culture are more likely to occur. By assessing what types of things, ideas, and behavior have been incorporated into a culture in recent years, strategic planners should better understand the relative ease or difficulty involved in initiating changes in consumer habits or workplace behavior.

So far we have examined how an understanding of the concept of culture change can facilitate the management of change that will inevitably occur in both the U.S. corporate culture operating abroad and the local indigenous culture. It must be pointed out, however, that such theoretical understanding does not relieve the corporation of its ethical responsibilities for influencing change in the most humane and nondestructive fashion. The creation of new markets solely for the sake of increasing markets, with no concern for the effects of those products on the local populations, is absolutely indefensible. Likewise, an overly heavy-handed approach in coercing local workers to change their attitudes and behaviors is both unethical and is likely to be counterproductive as well. In short, any conceptual understanding about culture change carries with it in the very strong imperative that it be applied in an ethical manner and with a genuine concern for the well-being of the people whose culture is being changed.

## ETHNOCENTRISM

*All cultures—to one degree or another—display ethnocentrism.* Perhaps the greatest single obstacle to understanding another culture is *ethnocentrism*—literally "culture centered"—which is the tendency for people to evaluate a foreigner's behavior by the standards of one's own culture and to believe that one's own culture is superior to all others. The tendency to be ethnocentric is universal. Since our own culture is usually the only one we learn (or at least the first), we take our culture for granted, assuming that our behavior is correct and all others are wrong. The extent to which ethnocentrism pervades a culture is clearly seen in our history textbooks. Take, for example, the historic event of the Holy Wars between the Christians and the Muslims during the Middle Ages. In our textbook accounts of the wars, we refer to the Christians as "crusaders" and the Muslims as religious "fanatics." Yet if we read the Islamic accounts of the wars, the terms "crusaders" and "fanatics" would be reversed.

A similarly poignant illustration of ethnocentric interpretations of the same historic events became apparent to me when I was doing fieldwork among the Kikuyu of Kenya and read approximately 60 years of colonial reports from the Kenya National Archives. The British District Commissioners, when describing any Kikuyu involved in the so-called Mau Mau rebellion of the 1950s, consistently used the term *terrorist*. However, when Kikuyu informants were asked about their lives during the 1950s, they would respond proudly that they were *freedom fighters*. Quite obviously, the connotations of these two terms are radically different. In this instance, both the British officials and the Kikuyu were seeing these tragic historical events from their own narrow cultural perspective.

No society has a monopoly on ethnocentrism, for it is found in all societies. Every society with its own distinct culture has the tendency to refer to themselves as "us" and everyone else as "them." People come to feel that they are the center of the world, and everyone and everything revolves around them. For example, there are a number of non-Western societies whose name for themselves means "man" or "people," the implication being that all outsiders are somewhat less than human. The ancient Chinese felt that unless a person spoke Chinese and observed Chinese customs, he or she was a barbarian. The Masai of East Africa have long felt that their god had given them all the cattle in the world. Whenever they encountered non-Masai with cattle, they felt perfectly justified in taking them back, thinking they must have been acquired illegally.

---

Ruhley (1982:29) tells a rather humorous story of ethnocentrism:

" . . . two U.S. tourists in Germany . . . were traveling on a public bus when one of them sneezed. A German turned around and said, sympathetically, "Gesundheit." The U.S. tourist commented, "How nice that he speaks English." If the German understood the comment, he may have had reason to question the tourist's intellect.

---

Sometimes our own ethnocentrism can startle us when we find ourselves in a different cultural setting. A particularly revealing episode occurred when an American visited a Japanese classroom for the first time. On the wall of the classroom was a brightly colored map of the world. But something was wrong: Directly in the center of the map (where he had expected to see the United States) was Japan. To his surprise, the Japanese did not view the United States as the center of the world.

A fundamental assumption of ethnocentric people is that their way of doing things is right, proper, and normal and those ways practiced by culturally different people are wrong and inferior. Such a blanket condemnation of cultural differences prevents us from seeing that other people view our customs as equally strange and irrational. For example, people in the United States think of themselves as being particularly conscious of cleanliness. As a nation we probably spend more money per capita on a whole host of commercial products designed to make ourselves and our environments clean, hygienic, and odor free. Yet a number of practices found in the United States strike people in other parts of the world as deplorably unclean. To illustrate, whereas most North Americans are repulsed by an Indonesian who blows his nose onto the street, the Indonesian is repulsed by the North American who blows his nose in a handkerchief and then carries it around for the rest of the day in his pocket; the Japanese consider the North American practice of sitting in a bathtub full of dirty, soapy water to be at best an ineffective way of bathing and at worst a disgusting practice; and East Africans think that North Americans have no sense of hygiene because they defecate in rooms (the bathroom) that are frequently located adjacent to that part of the house where food is prepared (the kitchen).

---

A particularly revealing illustration of how some Western customs can strike non-Westerners as offensive has been reported by E. Royston Pike in his discussion of kissing:

> What's so strange about a kiss? Surely kissing is one of the most natural things in the world, so natural indeed that we might almost ask, what are lips for if not for kissing? But this is what we think, and a whole lot of people think very differently. To them kissing is not at all natural. It is not something that everybody does, or would like to do. On the contrary, it is a deplorable habit, unnatural, unhygienic, bordering on the nasty and even definitely repulsive.
>
> When we come to look into the matter, we shall find that there is a geographical distribution of kissing; and if some enterprising ethnologist were to prepare a "map of kissing" it would show a surprisingly large amount of blank space. Most of the so-called primitive races of mankind, such as the New Zealanders (Maoris), the Australian aborigines, the Papuans, Tahitians, and other South Sea Islanders, and the Esquimaux of the frozen north, were ignorant of kissing until they were taught the technique by the white men. . . . The Chinese have been wont to consider kissing as vulgar and all too suggestive of cannibalism. . . . (1967:11–12)

---

All people in all societies are ethnocentric to some degree regardless of how accepting or open-minded they might claim to be. Our ethnocentrism should not be a source of embarrassment for it is a natural byproduct of growing up in our society. In fact, ethnocentrism may serve the positive function of enhancing group solidarity by discouraging assimilation into another culture and legitimizing the existing cultural group. On the other hand, ethnocentrism can contribute to prejudice, contempt for outsiders, and intergroup conflict. Although it is a deeply ingrained attitude found in every society, it is important that we become aware of it so that it will not hinder us in learning about other cultures. Awareness of our own ethnocentrism will never eliminate it but will enable us to minimize its negative effects. As businesspersons it is vital to refrain from comparing our way of life with those of our international business partners. Instead, we should seek to *understand* other people in the context of their unique historical, social, and cultural backgrounds.

## CULTURES ARE INTEGRATED WHOLES

*Cultures should be thought of as integrated wholes—that is, cultures are coherent and logical systems, the parts of which to a degree are interrelated.* Upon confronting an unfamiliar cultural trait, a usual response is to try to imagine how such a trait would fit into one's own culture. That is, we look at it ethnocentrically, or from our own cultural perspective. All too frequently we view an unfamiliar cultural item as simply a pathological version of one found in our own culture. We reason that if the foreign cultural item is different and unfamiliar, it must be deviant, strange, weird, irrational, and consequently inferior to its counterpart in our own culture. This ethnocentric interpretation, with its unfortunate consequences, is the result of pulling the item from its proper cultural context and viewing it from the perspective of another culture. It is also the result of the individual's inability to see the foreign culture as an integrated system.

When we say that a culture is integrated we are saying that its components are more than a random assortment of customs. It is rather an organized system in which particular components may be related to other components. If we can view cultures as integrated systems, we can begin to see how particular culture traits fit into the integrated whole, and consequently how they tend to make sense within that context. And of

*The various parts of a culture are all, to some degree, interrelated.*

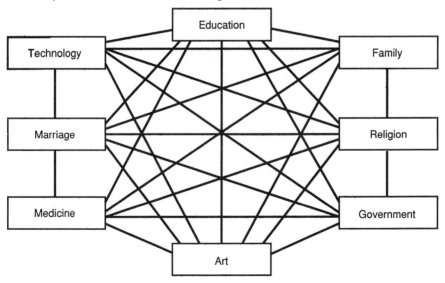

course, equipped with such an understanding, international businesspersons should be in a better position to cope with the "strange" customs encountered in the international business arena.

Perhaps a specific example will help to clarify this notion of integrated culture. Most Americans have difficulty identifying with the marital practice of polygyny (that is, a man having two or more wives at the same time). In addition to general misgivings about polygyny, there are a number of compelling reasons militating against its inclusion in the American cultural system. There are, in other words, other parts of U.S. culture that not only fail to support polygyny but also actually conflict with it. First, if a man attempts to have more than one wife at a time he runs the risk of finding himself behind bars, for it conflicts directly with our legal system. Moreover, the practice is counterproductive in a society based on a cash economy, for the more wives a man has the more money he needs to support them; and as a corollary, more wives mean more children, which require more visits to the pediatrician, Barbie dolls, hockey sticks, bicycles, swimming lessons, frozen pizzas, and eventually college tuition—all of which put additional strains on family income. In short, there is little in the American cultural configuration that would lend support to the practice of polygyny.

However, if we view polygyny within its proper cultural context, we will find that it is not only not immoral, illegal, or irrational but indeed is probably the most logical marital form that could be adopted. Clearly an ethnographic example of a polygynous society is required. Although literally hundreds of cultures could be used to illustrate the point, I have selected the traditional Kikuyu of East Africa because they are the people with whom I lived for 13 months.

For the Kikuyu, as is the case for many other peoples of the world, polygyny is the ideal marital form. Unlike American culture the Kikuyu cultural configuration contains a number of traits that tend to support polygyny and make it a viable marital alternative. First, the traditional Kikuyu economy is based on subsistence agriculture, which as practiced in fertile Kikuyuland is a relatively efficient means of livelihood. A single Kikuyu farmer can produce sufficient food for himself and several others. But the more hands contributing to the family farm, the better off economically the whole family would be. Thus, viewed from an economic perspective, it makes sense for the Kikuyu man to want more than one wife because the acquisition of new wives and children enhances the economic well-being of the household.

Second, the basic social unit of the Kikuyu is the patrilineage, a corporate group of male kinspeople ranging up to ten generations in depth, the members of which live together on lineage-controlled land. Since all lineage members want to see the lineage grow and prosper, there is considerable pressure put on Kikuyu to contribute male offspring to ensure the group's continued growth. What better way is there to increase one's chances of having male offspring than by maximizing the number of wives?

Third, the Kikuyu system of social status is based on the size of one's household, not on the household's material wealth. Simply put, prominent men are those with the greatest number of wives and children. Moreover, Kikuyu women also lend support to the practice of polygyny, for it is not at all unusual for Kikuyu wives to encourage their husbands to take additional wives to enhance the status of the household. Like their American counterparts, no Kikuyu woman wants to be married to a "nobody."

Fourth, polygyny as a marital form tends to be encouraged by the Kikuyu religion, one of the fundamental features of which is the belief in ancestor gods. When a prominent male Kikuyu dies, he is not buried and forgotten but is actually elevated to the status of deity and becomes an object of worship for the living members of his family. If his family consists of a single wife and child, he cannot expect to have much of a religious following. However, the larger his family (that is, wives and children), the greater the number of people worshipping him.

It would be possible to present a number of other explanations of why polygyny fits into the Kikuyu system. The point that should be emphasized, however, is that any cultural item, be it a learned behavioral response, an idea, or an object, must be viewed as a component of the total cultural system in which it is found. When items are wrenched from their proper cultural context and viewed from the perspective of another culture (that is, ethnocentrically), meanings and functions become distorted and the true nature of the item is, at best, imperfectly understood. But when we view a cultural item from within its proper or original cultural context, we have a much better chance of seeing how it logically fits into the integrated cultural system of which it is a part. And by so doing, we obtain a fuller understanding of how the culture functions.

If, in fact, cultures are coherent systems, with their constituent parts interrelated with one another, it follows logically that a change in one part of the system is likely to produce concomitant changes in other parts of the system. The introduction of a single technological innovation may set off a whole series of related changes. In other words, culture changes beget other culture changes.

To illustrate, one has only to look at the far-reaching effects on U.S. culture of a single technological innovation, which became widespread in the early 1950s—the TV set. This one single technological addition to our material culture has had profound consequences on the nonmaterial aspects of our culture, including our political, educational, and religious systems, to mention only three. For example, political campaigning for the presidency in 1948 and earlier had been conducted largely from the back end of a railroad car on so-called "whistle-stop" tours. By 1960, the year of the first televised presidential debates, television had brought the ideas, positions, speaking styles, and physical appearances of the candidates directly into the living rooms of the majority of voters. Today political candidates, because of the power of television, need to be as attentive to makeup, clothing, and nonverbal gestures as they are to the substantive issues of the campaign. In formal education, one of the many consequences of the widespread use of television has been to lower the age at which children develop "reading readiness" as a direct result of such programs as "Sesame Street." In terms of evangelical religion we must ask ourselves if there would even be an Oral Roberts University had it not been for television. Television has been described by various social commentators as both a blessing and a curse. Yet however we might feel about its pluses and minuses, we can hardly deny that it has contributed to profound changes in many other parts of the U.S. cultural system. And the reason for these changes is that cultures tend to be integrated systems with a number of interconnected parts, so that a change in one part of the culture is likely to bring about changes in other parts.

A particularly dramatic illustration of linked changes has been offered by Lauriston Sharp (1952) in his study of an aboriginal people in Australia, the Yir Yoront. Sharp shows how the introduction of steel axes to these stone-aged people by well-meaning but shortsighted missionaries altered significantly the relationship among family members and trading partners and eventually led to the disintegration of Yir Yoront culture.

To understand how this happened we must first understand the function of the stone axes that the steel axes replaced. First, since only men owned stone axes, women and children had to borrow them according to regular patterns of kinship interaction. This system of borrowing served to establish and maintain a well-defined system of sex, status, and role inequality. Second, since the stones used in making the stone axes were not available locally, Yir Yoront males had to obtain them by means of an elaborate trading network with neighbors located 400 miles to the south. These exchanges took place at large ceremonial gatherings, at which Yir Yoront met with other aboriginal peoples.

When the steel axes (which were clearly technologically superior to the stone axes) were dispensed by the missionaries, most of the traditional forms of social intercourse were disrupted. Kinship, age, and sex roles became confused because the existence of steel axes eliminated the necessity of going through traditional channels to borrow axes; traditional trading networks were abandoned, as were many of the aboriginal ceremonies where the trading took place; there was a loss of clearly defined authority patterns; and since the new steel axes had no origin myth or mythical ancestors associated with them, people became suspicious about all the various creation myths. In short, the introduction of a seemingly harmless innovation can lead to complex cultural repercussions.

The notion of integrated culture has several important implications for international businesspersons. First, when we understand that the parts of a culture are interrelated, we will be less likely to view foreign cultures ethnocentrically. Rather than wrenching a foreign cultural item from its original context and viewing it in terms of how well it fits into our own culture, we will be reminded to view it from within its proper cultural context. In other words, any cultural feature must be understood in terms of that culture. Thus we can begin to see how all cultures tend to be logical and coherent systems. Such an approach leads us to the inescapable conclusion that no cultures are inherently better or worse than any other, only different. This view of cultures as integrated wholes is not a value-laden philosophical rationalization for any type of behavior, however bizarre, destructive, or inhumane. Instead, such a culturally relativistic approach allows us to understand more fully why a particular cultural item is found in a society, even if it violates our sense of personal morality.

An understanding of the interconnectedness of the parts of culture can also help explain the nature of culture change. When systems are integrated it is impossible to change only one part of the system. Such an understanding would be critical for any responsible international businesspersons interested in expanding their markets into areas where their products (and perhaps ideas and behavior patterns associated with these products) are unknown. As was so dramatically shown with the case of the steel axes, some seemingly harmless commercial products could have profoundly disruptive effects on the very fabric of the society. By knowing the nature of the interconnectedness of the parts of a particular culture, the prudent, humane, and ultimately successful international businessperson will be able to predict the deleterious effects of a product in that cultural environment.

## THE CONCEPT OF CULTURE: MODEL OR REALITY?

Through the comparative study of a wide range of cultures throughout the world, cultural anthropologists have developed the general concept of culture and an understanding of those basic traits and processes shared by all specific cultures. This chapter has explored some of these cultural generalizations in an effort to provide a deeper appreciation of the cultural environment of international business. In addition to the various definitions of culture, this chapter has examined some of the basic characteristics that all cultures share, such as (1) the learned nature of culture; (2) how culture influences biological processes; (3) cultural universals; (4) the ubiquity of culture change; (5) ethnocentrism; and (6) the integrated nature of culture. It is assumed that an awareness of the concept of culture (what culture is and how it functions) is a necessary, yet not sufficient, prerequisite for an understanding of any particular culture.

Whenever dealing with any concept or generalization, such as the concept of culture, it is important to avoid viewing it in an overly rigid or concrete way. To arrive at statements that hold true for all cultures, anthropologists are operating at a relatively high level of abstraction. Since these generalizations are constructed from literally thousands of cultures in the world, there will be times when generalizations do not always jibe perfectly with reality. In no way does that fact invalidate the usefulness of the concept. The generalizations regarding culture discussed throughout this chapter should be viewed as *heuristic* in nature, rather than as exact representations of reality. They are generally valid descriptions of what happens most of the time. But even when discrepancies appear, the concept is still useful as a stimulant to further investigation.

When moving to the level of a specific culture, it is equally important to avoid overly rigid thinking. Anthropological statements about a particular culture are generalizations about what most of the people do and think most of the time. Although cultural norms exert a strong influence on behavior, they are hardly iron-clad propositions that can be used to predict with precision how people will respond in any given situation. Each culture must strike a balance between individual self-interests and the needs of the total society. Without denying the strong influence that culture has on behavior, people are nevertheless endowed with free will. That is, to one degree or another, individuals are free to go against their cultural norms, even though most do not. It is indeed the rare person in any society who complies totally with the social rules. As Barrett has pointed out, " . . . there is always a tendency to evade or stretch the meaning of the rules or to otherwise minimize their consequences" (1984:73). As a result, cultural anthropologists make the distinction between "ideal" behavior (what society says people should do) and "actual" behavior (what people in fact do).

The consequences of this fact is that in any given culture it is likely that individual variations in thought and action can be observed. To illustrate the nature and extent of this diversity, we can look at a familiar scene from our own culture, a high school classroom. In any given classroom even the most untrained observer will notice students behaving somewhat differently. As the teacher is lecturing, one male student may be flirting with the girl two rows over, another may be doodling, a third may be working on her unfinished homework for another class, and a fourth may actually be listening intently to extract some meaning from the lecture. Yet despite these individual variations, the students are nevertheless responding in *generally* similar ways. All remain seated; all are silent; all refrain from doing anything that would seriously interrupt the lecturer. Although the boy continues to flirt, he is not singing out loud or doing a handstand. The observable variations in behavior, in other words, are contained within socially accept-able limits. One of the tasks of the anthropologist—or any other cultural observer—is to determine where the normative limits are. It is the description of these *variations in behaviors within limits* that constitutes the patterns of any specific culture.

### CROSS-CULTURAL SCENARIOS

Read the following cross-cultural scenarios. In each mini-case study there is a basic cultural con-flict between the actors involved. Try to identify the source of the conflict and suggest how it could have been avoided or minimized. Then see how well your analyses compare to the explanations in the Appendix.

**2–1.** Sam Lucas, a construction supervisor for an international engineering firm, had the reputa-tion of being tough but fair-minded. Personally he was a very forceful, confrontive individual who always spoke his mind. He never hesitated to call on the carpet any worker who he felt was per-forming poorly. Even though during his six years with the company Sam had never worked outside of the United States, he was chosen to supervise construction on a new hotel project in Jidda, Saudi Arabia, primarily because of his outstanding work record. On this project Sam supervised the work of about a dozen Americans and nearly 100 Saudi laborers. It was not long before Sam realized that the Saudi laborers, to his way of thinking, were nowhere as reliable as the workers he had supervised in the United States. He was becoming increasingly annoyed at the seeming lack of competence of the local labor force. Following the leadership style that held him in such good stead at home, he would reprimand any worker who was not doing his job properly, and he would make certain that he did it publicly so that it would serve as an object lesson to all the other work-ers. He was convinced that he was doing the right thing and was being fair, for after all, he repri-manded both Americans and Saudis alike. He was troubled, however, by the fact that the problems seemed to be growing worse and more numerous.

WHAT ADVICE MIGHT YOU GIVE SAM?

**2–2.** Wayne Calder, a recent Harvard MBA and one of his organization's most innovative plan-ners, was assigned to the Paris office for a two-year period. Wayne was particularly excited about the transfer because he could now draw on the French he had taken while in school. Knowing that his proficiency in the French language would be an excellent entrée into French society, Wayne was looking forward to getting to know his French colleagues on a personal level. During the first week in Paris an opportunity to socialize presented itself. While waiting for a planning meeting with top executives to begin, Wayne introduced himself to Monsieur LeBec. They shook hands and exchanged some pleasantries, and then Wayne told LeBec how excited his family was to be in France. Wayne then asked LeBec if he had any children. LeBec replied that he had two daughters and a son. But when Wayne asked other questions about LeBec's family, his French colleague became quite distant and uncommunicative. Wayne wondered what he had done wrong.

HOW WOULD YOU EXPLAIN THIS BREAKDOWN IN COMMUNICATION?

**2–3.** For the past three years Ned Ferguson has served quite successfully as the manager of a U.S.–owned manufacturing company in Taiwan. Shortly after Ned's arrival in Taipei he instituted a number of changes in the plant operation that increased both production and worker satisfaction. However, within the last several months a series of what seemed to Ned to be unrelated incidents had occurred. First, there had been a fire in the warehouse, which fortunately was contained before too much damage had been done. On the following day the wife and two children of the local plant supervisor were killed in a spectacular automobile accident. And within the past several weeks there had been a rash of minor accidents on the assembly line, quite uncharacteristic given the plant's excellent past safety record. Ned heard that rumors were running rampant about the plant being cursed by evil spirits, and absenteeism had increased dramatically. To try to deal with these problems, Ned called together his chief supervisors. His American staff recommended that some experts from the insurance company come in to review the safety procedures, which, they argued, would show the workers that the company was taking their safety needs seriously. But the Taiwanese supervisors considered this step to be inadequate and instead suggested that a local religious priest be brought in, during company time, to pray for the workers and ward off any evil forces. Ned and his U.S. staff thought that such an action would do nothing but give official company support to superstition. The meeting ended without any substantial agreement between U.S. and Taiwanese supervisors.

HOW WOULD YOU EXPLAIN THIS BASIC CULTURAL CONFLICT?

**2–4.** Within the past decade Ray Cisneros had worked hard to become the top salesperson for the entire West Coast district of his company, which manufactures and distributes vinyl floor coverings. When his company received an invitation to make a marketing presentation to a large distribution firm in Buenos Aires, Ray's Hispanic background, fluency in Spanish, and excellent salesmanship all made him the logical choice for the assignment. Ray had set up an appointment to make his presentation on the same day that he arrived from Los Angeles. But upon arrival the marketing representative of the host firm, who met him at the airport, told him that the meeting had been arranged for two days later so that Ray could rest after the long trip and have a chance to see some of the local sites and enjoy their hospitality. Ray tried to assure his host that he felt fine and was prepared to make the presentation that day. Ray could see no good reason not to get on with the business at hand. Eventually the marketing representative (somewhat reluctantly) intervened on Ray's behalf, and the meeting was reset for later that afternoon. But once the meeting began Ray noticed that the Argentinean executives never really got beyond the exchange of pleasantries. Finally, the vice president in charge suggested that they meet again the next afternoon. Ray was feeling increasing frustration with the excruciatingly slow pace of the negotiations.

HOW COULD YOU HELP RAY GAIN SOME CLARITY ON THIS CROSS-CULTURAL SITUATION?

**2–5.** A U.S. fertilizer manufacturer headquartered in Minneapolis decided to venture into the vast potential of Third World markets. The company sent a team of agricultural researchers into an East African country to test soils, weather conditions, and topographical conditions in order to develop locally effective fertilizers. Once the research and manufacturing of these fertilizer products had been completed, one of the initial marketing strategies was to distribute, free of charge, 100-pound bags of the fertilizer to selected areas of rural farmers. It was thought that those using the free fertilizer would be so impressed with the dramatic increase in crop productivity that they would spread the word to their friends, relatives, and neighbors.

Teams of salespeople went from hut to hut in those designated areas offering each male head of household a free bag of fertilizer along with an explanation of its capacity to increase crop output. Although each head of household was very polite, they all turned down the offer of free fertilizer. The marketing staff concluded that these local people were either disinterested in helping themselves grow more food and eat better or so ignorant that they couldn't understand the benefits of the new product.

WHY WAS THIS AN ETHNOCENTRIC CONCLUSION?

# COMMUNICATING ACROSS CULTURES: LANGUAGE

*Americans who travel abroad for the first time are often shocked to discover that, despite all the progress that has been made in the past 30 years, many foreign people still speak in foreign languages. Oh, sure, they speak some English, but usually just barely well enough to receive a high school diploma here in the United States. (Barry, 1987:7)*

Business organizations, like other social systems, require effective communication in order to operate efficiently and meet their objectives. International business organizations require effective communication at a number of levels. The firm must communicate with its work force, customers, suppliers, and host government officials. Effective communication among people from the same culture is often difficult enough. But when attempting to communicate with people who do not speak English—and who have different ideas, attitudes, assumptions, perceptions, and ways of doing things—one's chances for miscommunication increase enormously.

Communication takes place in two ways: (1) through language (using words that have mutually understood meanings and are linked together into sentences according to consistently followed rules) and (2) through nonverbal communication, or what Edward T. Hall (1959) refers to as the "silent language." Chapters 3 and 4 examine the nature of communication in international business and how communication problems can develop when people communicate, or attempt to communicate, across cultures. This chapter will focus on language, and Chapter 4 will look at the nonverbal dimension of communication.

## THE NEED FOR LINGUISTIC PROFICIENCY
## IN INTERNATIONAL BUSINESS

If the success of the international businessperson is to be maximized, there is no substitute for an intimate acquaintance with both the language and the culture of those with whom one is conducting business. In fact, because of the close relationship between language and culture, it will be virtually impossible not to learn about one while studying the other. The argument in favor of foreign language competence for international businesspeople seems so blatantly obvious that to have to recount it here causes twinges of embarrassment. Yet the very fact that so many Westerners enter the international business arena without competence in a second language should help us overcome that embarrassment. A survey of U.S. firms conducting business in non–English-speaking countries revealed that only 31 percent considered a foreign language necessary for doing business abroad, and only 20 percent required their overseas employees to know the local language (Baker, 1984:69).

Most of the explanations offered for not learning to speak another language appear transparent and designed to justify past complacency and/or ethnocentrism. For example, we frequently hear that U.S. firms doing business abroad need not train their overseas personnel in a second language because English is rapidly becoming the international language of business. After generations of assuming that our goods and services were so desirable that the rest of the world would come to us, we now find ourselves in a highly competitive world marketplace with greater linguistic parity. English is now just one of the major languages of world trade and the mother tongue of only 5 percent of the world's population.

A host of other arguments have also been advanced to justify a monolinguistic approach to international business. For example, it has been suggested that Western businesspersons can avoid the time and energy needed to learn a second language by hiring in-country nationals who are well grounded in the local language and culture. Others have argued that a second language is not practical since most international businesspersons do not remain in the host country for more than a year or two. Moreover, it has even been suggested (Terpstra, 1978:21) that becoming proficient in a second language could actually hinder one's career advancement since that individual, spending most of his or her time out of the home country, would be away from the organization's political mainstream.

Despite these and other arguments (or perhaps post facto rationalizations) the simple fact remains that a fundamental precondition of any successful international business enterprise is effective communication. Whether dealing with international sales, management, or negotiations, the Western businessperson who must rely on translators is at a marked disadvantage. International business, like any business, must be grounded in trust and mutual respect. What better way to gain that trust and respect than by taking the time and energy to learn someone else's language? In terms of international marketing and negotiations, Theodore Huebener reminds us that

> . . . a knowledge of a customer's language has a distinct sales value. This is particularly true in Latin countries, where business conferences are conducted in a leisurely and unhurried way, in a highly social atmosphere. The American businessman who can speak the foreign tongue fluently and who can make intelligent comments on the art and literature of the country will gain not only the business but also the respect of the person he is dealing with. (1961:46)

Thus, proficiency in a second language enables the international businessperson to understand the communication patterns within their proper cultural context as well as increase general rapport with foreign business counterparts.

This in itself should be ample justification for Western businesspersons to have second language competence. But we can add a number of other compelling reasons as well. First, as Whorf (1956:212–14) has suggested, the only way to really understand the "world view" of another culture (that is, its system of categories for organizing the world) is through its language. Second, the experience of learning a second language is beneficial in the learning of third and fourth languages, so that the time spent today learning Spanish will facilitate the learning of Chinese or Arabic in the future. And third, learning another language (and culture) is the best way to gain a fuller appreciation of one's own language (and culture). With all these cogent arguments in favor of second language proficiency, one cannot help noticing the flagrant lack of attention foreign language competence has been given by Western business establishments.

> Even though English is the major *lingua franca* of international business, some American and British companies are beginning to realize that it pays to learn foreign languages. For example, in 1983, Jaguar, the British automobile manufacturer, started an in-house language center for the study of German. According to the *Economist* (May 16, 1987, pp. 67–68), Jaguar sales in West Germany the following year jumped a dramatic 60 percent against stiff competition from its local competitors, Mercedes and BMW.

With business becoming increasingly international, the role of language is becoming more important. American firms that in the past had exclusively domestic operations are now struggling with international correspondence, letters of credit, and customs regulations in a number of different languages; and multinational firms, which have had long histories of operating across linguistic boundaries, are having to add new languages to their repertoires. Some U.S. firms have taken the challenge of coping with other languages more seriously than others. Those U.S. firms that continue to work with their monolingual provincialism do so at a rather high risk to their own corporate health and longevity. Paul Aron, a high-level international businessman with Daiwa Securities America, perhaps put it most directly when he said: "American companies put little premium on language—and see how they're doing overseas" (Machan, 1988:140).

Yet even for those firms that take seriously the multilinguistic environment of international business, there are many hazards along the way. The literature is filled with examples of problems U.S. firms have had in their international advertising campaigns because of sloppy translations. One such example was reported by Slater:

> . . . an American ink manufacturer attempted to sell bottled ink in Mexico while its metal outdoor signs told customers that they could "avoid embarrassment" (from leaks and stains) by using its brand of ink. The embarrassment, it seems, was all the ink company's. The Spanish word used to convey the meaning of "embarrassed" was "embarazar," which means "to become pregnant." Many people thought the company was selling a contraceptive device. (1984:20)

In other instances of imprecise translations U.S. firms have advertised cigarettes with low "asphalt" (instead of tar), computer "underwear" (instead of softwear), and "wet sheep" (instead of hydraulic rams). As amusing as these examples may seem, such translation errors have cost U.S. firms millions of dollars in losses over the years, not to mention the damage done to their credibility and reputations.

It is important to keep in mind that U.S. firms do not have a monopoly on linguistic faux pas. Even when people *think* they know English, they frequently convey messages they don't particularly intend to send.

- A sign in a Romanian hotel informing the English-speaking guests that the elevator was not working read, "The lift is being fixed. For the next few days we regret that you will be unbearable" (Besner, 1982:53).
- A sign in the window of a Paris dress shop said, "Come inside and have a fit" (Besner, 1982:53).
- Reporting to his firm's headquarters, an African representative of an electronics firm referred to the "throat-cutting competition" when in fact he meant "cut-throat competition" (Salmans, 1979:46).
- A notice in a Moscow tourist hotel stated, "If this is your first visit to the U.S.S.R., you are welcome to it" (Besner, 1982:53).

In all these examples, it is clear that the translators know the language, but they still sent unintended messages. Even though they knew the meanings of all of the words used, and the grammatical rules for putting them together, communication was nevertheless short-circuited.

Not only do businesses face formidable problems when translating from one language into another, but confusion can also occur between two groups that ostensibly speak the same language. We often hear the comment "Fortunately we are being transferred by the company to London, so we won't have a language problem." It is true that they will not have to master a totally new language, complete with grammar, vocabulary, and sound system. But it is equally true that there are a number of significant differences between British and U.S. English that can lead to confusion and misunderstandings. In some cases the same word can have two very different meanings on either side of the Atlantic. The U.S. businessperson in London will be in for quite a jolt when his British counterpart, in a genuine attempt to pay a compliment, refers to the American's wife as "homely," for in the United States the word means "plain" or "ugly" but in the United Kingdom it means "warm" and "friendly." Another such misunderstanding actually occurred at a meeting of representatives from a U.S. firm and a British firm. According to Salmans, things were proceeding smoothly

> . . . until one of the . . . [British] executives suggested "tabling" a key issue. To his amazement, the Americans reacted with outrage. The reason, as he learned shortly, was that while in the UK "tabling" an item means giving it a prominent place on the agenda, in the US it means deferring it indefinitely. (1979:45)

And just imagine the look on the American businessperson's face when his female British counterpart asks him for a "rubber" (that is, an eraser) or invites him to "knock her up" (that is, stop by her house).

More frequently two different words refer to the same thing. To illustrate, the British live in "flats," not apartments; they "cue" up rather than line up; and they wear "plimsoles" rather than sneakers. When the North American steps into a British automobile, most parts of the vehicle have different names: To the British the trunk is the "boot"; the hood is the "bonnet"; the windshield is the "windscreen"; the horn is the "hooter"; and the vehicle runs on "petrol," not gas.

## LINGUISTIC DIVERSITY

Perhaps the most significant feature of being human is the ability to build and manipulate language and other symbolic codes. Other animal species communicate in a variety of ways: by means of nonlinguistic calls, body movements, gestures, olfactory stimuli, and other instinctive or genetically based mechanisms. Some nonhuman species, like certain of the great apes, have a limited capacity to learn symbolic codes (for example, American Sign Language), but they are unable to develop a language of their own. It is this ability to symbolize through language that is the hallmark of humanity. Language allows humans to transcend many of their biological limitations by building cultural models and transmitting them from generation to generation.

But what do we mean by language? A language (a universal found in all cultures of the world) is a symbolic code of communication consisting of a set of sounds (phonemes) with understood meanings and a set of rules (grammar) for constructing messages. The meanings attached to any word by a language are totally arbitrary. For example, the word *cat* has no connection whatsoever to that animal the English language refers to as cat. The word *cat* does not look like a cat, sound like a cat, or have any particular physical connection to a cat. Somewhere during the development of the English language someone decided that the word *cat* would refer to that particular type of four-legged animal, whereas other languages symbolized the exact same animal by using totally different words. Language, then, consists of a series of arbitrary symbols with meanings that, like other aspects of culture, must be learned and that, when put together according to certain grammatical rules, can convey complex messages.

Since languages are arbitrary symbolic systems, it is not surprising that there is enormous linguistic diversity on the face of the earth. There does not appear to be universal agreement as to how many languages there are in the world. Estimates range from several thousand to as many as 10,000. It seems reasonable to suggest 3,000 as a credible estimate. Even though exact numbers are not available, it is generally recognized that there are more than 1,000 languages among American Indians, about 750 in sub-Saharan Africa, over 150 on the subcontinent of India, and in excess of 750 on the single island of New Guinea. However, these estimates should be kept in their proper perspective. As Katzner has suggested,

> A single statistic tells a great deal: of the several thousand languages of the world, fewer than 100 are spoken by over 95 percent of the earth's population. One language, Chinese, accounts for 20 percent all by itself, and if we add English, Spanish, Russian, and Hindi, the figure rises to about 45 percent. German, Japanese, Arabic, Bengali, Portuguese, French and Italian bring the figure to 60 percent. . . . When we realize that the last five percent speak thousands of different languages, it is clear that the great majority of these languages are spoken by tiny numbers of people. . . . (1975:viii–ix)

There are several reasons for this vagueness in the number of discrete languages in the world. First, there is a question of whether to include in the total number all those languages that are dying out or have already died out. Second, certain remote areas of the world (such as New Guinea and parts of Brazil) have not been the subject of intensive descriptive linguistic study, and consequently, very little is known of the linguistic mosaics in these areas. And third, and by far the most problematic factor, is that linguists fail to agree on where to draw linguistic boundaries. Mutual unintelligibility is frequently used as the criterion for distinguishing between language groups. That is, if people can understand one another they speak the same language; if they can't, they don't. Yet, as is all too obvious, this criterion is hardly ironclad because there are varying degrees of intelligibility. Despite the fact that we cannot determine with absolute certainty the precise number of languages in the world today, the fact remains that the range of linguistic modes throughout the world is vast. And despite the claims by some U.S. businesspersons that English is widely used in international business, this enormous linguistic diversity in the world must be of concern to any U.S. businessperson attempting to compete in an increasingly interdependent marketplace.

The typical North American divides the great variety of cultures found in the world today into two categories: advanced civilizations like his or her own and so-called primitive cultures, which are frequently based on small-scale agriculture or hunting and gathering and have simple systems of technology. In keeping with this bipolar thinking, it is popularly held that technologically simple societies have equally uncomplex or unsophisticated languages. In other words, we frequently think that primitive people have primitive languages. Yet anthropological linguists tell us that this is not the case, for technologically simple people are no less capable of expressing a wide variety of abstract ideas than are people with high levels of technology.

To illustrate this point, we can consider the Navajo language spoken by Native Americans living in Arizona and New Mexico. When compared to English the Navajo language is no less efficient in terms of expressing abstract ideas. All we can say is that the two linguistic systems are different. It is true that Navajo does not have certain grammatical distinctions commonly found in English, as Beals, Hoijer, and Beals have noted:

> The Navajo noun has the same form in both the singular and the plural—there are no plural noun endings (such as the -s of book-s or the -en of oxen) in Navajo. Similarly, the third-person pronoun of Navajo is singular or plural and nondistinctive in gender: it can be translated *he, she, it,* or *they,* depending on the context. Finally, we find no adjectives in Navajo. The function performed by the English adjective is in Navajo performed by the verb. (1977:513)

Yet in another area of structure the Navajo language is considerably more precise than English. As Peter Farb (1968:56) reminds us, it is impossible for a Navajo speaker simply to say, "I am going." Rather, there will be considerably more information built into the verb form. For example, the verb stem would indicate whether the person is going on foot or by horseback, wagon, boat, or airplane. If the Navajo speaker is, in fact, going on horseback, she or he then must choose another verb form that will specify if the horse will walk, trot, gallop, or run. Moreover, the verb form chosen also will indicate if the speaker is "preparing to go," "going now," "almost at one's destination," or a number of other options. To be certain, the English speaker can convey the same information, but to do so would require a vast quantity of words. The Navajo language can provide an enormous amount of information by the proper verb form.

The central point is this: Despite the fact that the Navajo and English languages are very different, we can hardly conclude that one is any more efficient than the other at expressing a wide variety of abstract ideas. All cultural groups have symbolic systems that are, by and large, equally efficient at sending and receiving verbal messages. Such an understanding on the part of the international businessperson should serve as an important reminder that English is not inherently superior to the language of those with whom one is doing business and whose language one is learning.

## LANGUAGE AND CULTURE

A fundamental tenet of anthropological linguistics is that there is a close relationship between language and culture. It is generally held that it is impossible to understand a culture without taking into account its language; and it is equally impossible to understand a language outside of its cultural context. Yet despite the close connection between language and culture, we should not think of the relationship as being complete or absolute. There are societies, for example, that share common cultural traditions but speak mutually unintelligible languages. On the other hand, societies with quite different cultures may speak mutually intelligible languages. Nevertheless, culture influences language and language influences culture in a number of ways.

### The Influence of Culture on Language

Perhaps the most obvious relationship between language and culture is seen in vocabulary. The vocabularies of all languages are elaborated in the direction of what is considered adaptively important in that culture. In industrialized societies the vocabularies contain large numbers of words that reflect complex technologies and occupational specialization. The average speaker of standard American English knows hundreds of technological terms, such as *carburetor, microchip,* and *bulldozer,* as well as a myriad of terms designating occupational specialities, such as *accountant, philosopher, draftsman, clerk,* and *thoracic surgeon,* because technology and professions are focal concerns in U.S. culture. Thus, standard American English enables North Americans to adapt most effectively to their environment by providing a conceptual lexicon most suited to U.S. culture.

It is equally true for nonindustrialized societies that those aspects of environment and culture that are of special importance will be reflected in the vocabulary. The Koga of southern India have seven different words for bamboo, an important natural resource in their tropical environment, yet have not a single word for snow (Plog & Bates, 1980:209). The pastoral Nuer of the Sudan, whose everyday lives revolve around their cattle, have words in their language that enable them to distinguish between hundreds of types of cows, based on color, markings, and configuration of horns. This elaborate vo-

*The importance of snow in Eskimo culture is reflected in its language.*

cabulary is an indication of the central economic and social role that cattle play in their society (Hickerson, 1980:112). The Eskimos' complex classification of types of snow is a classic example of the close connection between language and culture. Whereas the typical New Yorker has a single word for snow, the Eskimos have a large number of words, each designating a different type of snow, such as drifting snow, softly falling snow, and so on. Even though the New Yorker can express the same ideas with a number of modifiers, the Eskimos view snow as categorically different substances because their very survival requires a precise knowledge of snow conditions. Whether we are looking at the Koga, the Nuer, or the Eskimo language, the point remains the same: In all languages points of cultural emphasis are directly reflected in the size and specialization of the vocabularies. In other words, a language will contain a greater number of terms, more synonyms, and more fine distinctions when referring to features of cultural emphasis.

Although it is frequently more difficult to find points of cultural emphasis in large, highly differentiated societies, one area of cultural emphasis in the United States is sports. To illustrate, Hickerson (1980:118) reminds us that standard American English contains a number of colloquialisms that stem from the popular sport of baseball:

1. He made a grandstand play.
2. She threw me a curve.
3. She fielded my questions well.
4. You're way off base.
5. You're batting 1000 (500, zero) so far.
6. What are the ground rules?

7. I want to touch all the bases.
8. He went to bat for me.
9. He has two strikes against him.
10. That's way out in left field.
11. He drives me up the wall.
12. He's a team player (a clutch player).
13. She's an oddball (screwball, foul ball).
14. It's just a ball park estimate.

### The Influence of Language on Culture

We have just seen how languages tend to reflect cultural emphases. On the other side of the linguistic coin, however, some linguists have posited that language may actually influence certain aspects of culture. Language, they suggest, establishes the categories on which our perceptions of the world are organized. According to this theory, language is more than a system of communication that enables people to send and receive messages with relative ease. Language also establishes categories in our minds that force us to distinguish those things we consider similar from those things we consider different. And since every language is unique, the linguistic categories of one language will never be identical to the categories of any other. Consequently, speakers of any two languages will not perceive reality in exactly the same way. Edward Sapir was one of the first linguists to explain how language tends to influence our perceptions:

> The fact of the matter is that the real world is to a large extent unconsciously built up on the language habits of the group. No two languages are ever sufficiently similar to be considered as representing the same social reality. The worlds in which different societies live are distinct worlds, not merely the same world with different labels attached. (1929:214)

Along with the amateur linguist Benjamin Lee Whorf, Sapir developed what has been referred to as the Sapir-Whorf hypothesis. This hypothesis, dealing with the relationship between language and culture, states that language is not merely a mechanism for communicating ideas but rather is itself the shaper of ideas. There is no general agreement among scholars concerning the validity of the Sapir-Whorf hypothesis. Although it has been shown that in some languages some correspondence does exist between grammatical categories and cultural themes, linguistic determinism is not an established fact. For example, the gender distinction made in English is *not* indicative of the relative importance of gender in other parts of the culture. Yet some tests of the hypothesis have suggested that language indeed can influence perceptions or world view.

One of the more ingenious attempts at testing the Sapir-Whorf hypothesis was devised by anthropologist Joseph Casagrande (1960) of the Southwest Project in Comparative Psycholinguistics. The study used a sample of over 100 Navajo children divided into two groups: those who spoke only Navajo and those who spoke both Navajo and English. Since the two groups were similar in all other major sociocultural variables except language (that is, education, family income, religion, and so on), it was assumed that whatever differences in perception emerged among the two groups could be attributed to the variable of language.

Having a thorough knowledge of the Navajo language, Casagrande understood that Navajo speakers, when referring to an object, are led by their linguistic categories to choose among a number of different verbs depending on the shape of the object. That is, when asking to be given a particular object, a Navajo speaker will use one verb form if the object is long, thin, and flexible (like a rope) and another if the object is long, thin, and rigid (like a stick). This feature of the Navajo language led Casagrande to hypothesize that Navajo-speaking children would be more likely to sort or discriminate according to shape than English-speaking children, who would be more likely to sort according to other criteria such as size or color. To test the hypothesis, the children from both groups were shown two objects (a yellow stick and a blue rope) and then asked to tell which of these objects was most like a third object (a yellow rope). In other words, all of the children were asked to tell whether the yellow rope was more like the yellow stick or the blue rope. As the hypothesis had predicted, Casagrande found that those children who spoke only Navajo were more likely to sort according to shape (that is, blue rope and yellow rope) whereas those who were bilingual more often sorted according to color.

Thus, the Sapir-Whorf hypothesis (that is, that the structure of a language can significantly influence perception and categorization) seems to have been supported by this series of experiments. Although it is considerably easier to demonstrate the cultural influence on language, the Sapir-Whorf hypothesis continues to remind us that the relationship can also flow in the other direction.

The implications of the Sapir-Whorf hypothesis for the international businessperson are obvious. The hypothesis states that linguistically different people not only communicate differently but also think and perceive reality differently. Thus, by learning the local language, the international businessperson will acquire a vehicle of communication as well as a better understanding of why people think and behave as they do.

## EXPLICIT VERSUS IMPLICIT COMMUNICATION

Cultures also vary in terms of how explicitly they send and receive verbal messages. In the United States, for example, effective verbal communication is expected to be explicit, direct, and unambiguous. Good communicators are supposed to say what they mean as precisely and straightforwardly as possible. Speech patterns in some other cultures are considerably more ambiguous, inexact, and implicit. Bernstein's (1964) distinction between elaborated and restricted codes provides a conceptual framework to better understand the differences between these two fundamentally different types of speech patterns. Restricted codes use shortened words, phrases, and sentences and rely heavily on hidden, implicit, contextual cues such as nonverbal behavior, social context, and the nature of interpersonal relationships. Restricted codes are a form of "shorthand" communication which do not rely on verbal elaboration or explication. Elaborated codes, on the other hand, emphasize elaborate verbal amplification and place little importance on nonverbal or other contextual cues.

Bernstein's notion of restricted and elaborated codes is quite similar to Edward Hall's conceptualization of high-context cultures and low-context cultures:

> A high-context (HC) communication or message is one in which most of the information is either in the physical context or internalized in the person, while very little is in the coded, explicit, transmitted part of the message. A low-context (LC) communication is just the opposite; i.e., the mass of the message is vested in the explicit code. (1976:79)

To combine these two schemes of Bernstein and Hall, high-context cultures, relying heavily on restricted codes and contextual cues, demonstrate inexact, implicit, and indirect communication patterns. In contrast, low-context cultures, relying on elaborated verbal messages, demonstrate precise, explicit, and straightforward communication patterns.

Like so many other bipolar typologies found in the social science literature, the notions of restricted vs. elaborated codes or high-context vs. low-context cultures are not "either-or" categories. Relatively restricted or elaborated codes can be found in any speech community, although one or the other mode is likely to predominate. Whereas the United States is not the best example of a low-context culture, it is clearly near the low-context end of the continuum. Based on the writings of Edward Hall (1976) and L. R. Kohls (1978) it is possible to place 12 nationalities on a high- versus low-context continuum:

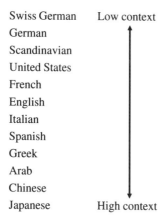

As would be predicted, low-context cultures, relying on elaborated verbal codes, demonstrate high value and positive attitudes toward words. The Western world (northern Europe and the United States, specifically) has had a long tradition of rhetoric, a tradition that places central importance on the delivery of verbal messages. According to Gudykunst and Kim (1984:140), "a primary function of speech in this tradition is to express one's ideas and thoughts as clearly, logically, and persuasively as possible, so the speaker can be fully recognized for his or her individuality in influencing others." In contrast, in such high-context cultures as Japan and China, verbal messages, although important, are only a part of the total communication context. It is not that words are unimportant in Eastern cultures, but rather that the words are inseparably interrelated to social relationships, politics, and morality. Given this more holistic approach to communication, its purpose in many Eastern cultures is not to enhance the speaker's individuality through the articulation of words but rather to promote harmony and social integration. According to Gudykunst and Kim,

> The primary emphasis is placed not on the technique of constructing and delivering verbal messages for maximum persuasiveness but on conformity to the already established social relationships defined by the position of the individual speaker in the society. In such a rhetorical context, one is expected to possess a moral and intellectual integrity and a keen sensitivity to subtle and implicit contextual cues surrounding the total communication process. Without the contextual base, the speaker's verbal articulation and delivery are perceived as less meaningful, if not superficial or even deceitful. (1984:141)

Thus, whereas Western cultures place a great deal of power in words, many Asian cultures show a certain mistrust or skepticism of words or at least have a keen awareness of the limitation of words alone.

---

Chinese scholar Robert Kapp describes the indirect style of communicating found among the Chinese, which can affect business negotiations between U.S. and Chinese businesspeople.

> The indirection that permeates Chinese speech even in English translation, can be particularly disconcerting to Americans. "Perhaps" and "maybe" are cultural stock-in-trade. "Maybe I will come with you" usually means "I'm coming." "Perhaps it is too far for you to walk" means "There's no way I'll let you walk." When something is "inconvenient," it most likely is impossible. But more than verbal indirection is at work here. The absence of a categorical statement implies that "perhaps" some room for discussion remains; and, in any case, a subsequent reversal will not represent a clear backing-down. Despite the firm signal that conditional speech often implies, negotiation is never totally foreclosed and dignity is maintained, at the expense of American patience. (1983:20–21)

---

This cautious approach can be seen in the general suppression of negative verbal messages. As a result, politeness and the desire to avoid embarrassment often take precedence over the truth. This approach, at least in part, explains why Eastern cultures have so many nonverbal ways of saying "no" without directly or unambiguously uttering the word. Needless to say, this practice has caused considerable misunderstanding when North Americans try to communicate with Japanese. To illustrate, the Japanese in everyday conversation frequently use the word *hai* ("yes") to convey not agreement necessarily, but rather that they understand what is being said.

When negotiating with Asians, it is important to understand that "yes" is not always an affirmative response. Before taking "yes" for an answer, one must ascertain if in fact it was merely a polite response that really meant "no." Asian businesspersons, for example, are not likely to say "no" directly to a proposal but rather will reply in ways that are synonymous with "no." To illustrate, Engholm (1991:115–16) suggests a number of ways that Asians say "no" without coming right out and saying it. In response to a Westerner's question: "Has my proposal been accepted?" an Asian businessperson is likely to reply in a number of different ways:

*The conditional "yes":* "If everything proceeds as planned, the proposal will be approved."

*The counterquestion:* "Have you submitted a copy of your proposal to the Ministry of Electronics?"

*The question is criticized:* "Your question is difficult to answer."

*The question is refused:* "We cannot answer this question at this time."

*The tangential reply:* "Will you be staying longer than you originally planned?"

*The "yes, but . . . " reply:* "Yes, approval looks likely, but. . . . The meaning of "but" could mean "it might not be approved."

*The answer is delayed:* "You will know shortly."

*The Japanese use verbal understatement, while Arabs frequently use "verbal overkill."*

In these same high-context societies that rely on relatively restricted codes, it is not unusual to leave sentences unfinished or to tolerate intermittent periods of silence. Whereas most Westerners try to make their point as quickly and straightforwardly as possible, many Eastern cultures value silence as a major element of their rhetorical styles. Silence allows Japanese communicators, for example, to gain a better feel for their partners, and for this reason, they are not reluctant to let long silences develop. The radically different meaning of silence in Japan as compared to the West is well described by Morsbach:

> These silences are frequently misunderstood by Westerners, who tend to interpret them as noncomprehension, and therefore try to shorten the silence by explaining their point once again, or by moving on to the next topic. Well meaning attempts to make the Japanese partner(s) "speak up" often tend to cause silent frustration and resentment since, from the Japanese viewpoint, the Westerners are often seen as being the culprits who should rather be taught how to "shut up." (1982:310)

Simply put, in certain Asian societies rhetorical ambiguity results from restricted codes, and successful communication depends on a sensitivity to the nonverbal context. Other speech communities, such as certain Arabic cultures, are equally imprecise, but for exactly the opposite reason. That is, they engage in overassertion, exaggeration, and repetition. The Arabic language is filled with forms of verbal exaggeration. For example, certain common ending words are meant to be emphasized; frequently certain pronouns will be repeated in order to fully dramatize the message; highly graphic metaphors and similes are common; and it is not at all uncommon to hear an Arabic speaker use a long list of adjectives to modify a single noun for the sake of emphasizing the point.

This linguistic propensity for verbal overkill was the subject of research conducted by Prothro (1955), who rated groups of Arabs and North Americans on a continuum of understatement and overstatement. This study concluded that Arabs were considerably more likely to overstate the case than were North Americans. What would be an assertive statement to a North American might appear to be weak and equivocating to an Arab. Even though verbal threats are commonplace in the Arabic language, they tend to function more as a psychological catharsis than as an accurate description of the speaker's real intentions. It should be kept in mind that this rhetorical feature of linguistic overassertion is just another form of verbal ambiguity or inexactness because it fails to send direct, precise messages.

## LANGUAGE AND SOCIAL CONTEXT

The understanding of linguistic differences in international business can be further complicated by the fact that people frequently speak several different languages or different forms of the same language *depending on the social situation*. Bilingualism (or multilingualism) is the most obvious form of situational language use, for a person may speak one language at home, another language at work, and still another language in the marketplace. But people who speak only one language also switch styles of language. For example, the expressions college students use when speaking to one another in the dormitory are noticeably different from the forms of expression they use when they are conversing with their ministers, their grandparents, or their professors. Levels of formality between speakers, relative status, and sex and age of the speakers can frequently determine what is said and how it is said. As Farb (1974:43) has put it, "between the grammar of my language and its expression in audible speech lies the filter of the social system in which I live."

Depending on who is addressing him, a man could be referred to as *Dr. Allen, Richard, Dick, Sir, Sweetheart, Doc,* or *Fella,* among others. It is not likely that his wife or mother would address him as *Dr. Allen,* nor is it likely that the nurses at the hospital would refer to him as *Dick* or *Fella.* Moreover, the same person may use different terms of address in different social situations. His wife may address him as *Dick* at the dinner table, *Sweetheart* while making love, and *Richard* if they are engaged in an argument.

It has been shown (Brown & Ford, 1961) that in the United States people are addressed by either (FN) first name (*Richard*) or by (TLN) title and last name (*Dr. Allen*), depending on the level of formality and relative social status between the speakers. In the American English context there are only three possible combinations of address between two people: (1) reciprocal use of TLN, as in the exchange "Hello, Professor Davis"; "Good evening, Mrs. Bolton"; (2) reciprocal use of FN, as in the exchange "What's happening, Jack?"; "Not much, Norm"; and (3) nonreciprocal use of TLN and FN, as in the exchange "Good morning, Dr. Graves"; "Hello, Ricky." The first two exchanges—both reciprocal—imply relatively equal status between the speakers. The first situation indicates a formal, nonintimate relationship, whereas the second situation indicates an informal, more intimate relationship. Unlike the first two cases, the third case (TLN/FN) is indicative of marked status inequality, either differences in age (that is, children and adults) or differences in rank within an organization (teacher/student; executive/secretary; surgeon/nurse).

In the Javanese language every speech situation (not just terms of address) re-

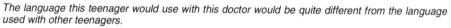

*The language this teenager would use with this doctor would be quite different from the language used with other teenagers.*

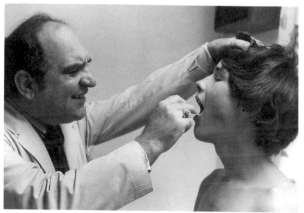

quires the speaker to make choices that reflect the relative social status of the person being addressed. Before a word is uttered the speaker must choose one of three basic linguistic styles: the plain, the fancy, and the elegant. In addition, the Javanese speaker can use special terms known as "honorifics," which enable the speaker to express minute gradations of social respect within each of these three styles. As Farb has noted

> He has no choice but to inform his listener exactly what he thinks of him—because the style he selects reveals whether he considers the listener worthy of low speech, the middle-ground fancy speech, or elegant speech, with or without honorifics. (1974:44)

Not only is social status reflected in speech patterns, but frequently linguistic differences can be observed in the same speech community between men and women. Sometimes the distinctions between the sexes are reflected in vocabulary. In some languages these vocabulary differences are not simply a matter of relative frequency of usage; rather there are pairs of words (doublets) carrying the same meanings, one word being a male word and one word being a female word. To illustrate, among the Island Carib of the West Indies, women use the word *kuyu* for rain and men use the word *kunobu;* many more doublet nouns are found in this language (Hickerson, 1980:91). In Koasati, a native language of southwestern Louisiana, differences appear in certain indicative and imperative verb forms depending on the sex of the speaker. Koasati men say *lakawho's* to mean "lift it," whereas Koasati women would use the word *lakawhol* (Haas, 1964:228). Thus, in this case grammatical forms are chosen to match the sex of the speaker rather than the referent.

Sex differences can also be seen in more subtle areas of language such as intonation, loudness, assertiveness, and style. For example, according to Kramer (1974) women in the United States speak less forcefully than men as evidenced by their more frequent use of qualifiers (for example, "It may just be my opinion but . . . ") or the practice of following a declarative statement with such questions as "isn't it?" or "wouldn't you agree?" Moreover, women in the United States tend to speak more "properly" than men by using less profanity, by using certain polite expletives such as "my gracious," and by using such intensifiers as *so* and *such* (as in the expression "I am *so* delighted to see you").

---

Sometimes U.S. businesspersons can get themselves into hot water by assuming that foreigners are unable to understand English. Barnum and Wolniansky (1989:53) tell of a representative of a U.S. aircraft manufacturer riding into Cairo from the airport with his American colleague and an Egyptian chauffeur. As the two Americans chatted, one made a somewhat disparaging remark about Egyptians' ability to handle the aircraft they were purchasing from the American firm. Unfortunately, the Egyptian chauffeur's understanding of English was much better than the American had thought. The chauffeur relayed the contents of this remark to a colleague, who contacted the minister of defense, who, in turn, contacted the U.S. ambassador. Within 48 hours, the insensitive businessman had been deported from Egypt.

---

Variations in language usage according to age appear to be even more widespread than those based on sex. One particularly commonplace occurrence is "baby talk," a specialized form of language used to communicate with children. In the English language we sometimes hear adults use such terms as *night-night* (for *good night*), *choo-choo* (for *train*), or *woof-woof* (for *dog*). Although English baby talk is quite unsystematic (to the extent that it is used inconsistently), other languages, such as Comanche, have a very well defined and consistently used form of baby talk. According to Casagrande (1948:11–14) the Comanche use about 40 words and phrases covering general topics of communication such as *nana* (meaning "it might hurt") and *koko* (referring to candy, cookies, or between-meal snacks). Interestingly enough, these Comanche words have several things in common with the baby talk found in most other parts of the world: They use simple sounds in a repetitive fashion. Regardless of where we might find it, the relatively widespread occurrence of baby talk serves to remind us that variations of a language can depend on the age of the speaker or the age of the person being addressed.

## SOME ADDITIONAL COMPLICATING FACTORS:
## SLANG, EUPHEMISMS, PROVERBS, AND VERBAL DUELING

To function effectively in any language community it is necessary to know not only the formal structure of the language (vocabulary and grammar, for example) but also how it is used in different social situations. We have seen that what is said and how it is said can vary depending on the sex, age, or relative social status of the speakers. In other words, to understand linguistic communication in an international business context, it is necessary to understand the social context in which the communication is taking place, or as the anthropological linguist would put it, the ethnography of speaking.

To further complicate the learning of another language, most languages, for a variety of cultural reasons, employ certain nonstandard forms such as slang, word avoidances, euphemisms, proverbs, and various types of verbal dueling.

### Slang

Slang has been defined as "very informal usage in vocabulary and idiom that is characteristically more metaphorical, playful, elliptical, vivid, and ephemeral than ordinary language" (Stein, 1979:1235). This definition should not lead us to conclude that slang is the language of the common people. Instead, slang should be viewed as the speech of those who consider themselves to be part of a particular subgroup within the wider linguistic community. In certain northern U.S. cities, blacks use such slang terms as *hawks* ("strong winds"), *oreo* ("a person who is black on the outside but white on the inside"), and *bad* ("good"). Jazz musicians, computer buffs, teenagers, hookers, psychologists, and truck drivers are just several subgroups within the United States that have their own slang. The importance of slang, whether we are referring to the speech of black New Yorkers or that of truck drivers, is that it helps determine who is a member of an in-group and who is not. Slang presents several important problems for the person trying to learn a second language. First, slang increases the possible variations of expressions in any given speech community. And second, since many slang words are used for only several years before disappearing or becoming incorporated into the standard form of the language, it is difficult to keep up with current slang trends.

### Euphemisms

Behavioral and verbal taboos exist in all known societies. That is, there are certain categories of words that should be avoided in normal, polite parlance. In many, but certainly not all, cases, the prohibited words are associated with sexual relations and everyday bodily functions such as menstruating, urinating, and defecating. Whatever words may be deemed to be taboo by a language, it is a fairly arbitrary process, for a word prohibited in one speech community may be perfectly acceptable in another. Taboo words are dealt with through the use of euphemisms—that is, by substituting a bland, vague, or indirect expression for one thought to be too direct, harsh, or blunt. In the English language, for example, the subject of death is so unpleasant that we have developed an entire system of euphemisms to avoid dealing with the subject in a direct way. People don't die, they "pass away." Those in charge of burials are no longer undertakers but are now "funeral directors." Corpses are not buried in graves, but rather the "dearly departed" are "interred" in "memorial parks." And hearses, which clearly are single-purpose vehicles, are now euphemistically called "coaches."

Even though the English language has more than its share of euphemisms, this practice of substituting vague words for more precise ones can be found to some degree in all languages. Again, the existence of taboo words and euphemisms presents yet another obstacle to second language learning for the international businessperson. The learner must become familiar with the prevailing value system of the particular speech community to understand which topics can legitimately be dealt with in a direct and straightforward manner. Without such an understanding it will be impossible to know when to use a bland expression and when not to.

### Proverbs

Another nonstandard form of language that must be mastered is the general category of proverbs, aphorisms, and maxims. These wise sayings, regardless of where they might be found, have certain things in common with one another: (1) They deal with the essential truths as defined by the culture; (2) they are usually expressed simply and concretely, though often metaphorically; and (3) they advise and instruct how people should comport themselves. The English language is filled with pithy proverbial expressions (for example, Burton Stevenson's *The Home Book of Proverbs, Maxims and Familiar Phrases,* 1948, contains 2,666 pages of English proverbs) that are widely understood if not always used on a regular basis:

The early bird catches the worm.

All that glitters is not gold.

He who lingers is lost.

A penny saved is a penny earned.

Too many cooks spoil the broth.

It is wise to risk no more than one can afford to lose.

Early to bed, early to rise, makes a man healthy, wealthy and wise.

Proverbs are found in all languages and are related to other forms of folk literature, such as riddles, fables, and myths. A cross-cultural examination of proverbs reveals that the same basic idea can appear in two widely divergent and unrelated languages. For example, the biblical injunction "an eye for an eye, a tooth for a tooth" can be found in the Nandi (East African) proverb "A goat's hide buys a goat's hide and a gourd a gourd." And of course, many similarities in the style and substance of proverbs can be identified in geographically contiguous speech communities. The proverb "A bird in the hand is worth two in the bush" originated with Latin but can be found today in the Romanian, Spanish, Portuguese, German, and Icelandic languages.

Since proverbs tend to be recited in the present tense, people tend to think of them as being universally applicable, as relevant guides for living today as they have been in the past and will continue to be in the future. Different societies rely on proverbs to varying degrees as guides for present behavior. An important part of mastering a second language is understanding both the meanings of proverbs and how seriously they are taken as prescriptions for behavior.

### Verbal Dueling

In certain speech communities, and under specified conditions, people are encouraged to engage in competitive communication, in which the speakers are more concerned with asserting their dominance than with imparting information. One particularly well documented example of verbal dueling from our own society is an institutionalized form of insult contest played by urban black adolescent males—"playing the dozens." This form of verbal dueling begins when one player insults a member of the opponent's family, in most cases his mother. Although the person whose family member has been disparaged can choose not to play, in most cases he will retort with a counter insult of his own. These insulting verbal thrusts and parries will continue until the participants get bored or someone emerges victorious, with both participants being incited by an attentive audience.

A similar type of verbal game is played by Turkish male adolescents. The objective of the Turkish version is to call into question a young man's virility, thereby forcing him into a subordinate role. Even societies that have reputations for being particularly peaceful in nature, such as the Eskimos, engage in verbal dueling. In fact, it is not surprising to find verbal dueling in nonaggressive societies, for its serves as an effective mechanism for diffusing personal enmity by the use of words rather than weapons.

In some cases verbal dueling can be carried out at a national level. According to Ya'ari and Friedman (1991), all three of the major players in the 1991 Gulf War (Iraq, Kuwait, and Saudi Arabia) used an archaic rhetorical art form to exchange insults over the airwaves. This traditional form of verbal dueling, known as *hija,* dates back to biblical times when warriors (such as Goliath) would loudly ridicule their opponents while boasting of their own prowess. This ancient literary tradition of "cursing in verse" was based on the notion that one could gain a supernatural advantage by insulting one's adversaries in rhyme. The *hija* form of verbal dueling—which has its own format, meters, and rhyming patterns—begins with boastful self-praise and then proceeds to vitriolic insults. Immediately after the Iraqi invasion of Kuwait in August 1990, the Saudi, Iraqi, and Kuwaiti television stations broadcasted hours of uninterrupted *hija* poetry, praising themselves while berating the opposition. The content of the dueling poets was scathing. To illustrate, because the allied forces included some women, the Iraqi *hija* poets ridiculed the Saudis for hiding behind the skirts of women, a direct and unequivocal insult to their virility. On the other side, Saudi *hija* poets composed brutal verses that accused Saddam Hussein of attacking his neighbors at night, of being ungrateful for the help given him in his earlier efforts against the Iranians, and, the ultimate insult, of being a Jew.

All of these forms of verbal dueling—be they found in a Philadelphia ghetto, a Turkish village, the Alaskan tundra, or in the Middle East—are examples of nonstandard forms of language use that must be understood if the second-language learner is to appreciate fully the subtleties of the communication patterns in the international marketplace.

## CONCLUSION

It has been estimated conservatively that there are some 3,000 mutually unintelligible languages in the world today. Some of them have hundreds of millions of speakers, whereas some have only hundreds. Yet despite the diversity in the size of different linguistic communities, no languages are inherently more efficient at expressing a wide range of ideas than others. Thus, there is no reason for English-speaking businesspeople to harbor a linguistic superiority complex.

As has been pointed out in this chapter, learning a language requires time, hard work, and dedication on the part of the learner and a sense of commitment on the part of the employer. Even after one masters the vocabulary, grammar, and syntax of a second language it is still possible, even likely, to engage in verbal miscommunication. First, it is frequently impossible to translate some ideas from one language into another without a loss of some meaning. Second, some languages rely more on the explicit spoken word, whereas others rely more on the use of nonverbal cues and communication context. Third, people frequently speak different forms of the same language, depending on the social situation in which the communication takes place. And finally, to further complicate communication, all languages, to some extent, use nonstandard forms such as slang and euphemisms.

Yet despite the formidable task learning a second language is for most people in the United States, there are many good reasons to justify the effort:

- Learning the host language builds rapport and sets the proper tone for doing business abroad.
- Knowledge of the local linguistic categories greatly helps to understand the world view of the culture.

- Learning a second language facilitates learning other languages.
- To provide the best possible medical care for oneself and one's family it is vital to be able to communicate clearly the nature of a medical problem to local medical personnel that do not speak English.
- With the increasing threat of terrorism against U.S. citizens, a knowledge of the local language might prevent involvement, injury, or death.

In addition to all these cogent reasons, perhaps the best reason for learning a second language is for personal enjoyment. Since language is the best way to get "inside" another culture, the time and effort spent on language training can mean the difference between a hardship assignment and an intellectually and personally rewarding overseas business assignment.

### CROSS-CULTURAL SCENARIOS

Read the following cross-cultural scenarios. In each mini-case study there is a basic cultural conflict between the actors involved. Try to identify the source of the conflict and suggest how it could have been avoided or minimized. Then see how well your analyses compare to the explanations in the Appendix.

**3–1.** Frank McDougal had been chosen to set up a branch office of his engineering consulting firm in Seoul, Korea. Although the six engineering consultants who would eventually be transferred to Seoul were Americans, Frank was interested in hiring local support staff. He was particularly interested in hiring a local person with excellent accounting skills to handle the company's books. He was quite confident that he would be able to find the right person for the job because his company was prepared to offer an excellent salary and benefits package. After receiving what he considered to be several excellent leads from a friend at the Rotary Club, he was quite surprised to be turned down by all four prospective candidates. They were very appreciative of being considered for the position but all preferred to stay with their current employer. Frank just couldn't understand why all four of these Koreans chose to pass up an increase in salary and fringe benefits.

HOW WOULD YOU EXPLAIN THIS SITUATION TO FRANK?

**3–2.** Tom Forrest, an up-and-coming executive for a U.S. electronics company, was sent to Japan to work out the details of a joint venture with a Japanese electronics firm. During the first several weeks Tom felt that the negotiations were proceeding better than he had expected. He found that he had very cordial working relationships with the team of Japanese executives, and in fact, they had agreed on the major policies and strategies governing the new joint venture. During the third week of negotiations Tom was present at a meeting held to review their progress. The meeting was chaired by the president of the Japanese firm, Mr. Hayakawa, a man in his mid-40s, who had recently taken over the presidency from his 82-year-old grandfather. The new president, who had been involved in most of the negotiations during the preceding weeks, seemed to Tom to be one of the strongest advocates of the plan that had been developed to date. Also attending the meeting was Hayakawa's grandfather, the recently retired president. After the plans had been discussed in some detail, the octogenarian past president proceeded to give a long soliloquy about how some of the features of this plan violated the traditional practices on which the company had been founded. Much to Tom's amazement, Mr. Hayakawa did nothing to explain or defend the policies and strategies that they had taken weeks to develop. Feeling extremely frustrated, Tom then gave a fairly strongly argued defense of the plan. To Tom's further amazement, no one else in the meeting spoke up in defense of the plan. The tension in the air was quite heavy and the meeting adjourned shortly thereafter. Within days the Japanese firm completely terminated the negotiations on the joint venture.

HOW COULD YOU HELP TOM BETTER UNDERSTAND THIS BEWILDERING SITUATION?

**3–3.** After graduating fourth in his class from a highly ranked engineering school, Eric Anderson took a job with an international construction company that had major contracts throughout the world. As a child Eric had traveled widely with his parents and had never lost his interest in other cultures and other parts of the world. After a six-month orientation in the home office in California, Eric was excited about his assignment as a consulting engineer on a new multi-million-dollar government office building in a West African country. For the first several months Eric worked with a team of people planning the project before the actual construction began. Since Eric had shown a high aptitude for learning foreign languages in college, he was seen as the most "international" of all the American engineers on the project and was asked by the project manager to enroll in a full-time language course so that he would be able to communicate directly with the local construction workers and supervisors.

The intensive language training went reasonably well for the first several weeks, but after the first month Eric's interest in the course declined considerably. After six weeks, despite the fact that the instructor had nothing but praise for Eric's progress, Eric became increasingly discouraged with the language training and eventually asked to be transferred to another project.

WHY DID ERIC BECOME SO DISSATISFIED?

**3–4.** A large Baltimore manufacturer of cabinet hardware had been working for months to locate a suitable distributor for its products in Europe. Finally invited to present a demonstration to a reputable distributing company in Frankfurt, it sent one of its most promising young executives, Fred Wagner, to make the presentation. Fred not only spoke fluent German but also felt a special interest in this assignment because his paternal grandparents had immigrated to the United States from the Frankfurt area during the 1920s. When Fred arrived at the conference room where he would be making his presentation he shook hands firmly, greeted everyone with a friendly *Guten Tag,* and even remembered to bow the head slightly as is the German custom. Fred, a very effective speaker and past president of the Baltimore Toastmasters Club, prefaced his presentation with a few humorous anecdotes to set a relaxed and receptive atmosphere. However, he felt that his presentation was not very well received by the company executives. In fact, his instincts were correct, for the German company chose not to distribute Fred's hardware products.

WHAT WENT WRONG?

**3–5.** Betty Carpenter, president of a cosmetics firm headquartered in Chicago, was interested in expanding its European markets. After attending a four-day trade show in London, she decided to spend several days in Paris talking to some potential distributors of their more popular product lines. She figured that the three years of college French she had taken while an undergraduate at Radcliffe would hold her in good stead with her business contacts in Paris. Upon arrival she felt quite confident with her proficiency in French in getting from the airport and checking into her hotel. The next morning she met with Monsieur DuBois, vice president of a large French department store chain. Although their initial conversation went quite well, when the subject turned to business Betty felt that she was not communicating very effectively with DuBois. He seemed to be getting mildly annoyed and showed little interest in continuing the discussions.

WHAT WAS BETTY'S PROBLEM?

# 4

# COMMUNICATING ACROSS CULTURES: THE NONVERBAL DIMENSION

Successful communication in the international business environment requires not only an understanding of language but also the nonverbal aspects of communication that are part of any speech community. Nonverbal communication has been referred to as *metacommunication, paralinguistics, second-order messages,* the *silent language,* and the *hidden dimension* of communication, among other terms. As important as language is to the sending and receiving of messages, nonverbal communication is equally important because it helps us interpret the linguistic messages being sent. Nonverbal cues frequently indicate whether verbal messages are serious, threatening, jocular, and so on. In addition, nonverbal communication is responsible in its own right for the majority of messages sent and received as part of the human communication process. In fact, it has been suggested on a number of occasions that only about 30 percent of communication between two people in the same speech community is verbal in nature. In a cross-cultural situation (as is likely in international business), when people are not from the same speech community, they will rely even more heavily on nonverbal cues.

## THE NATURE OF NONVERBAL COMMUNICATION

Nonverbal communication functions in several important ways in regulating human interaction. It is an effective way of (1) sending messages about our feelings and emotional states, (2) elaborating on our verbal messages, and (3) governing the timing and turn taking between communicators. Even though some nonverbal cues function in similar ways in many cultures, there are also considerable differences in nonverbal patterns that can result in breakdowns in communication in a cross-cultural context. The literature is filled with scenarios of how a misreading of nonverbal cues leads directly to cross-cultural friction. The need to master the nonverbal repertoire of another culture—in addition to gaining linguistic competence—increases the challenge of working successfully in an international business setting. Yet, as has been suggested by Collett (1971), people who know the nonverbal cues of another culture will be better liked by members of that culture, and by implication, will have a greater chance for successful interaction.

In much the same way that languages are arbitrary systems of communication, the nonverbal aspects also display a certain arbitrariness, to the extent that there is a wide range of alternative ways of expressing ideas and emotions nonverbally. The enormous range of nonverbal expressions found throughout the world clearly demonstrates two broad categories of differences: (1) when the same nonverbal cue carries with it very different meanings in different cultures and (2) when different nonverbal cues carry the same meaning in different cultures.

Often the same gesture has different, or even opposite, meanings. Hissing, for example, used as a somewhat rude way of indicating disapproval of a speaker in U.S. society, is used as a normal way to ask for silence in certain Spanish-speaking countries and as a way of applauding among the Basuto of southern Africa. In U.S. society protruding one's tongue is an unmistakable gesture of mocking contempt, whereas in southern China it is an expression of embarrassment over a faux pas (LaBarre, 1947:57). The hand gesture of inserting the thumb between the index and third fingers is a sign for good luck in Portugal but an invitation to have sex in Germany. And the hand gesture of putting one's index finger to the temple communicates "he is smart" in the United States but can mean just the opposite—"he is stupid"—in certain western European cultures.

In contrast, the same message can be sent in various cultures by very different nonverbal cues. To illustrate, in the United States and most western European societies the nonverbal cue for affirmation (that is, signifying "yes" or agreement) is nodding the head up and down. Despite contentions by early twentieth-century psychologists that such a nonverbal gesture is natural or instinctive to all humans, we now know that affirmation is in fact communicated nonverbally in a variety of different ways. For example, affirmation is signaled among the Semang of Malaya by thrusting the head forward sharply, in Ethiopia by throwing the head back, among the Dyaks of Borneo by raising the eyebrows, among the Ainu of northern Japan by bringing both hands to the chest and then gracefully waving them downward with palms up, and by rocking the head from shoulder to shoulder among the Bengali servants of Calcutta (Jensen, 1982:264–65).

The last decade has witnessed a dramatic increase in research on the general topic of nonverbal communication. Like any new field of study, what constitutes the subject matter of nonverbal communication has not always met with widespread agreement. Classifications of nonverbal behavior vary from the threefold scheme of Eisenberg and Smith (1971) to the typology of Condon and Yousef (1975:123–24), which includes 24 categories. Despite the many alternative ways of categorizing the domain of nonverbal communication, the following topics are found widely in the literature:

- Facial expressions (smiles, frowns)
- Hand gestures
- Walking (gait)
- Posture
- Space usage (proxemics)
- Touching

- Eye contact
- Olfaction (scents or smells such as perfume)
- Color symbolism
- Artifacts ( jewelry, fly wisks, lapel pins, etc.)
- Clothing
- Hairstyles
- Cosmetics
- Time symbolism
- Graphic symbols
- Silence

A thorough discussion of all these aspects of nonverbal communication would take us beyond the scope of this book. However, to convey the importance of nonverbal communication in an international business context, we will examine some of the more obvious domains in some detail. This discussion will be limited to those nonverbal phenomena that most significantly affect interpersonal communication, including posture, gestures, touching, facial expressions, eye contact, and the use of space. Before such a discussion, however, it is imperative that we first understand some of the potential pitfalls of studying nonverbal communication in the international business environment.

First, there is the potential hazard of overgeneralization. We frequently hear references made to such geographical areas as the Middle East, Latin America, or sub-Saharan Africa, yet these are hardly appropriate units of analysis for observing patterns of nonverbal communication. In sub-Saharan Africa alone there are over 40 independent nation-states and more than 800 different linguistic communities that speak mutually unintelligible languages. Yet we cannot count on uniformity even within a single speech community, for even here there are likely to be internal variations in nonverbal communication patterns depending on such variables as class, education, occupation, and religion. For example, many of Edward Hall's insightful conclusions on Arab nonverbal communication (discussed subsequently) are based on the observations of middle- and upper-class males, largely students and businesspersons. It is not very likely that Arab females would conform to the same patterns of nonverbal communication as the Arab males that Hall describes. Thus, it is advisable to exercise some caution when generalizing even within a single culture or speech community.

A second potential obstacle is the unwarranted assumption that within any given speech community all nonverbal cues are of equal importance. Some nonverbal patterns may be rarely used and imperfectly understood, whereas others are more widely used and universally understood.

A third possible pitfall lies in overemphasizing the differences between cultures in terms of their nonverbal communication patterns. Although this chapter focuses on the great variety of nonverbal patterns found throughout the world, it should be remembered that there are also many nonverbal similarities between different speech communities. The problem, of course, for the international businessperson is to distinguish between them.

Finally, we should avoid thinking that the consequences of misunderstanding nonverbal cues are always catastrophic. To be certain, the misreading of some nonverbal cues can lead to the misinterpretation of social meanings, which in turn can result in serious breakdowns in communication and the generation of hostility. Many other nonverbal cues, on the other hand, have no such dire consequences but rather can lead to minor irritations or even amusement. Although it is necessary to remember that the misreading of all nonverbal cues is not a matter of life and death, it is equally important to remember that the greater knowledge we have of the nonverbal cues found in the international business environment, the greater will be our chances of successful communication and the achievement of our personal and professional objectives.

Having mentioned these methodological caveats, we can now turn to a brief examination of some of the more salient areas of nonverbal communication. The following discussion of such subdivisions as posture, gestures, and space usage should not suggest that these points are isolated or unrelated to one another. This approach is used here solely for purposes of presentation and should not be interpreted as denying or overlooking the very real connections between these aspects of nonverbal communication found in any speech community.

## BODY POSTURE

The way that people hold their bodies frequently communicates information about their social status, religious practices, feelings of submissiveness, desires to maintain social distance, and sexual intentions, to mention only several areas. When communicating, people tend to orient their bodies toward others by assuming a certain stance or posture. A person can stand over another person, can kneel, or can "turn a cold shoulder," and in each case something different would be communicated by the body posture. Postural cues constitute very effective signs of a person's inner state as well as his or her behavioral expectations of others.

It has been suggested (Hewes, 1955:231) that the human body is capable of assuming approximately a thousand different body postures. Of course, which body position any given culture chooses to emphasize will be learned by the same process by which other aspects of culture are internalized. To illustrate this point, we can look at differences in body posture that people assume when relaxing. People in the United States, for example, are sitters, whereas people in some rural parts of Mexico are squatters. This basic cultural difference has actually been used by the U.S. Border Patrol to identify illegal migrants. According to Samovar and Porter (1991:192), by flying surveillance planes at low altitudes over migrant worker camps in southern California, the Border Patrol can tell which groups of campers are squatting and which are sitting, the implication being that the squatters are the illegal aliens.

When people are interacting in a cross-cultural environment, sharp differences can be seen in terms of what postures are taken and what meanings they convey. For example, in the United States we stand up to show respect, whereas in certain Polynesian cultures people sit down. We frequently lean back in our chairs and put our feet on our desks to convey a relaxed, informal attitude, but the Swiss and Germans would think such posture rude. And for many people squatting is the most normal position for relaxing, yet for the typical North American it seems improper, "uncivilized," or at least not terribly sophisticated.

Sometimes we can inadvertently choose a body posture that will have disastrous results. Condon and Yousef describe such a case:

The British professor of poetry relaxed during his lecture at Ain Shams University in Cairo. So carried away was he in explicating a poem that he leaned back in his chair and so revealed the sole of his foot to an astonished class. To make such a gesture in a Moslem society is the worst kind of insult. The Cairo newspapers the next day carried banner headlines about the student demonstration which resulted, and they denounced British arrogance and demanded that the professor be sent home. (1975:122)

Perhaps one of the most visible and dramatic nonverbal messages sent by posture or body stance is that of submissiveness. Generally, submissiveness is conveyed by making oneself appear smaller, by cringing, crouching, cowering, or grovelling. The idea behind this submissive posture is that the submissive individual is so weak, small, and nonthreatening that he or she is hardly worth attacking. In its most extreme form, we can see prisoners of war crouching before their captors in a squatting position, heads lowered, with their bodies curled up. In its mildest form we can notice a subordinate person bending ever so slightly at the waist (bowing) in the direction of the superordinate person. This form of bowing is a very subtle and temporary lowering of the body in deference to the higher-status person.

The degree to which a bowing or lowering of the body is emphasized varies from one culture to another. In many cultures today the full bow or other dramatic lowering of the body is generally reserved for formal occasions such as greeting a head of state or monarch or as part of certain religious ceremonies. For example, British commoners standing before the queen or being honored by royalty in a ceremony of knighthood would be expected to bow, curtsey, or kneel. As part of their religious practices some Christians kneel, Catholics genuflect, and Muslims kowtow, an extreme form of body lowering in which the forehead is brought to the ground. Although bowing as a world-wide phenomenon has been on the decrease in recent decades, it has survived in German culture and exists to an even greater degree in modern Japan, where bows are an integral part of everyday social interaction. In the United States, however, bowing or any type of submissive body posture is particularly irritating, for it tends to connote undue formality, aristocracy, and a nonverbal denial of egalitarianism.

Nowhere is bowing more important to the process of communication today than in Japanese society. As an indication of how pervasive bowing is in present-day Japan, Morsbach reports that "some female department store employees have the sole function of bowing to customers at department store escalators" and that many Japanese "bow repeatedly to invisible partners at the other end of a telephone line" (1982:307). Bowing initiates interaction between two Japanese, it enhances and embellishes many parts of the ensuing conversation, and it is used to signal the end of a conversation. Although

*How deeply a person bows in Japan communicates relative social status.*

Westerners, in a very general sense, understand the meaning attached to bowing, appropriate bowing in Japan is an intricate and complex process. Reciprocal bowing is determined largely by rank. In fact, it is possible to tell the relative social status of the two communicators by the depth of their bows (the deeper the bow, the lower the status). When bowing deeply, it is conventional to lean slightly to the right to avoid bumping heads. The person of lower status is expected to initiate the bow, and the person of higher status determines when the bow is completed. People of equivalent status are expected to bow at the same depth while starting and finishing at the same time. And as Befu relates, this synchronization is an important feature:

> . . . the matter of synchrony, in fact perfect synchrony, is absolutely essential to bowing. Whenever an American tries to bow to me, I often feel extremely awkward and uncomfortable because I simply cannot synchronize bowing with him or her . . . bowing occurs in a flash of a second, before you have time to think. And both parties must know precisely when to start bowing, how deep, how long to stay in the bowed position, and when to bring their heads up. (1979:118)

How we position ourselves when communicating with another person is also culturally variable. To turn one's back on someone is a clear nonverbal indicator in the United States (and in many other societies as well) of an unwillingness to converse at all. But the degree to which two people are expected to face one another in normal conversation is not the same in all cultures. Even though two white, middle-class North Americans have no difficulty conversing while walking next to each other with an occasional turn of the head, Edward Hall (1966:160–61) found it to be a major problem when attempting to walk and talk in this fashion with an Arabic friend. While they walked the

Arab stopped to face Hall each time he spoke. Since many Arabic cultures insist on a high degree of eye contact when conversing, conversants must be facing one another directly. Hall soon discovered that to talk while walking side by side without maintaining intense eye contact was considered rude by the Arab's standards. This example illustrates not only how body stance or position communicates different messages but also how two domains of nonverbal communication—body position and gaze—are intimately interconnected.

## HAND GESTURES

Until very recently the importance of hand gestures has been largely unnoticed. Nonverbal communication in general and hand gestures in particular have long been considered a trivial aspect of communication, especially in the Western world. Since we are told that language (that is, the capacity to use words to symbolize) is the hallmark of our humanity, we tend to consider all other forms of communication as pedantic and unimportant. But human communication is greatly enriched by the nonverbal component, and in fact the very meaning of words can change depending on the accompanying hand gestures. Harrison (1974:135) offers an illustration from the English language. The words "Just let me say . . ." when used with the gesture of the hand up, palm facing the addressee, are likely to mean "Wait, let me say. . . ." These same words with the gesture of the hand out, palm facing downward, would most likely imply "Let me tell you how it really is. . . ." And finally to utter these words with the hand out, palm facing upward, would mean "It seems to me. . . ." Thus, these three different palm orientations can provide three quite different meanings to the same words. Obviously, words are nearly indispensable for the communication of facts, but without hand gestures the human communication process would be mechanical and less capable of subtle nuances.

The use of fingers, hands, and arms for purposes of communicating varies considerably from one culture to another. Some cultures (for example, those located in southern Europe and the Middle East) employ a wide variety of gestures frequently and with considerable force and purposefulness. The half-jocular notion that Italians would be unable to express themselves if their hands were tied behind their backs is more than a vulgar stereotype. Based on research conducted on Italian and Jewish immigrants in New York City, Efron (1941) found that Italians used broad, full-arm gestures with relative frequency. At the other extreme some indigenous Indian groups in Bolivia use hand gestures very sparingly because the cool highland climate requires them to keep their hands under shawls or blankets (Jensen, 1982:266). And still other cultures, like our own and those found in northern Europe, illustrating a middle position, tend to be more reserved in their use of gestures. These cultures place a higher value on verbal messages and no doubt consider excessive gesturing to be overly emotional, nonrational, and socially unsophisticated.

Unlike verbal communication, which is usually well documented in structure and meaning, the nonverbal aspects of communication in most language communities are very infrequently described, and when they are, those descriptions are usually superficial and incomplete. One of the rare exceptions is the study conducted by Morris et al.

(1979) of 20 major gestures found in western Europe. Data were collected from 40 localities, using 25 languages, in 25 different countries. A sizable number of these gestures, used and understood widely in contemporary Europe, are also used and understood in the United States. There is, for example, general consensus in both the United States and western Europe about the meaning of crossed fingers (good luck), the contemptuous nose thumb, and the sexually insulting forearm jerk. Given our strong European heritage it is not surprising that many European gestures have survived the Atlantic crossing. Yet despite these similarities on both sides of the Atlantic, there are far more gestures used commonly in Europe that have little or no meaning in the United States. Morris and his associates cite the following hand gestures, which are widely used in Europe but have little meaning to the person on the streets of Chicago, Atlanta, or Phoenix:

> *The eyelid pull* (the forefinger is placed below one eye, pulling the skin downward and thereby tugging on the lower eyelid—meaning "I am alert" or "Be alert" in Spain, France, Italy, and Greece.
>
> *The chin stroke* (the thumb and forefinger, placed on each cheek bone, are gently stroked down to the chin)—meaning "thin and ill" in the southern Mediterranean area.
>
> *The earlobe pull or flick* (the earlobe is tugged or flicked with the thumb and forefinger of the hand on the same side of the body)—a sign of effeminacy found predominantly in Italy, meaning "I think you are so effeminate that you should be wearing an earring."
>
> *The nose tap* (the forefinger in a vertical position taps the side of the nose)—meaning "Keep it a secret."

One of the sources of confusion when trying to understand hand gestures in other cultures is that different cultures can use quite different gestures to signify the same idea. Morris (1977:41–42) illustrates this notion by looking at how men in different parts of the world signal their appreciation of a physically attractive female:

> *The cheek stroke* (Greece, Italy, and Spain)—the gesturer places his forefinger and thumb on his cheekbone and strokes them gently toward the chin.
>
> *The cheek screw* (Italy, Sardinia)—the forefinger is pressed into the cheek and rotated.
>
> *The breast curve* (found in a wide range of cultures)—hands simulate the curve of the female breast.
>
> *The waist curve* (common in English-speaking countries)—the hands sweep down to make the curvacious outline of the female trunk.
>
> *The eye touch* (South America, Italy)—a straight forefinger is placed on the lower eyelid and pulled down slightly.
>
> *The two-handed telescope* (Brazil)—the hands are curled one in front of the other as the man looks through them in telescope style.
>
> *The moustache twist* (Italy)—the thumb and forefinger twist an imaginary moustache.
>
> *The hand on heart* (South America)—the right hand is placed over the heart, signifying a "heart throb."
>
> *The fingertip kiss* (France)—the fingertips are kissed and then spread out in the direction of the woman.

*The air kiss* (English-speaking countries)—a man kisses the air in the direction of the woman.

*The cheek pinch* (Sicily)—a man pinches his own cheek.

*The breast cup* (Europe in general)—both hands make a cupping movement in the air, simulating the squeezing of the woman's breast.

By researching the ethnographic literature we could no doubt identify many other hand gestures found in different cultures to signify female attractiveness. However, the major point has been made: that since the human hand is such a precision instrument, and since communication patterns are so arbitrary, there are a vast array of alternative hand gestures to convey any given idea.

Those in high offices are not immune from sending unintentional messages nonverbally when traveling abroad. As his limousine passed a group of protestors in Canberra, Australia, President George Bush early in 1992 held up his first two fingers with the back of his hand toward the protestors. Thinking that he was giving the nonverbal gesture meaning "victory," he failed to realize that in Australia that same hand gesture is equivalent to holding up the middle finger in the United States.

But cross-cultural misunderstandings can also occur when a single hand gesture has a number of different meanings in different parts of the world. For example, most people in the United States know that to signify that something is OK or good one raises one's hand and makes a circle with the thumb and forefinger. However, this very same hand gesture means "zero" or "worthless" to the French, "money" to the Japanese, "male homosexual" in Malta, and a general sexual insult in Sardinia and Greece. Another example—and one that had some serious diplomatic repercussions—is the

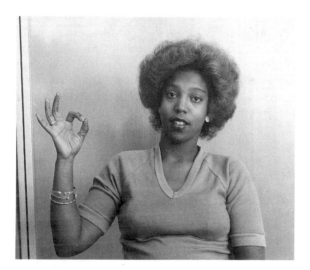

*This gesture has different meanings in different cultures.*

clasped-hands-over-the-head gesture made famous by Soviet Premier Khrushchev on his visit to the United States in the 1960s. Interpreted by North Americans as an arrogant gesture used by victorious prizefighters, it was used by Khrushchev as a gesture of international friendship.

## FACIAL EXPRESSIONS

The face is perhaps the single most important part of the body for channeling nonverbal communication. It is particularly rich in its potential for communicating emotional states, and it has been suggested that next to speech, the face is the "primary source of giving information" (Knapp, 1972:68–69). Although in English, and in most other languages as well, there are only a handful of words to refer to specific facial expressions (for example, *smile, frown, grimmace, squint*), human facial muscles are so complex that approximately a thousand different facial expressions are possible (Ekman, Friesen, & Ellsworth, 1972:1). The face is, in fact, so central to the process of communication that we speak of "face-to-face" communication, and English speakers to some extent, and Japanese to a far greater degree, speak of "losing face" in certain unfortunate situations.

There is little question about the importance of the face as a source of nonverbal communication. The face is capable of conveying emotional, attitudinal, and factual information in short periods of time. In addition, the question of facial expressions has been central to the nature-nurture debate surrounding all nonverbal communication. Unlike every other form of nonverbal communication—which tends to be largely culture bound—a substantial body of literature claims that some facial expressions may be innate human traits, regardless of cultural context. Charles Darwin (1872) was the first to propose the notion of certain universal facial expressions, an idea supported more recently by Allport (1924) and Ekman, Friesen, and Ellsworth (1972). All these researchers have attempted to demonstrate that certain emotions are expressed by the same facial expressions in widely diverse cultures, including isolated, preliterate cultures having no contact with the Western world. Some researchers have traveled the globe in search of remote tribal groups that have facial expressions identical to our own. For example, Eibl-Eibesfeldt (1971) contends that all people give a rapid "eyebrow flash" when greeting someone (the eyebrows are instantaneously raised and then lowered). Although this research is not exhaustive, the wide global distribution of this particular facial movement strongly suggests that the behavior is inborn. Moreover, children who were born blind and deaf exhibit the normal repertoire of facial expressions, which would tend to eliminate the possible explanation that they were acquired through the process of learning (Eibl-Eibesfeldt, 1972).

The nature-nurture question has not been settled, and others contend that facial expressions are culture bound. Birdwhistell (1963) has advanced the position that there are no facial expressions with universal meanings and that they are instead the result of cultural, not biological, inheritance. To substantiate this position one has only to examine the variations in smiling behavior throughout the world. LaBarre (1947:52) has distinguished between two well-described cultures in the southwest Pacific—the Papuans, known for their wide use of smiling, and the Dobus, where "dourness reigned." Gorer (1935:10) reports that in certain parts of Africa laughter and smiling are used to express surprise, wonder, and embarrassment, not amusement or happiness. Morsbach (1982:307) has suggested that although smiling can be a sign of joy in Japan, it can also be used to hide displeasure, sorrow, or anger, and the trained observer should be able to distinguish between these two types of smiling. Jensen (1982:265) contends that in some Asian cultures smiling is a sign of weakness, and it is for this reason that teachers avoid smiling in class lest they lose control over their students. Thus, it would appear that despite the fact that all people smile, the meanings attached to this particular facial expression vary widely.

---

Smiles don't always indicate happiness. Engholm (1991:134) relates a personal experience that illustrates the meaning of a smile in China:

> One morning, standing in front of our hotel in Korla, a desert town in the Xinjiand province of China, a United Nations consultant and I saw a tractor-wagon, loaded with masonry rock, hit a ditch and dump its contents upon its driver. . . . Our hotel concierge ran over to examine the situation and gave us the lowdown with a toothy smile: "He dead for sure. Hit his head very hard, I think." We stood there horrified at his seeming indifference, until we remembered that his smile was a shield to protect us—the honored foreign guests—from being disturbed by the event.

---

In some parts of the world it is considered highly desirable to maintain an expressionless face. Nowhere is this ideal more widely adhered to than in Japan, which no doubt accounts for the contention by many Westerners that the Japanese are "inscrutable." According to Morsbach,

> Self-control, thought of as highly desirable in Japan, demands that a man of virtue will not show a negative emotion in his face when shocked or upset by sudden bad news; and if successful, is lauded as *tiazen jijaku to shite* (perfectly calm and collected), or *mayu hitotsu ugokasazu ni* (without even moving an eyebrow). . . . The idea of an expressionless face in situations of great anxiety was strongly emphasized in the *bushido* (way of the warrior) which was the guideline for samurai and the ideal of many others. (1982:308)

This ideal of masking one's emotions is well supported by research conducted by Shimoda, Argyle, and Bitti (1978). English, Italian, and Japanese judges were asked to read or "decode" the nonverbal facial expressions of performers from these three cultural groups. All three sets of judges had the least accuracy reading the facial expressions of the Japanese performers, a result explained by the lack of negative facial expressions.

It is not necessary here to decide which side in this nature-nurture debate is most correct; reality exists somewhere in between these two polarized positions. In other words, no facial expressions are either totally innate or totally acquired by learning. A more reasonable interpretation of the data would be that although certain facial expressions may be universally found throughout the world, specific cultural norms may influence how, when, and why they are used. For example, the stimulus that elicits a particular facial expression may differ from culture to culture. In the United States the sight of a rat running through one's kitchen might elicit fear and/or disgust. In another culture, where rodents are routinely eaten, such a sight might provoke pure joy and delight.

Another factor that would tend to produce cultural differences is that facial expressions are filtered through one's culturally learned display rules. Our culture teaches us what we should feel and how we should show it. It might be appropriate to *intensify* a felt emotion because it is socially expected, such as a display of exaggerated pleasure over receiving a Christmas present that was not particularly attractive or desirable. On other occasions, it might be socially appropriate to *deintensify* or deemphasize an emotion, such as repressing one's delight over winning a large pot in a poker game. In addition, in some situations a culture requires one emotion to mask another, as exemplified by the runner-up in a beauty contest who is expected to suppress her own disappointment by showing happiness for the winner. Or looked at from an intercultural perspective, Morsbach (1982:307) reminds us that the Japanese often mask their sorrow or anger by laughing and smiling. Thus, these socially learned display rules of intensification, deintensification, and masking can modify facial expressions from one cultural context to another. If in fact cultural learning can affect how and to what extent messages are sent by facial expressions, it behooves international businesspeople to become familiar with this critical aspect of nonverbal communication.

## GAZE

All cultures use gaze (eye contact) as a very important mechanism of communicating nonverbally. Heron refers to gaze as "the most fundamental primary mode of interpersonal encounter," for it is where two pairs of eyes come together "that people actually meet (in the strict sense)" (1970:244). Unlike other forms of nonverbal communication, the gaze is particularly salient because it is so noticeable. As Ellsworth has noted,

> For a behavior that involves no noise and little movement, it has a remarkable capacity to draw attention to itself even at a distance. . . . People often use a direct gaze to attract another person's attention in situations where noise or gesticulation are inappropriate. The fact that we expect others to be responsive to our gaze is illustrated by our exasperation when dealing with people who have learned immunity to the effects of a stare, such as waiters. (1975:5–6)

The communicative function of the eyes has not escaped the nonsocial scientists, for as Ralph Waldo Emerson wrote, "One of the most wonderful things in nature is a glance of the eye; it transcends speech; it is the bodily symbol of identity" (cited in Champness, 1970:309). In fact, the eyes are such a powerful force for interpersonal interaction that it is impossible not to communicate through visual behavior. That is, if we maintain eye contact with someone we are communicating just as much as if we avoid eye contact.

Although some aspects of eye communication are partially controlled by physiology, such as pupil dilation, much of the meaning attached to gaze and gaze avoidance is culturally determined. Like many other forms of learned behavior, gaze can be affected by early childhood socialization, as exemplified by Japanese infants who are carried on their mothers' backs and thus have little contact with the mothers' faces. And in later life, cultures tend to be extremely efficient at instilling certain values concerning gaze or its avoidance. Yet whenever it may be internalized, how, when, and to what extent people in different parts of the world use gaze as a communication mechanism varies widely.

One of the best scientifically controlled studies of eye contact in a number of different cultures was conducted by Watson (1970) among foreign exchange students in the United States. Pairs of students were invited into a laboratory and asked to talk on any subject in their native language while being observed from a one-way screen. Watson found that the highest levels of gaze were recorded for Arabs and people from Latin America, and the lowest levels were found among Indians and northern Europeans. These findings lend credence to the earlier statement made by Edward Hall that "Arabs look each other in the eye when talking with an intensity that makes most Americans highly uncomfortable" (1966:161). In addition, Watson also found that within any given group, gaze did not vary according to overseas cultural experience, such as length of time in the United States. This is a good indicator that gaze patterns are fairly rigidly fixed early in life and are relatively unaffected by adult experiences.

There are a number of cultures in which gaze tends to be more important than among middle-class North Americans. For example, in Greece it is customary to look at people in public places, a practice that would make the typical resident of Kansas quite uncomfortable. And in North Africa the Taureg place considerable emphasis on gaze because the other channels of nonverbal communication, such as hands and arms, are covered with clothing. In such cultures a lesser degree of eye contact (such as might be found in the United States) can be viewed as impolite, inattentive, insincere, and aloof.

On the other hand, many societies teach their children to avoid direct eye contact in general or in specific social situations. Argyle and Cook (1976:29) report that among the Wituto and Bororo Indians of South America both parties in a conversation must avoid direct eye contact by looking at some external object while talking. In Japan, rather than looking a person straight in the eyes, one should focus the gaze somewhat lower, around the region of the Adam's apple (Morsbach, 1982:308). The Navajo define eye contact so negatively that they have as part of their folklore a mythical monster named He-Who-Kills-With-His-Eyes who serves to teach Navajo youngsters that to stare can actually kill another person. And in many parts of sub-Saharan Africa direct eye contact must be avoided when addressing a higher-status person. When we interact in an international business context with people from such cultures, we must realize that our insistence on maintaining a relatively high level of gaze could be interpreted as threatening, disrespectful, haughty, or insulting.

Just as there are considerable verbal differences between the English spoken in

England and in the United States, there are also differences in certain nonverbal aspects of communication, such as the use of eyes to send and receive messages. According to Edward Hall,

> Englishmen in [the United States] have trouble . . . when they want to interact. They never know for sure whether an American is listening. We on the other hand, are equally unsure as to whether the English have understood us. Many of these ambiguities in communication center on differences in the use of the eyes. The Englishman is taught to pay strict attention, to listen carefully, which he must do if he is polite and there are not protective walls to screen out sounds. He doesn't bob his head or grunt to let you know he understands. He blinks his eyes to let you know that he has heard you. Americans on the other hand, are taught not to stare. We look the other person straight in the eye without wavering only when we want to be particularly certain that we are getting through to him. (1966:143)

Rules for eye contact in public places also vary from one culture to another. In France, for example, it is quite acceptable for a man to stare blatantly at a woman on the street. In fact, according to Davis, "some French women complain that they feel uncomfortable on American streets—as if they had suddenly become invisible" (1971:68). This is understandable because public eye behavior in the United States is considerably more restricted than in France or in other parts of the world as well. In the United States staring openly at someone in a public place is considered rude and an infringement on his or her privacy. Instead, North Americans practice what Goffman (1963) refers to as "civil inattention," a very subtle practice whereby people give others just enough eye contact to acknowledge their presence but at the next moment withdraw that eye contact so they are not singled out as an object of particular curiosity. When two people are walking toward each other, civil inattention permits eye contact up to approximately 8 feet before the eyes are cast downward as they pass, or as Goffman (1963:84) puts it, "a kind of dimming of lights." Like so many other aspects of nonverbal behavior, civil inattention is such a subtle social ritual that most middle-class North Americans are barely aware of it. Nevertheless, it remains an important nonverbal behavior that regulates interaction in the United States.

## PROXEMICS

How people use personal space in their interactions with others is another "silent language" that must be understood to achieve clear communication within an international business setting. This area of nonverbal communication is known as the study of *proxemics,* a term introduced by anthropologist Edward Hall, most notably in his book *The Hidden Dimension* (1966). Although other researchers have developed similar concepts to Hall's notion of personal space (Sommer, 1959; Kuethe, 1962; Little, 1965), his observations and theories are not only clearly presented but also rich in cross-cultural insights. Hall's major contribution to our understanding of intercultural communication has been to demonstrate that people follow predictable cultural patterns when establishing distance between themselves and others. How close a person gets to another in normal conversation will depend on the nature of the social interaction, but in all cases the specific magnitude of the distance will be dictated by *cultural* norms.

According to anthropologist Conrad Kottak,

> The world's cultures have strikingly different opinions about matters of personal space. When Americans talk, walk, and dance, they maintain a certain distance from others—their personal space. Brazilians, who maintain less physical distance, interpret this as a sign of coldness. When conversing with an American, the Brazilian characteristically moves in as the American "instinctively" retreats. In these body movements, neither Brazilian nor American is trying consciously to be especially friendly or unfriendly. Each is merely executing a program written on the self by years of exposure to a particular cultural tradition. Because of different cultural conceptions of proper social space, cocktail parties in such international meeting places as the United Nations can resemble an elaborate insect mating ritual, as diplomats from different cultures advance, withdraw, and sidestep. (1987:210)

An important part of Edward Hall's (1966) typology of proxemics is his delineation of four categories of distance based on his observations of middle-class North Americans:

1. Intimate distance: ranging from body contact to 18 inches, a distance used for lovemaking, comforting, and protecting, at which olfactory and thermal sensations are at their highest.
2. Personal distance: from 18 inches to 4 feet depending on the closeness of the relationship. At this distancing mode people have an invisible "space bubble" separating themselves from others.
3. Social distance: from 4 to 12 feet, a distance used by acquaintances and strangers in business meetings and classrooms.
4. Public distance: from 12 to 25 feet, at which the recognition of others is not mandatory and the subtle shades of meaning of voice, gesture, and facial expression are lost.

Although the specific distances described apply to middle-class North Americans, all cultures have accustomed their people to feel comfortable at a specific distance. What is appropriate distance for one cultural group might appear to be "crowding" to another or "standoffish" to a third. For example, operating within Edward Hall's (1966) category of personal space, most middle-class North Americans choose for normal conversations a distance of approximately 20 inches, with minor variations depending on sex and level of intimacy. For certain cultural groups in South America and the Caribbean the normal conversational distance is in the range of 14 to 15 inches. And for certain cultures in the Middle East that distance is as small as 9 to 10 inches. These appreciable differences should make it painfully obvious just how important an understanding of proxemic variables is to effective intercultural communication. To stand 20 inches from a Saudi Arabian, although normal for a North American, communicates reserve, unfriendliness, and a sense of superiority. Yet when the Saudi moves closer, to establish what for him or her is a more comfortable conversational distance, the typical

*Arabs and westerners have different definitions of how closely people should stand to one another in normal conversation.*

North American interprets it as pushy or aggressive. Because of these culturally produced perceptions of space, it has not been unusual for North Americans, when conversing with South Americans or Middle Easterners, to find themselves continually backpedaling in an attempt to maintain their 20-inch distance as their foreign acquaintances continue to move closer. Although both conversants are simply trying to establish the normal conversational distance as determined by their cultural upbringing, considerable misunderstandings can occur.

Proxemic patterns are so important for cross-cultural communication largely because they represent such a subtle, and frequently overlooked, form of nonverbal communication. Each culture develops its own set of rules and uses of space, which like other aspects of culture are learned, but learned in an unconscious manner. It would be hard to find anyone in the United States who could testify that while growing up his or her adult role models explicitly taught him or her to maintain a conversational distance of 20 inches. Nevertheless, according to the findings of Hall and others, middle-class North Americans have learned what "proper" distance is, and they have learned it with remarkable consistency.

Although Edward Hall's (1966) descriptions of cultural differences in space usage are anecdotal, other, more empirically based research has come to essentially the same conclusions. Watson and Graves (1966), testing Hall's theories in a comparative study of North American and Arab students, found that the Arab students not only stood closer to one another than did the North Americans but also talked more loudly, touched each other more often, maintained a higher degree of eye contact, and faced each other more directly. In another study, Little (1968) used doll figures as a simulated measure of personal space among five cultural groups: North Americans, Swedes, Scots, Greeks, and southern Italians. As Hall's theories predicted, the southern European cultures chose social schemes reflecting less interpersonal distances than northern European cultures. Later empirical research by Watson (1970) concluded that South Americans, Asians, and people from the subcontinent of India normally choose spatial distances that are midway between Arabs and northern Europeans. Finally, Baxter (1970), observing 859 pairs of people in a New York City zoo, found that Mexicans stood appreciably closer to one another than did white North Americans, and black North Americans stood further apart than the other two groups.

An awareness of proxemics has important implications for the conduct of international business. How different cultural groups use their office space, for example, can lead to breakdowns in communications between business partners. Whereas many North Americans are accustomed to having a desk between themselves and their business partners, many South Americans see a desk as an unnecessary barrier and may try to crowd into the North American's personal space. At the other extreme, Germans, who see their personal space as an extension of their egos, tend to be very protective of it. Unlike North Americans, who generally close their office doors only for private conferences, Germans are likely to keep their office doors closed all the time, for to do otherwise is considered to be exceedingly unbusinesslike. Moreover, Germans become uncomfortable when someone moves his or her office chair closer to adjust the social situation. This cultural norm, at least in part, explains why Germans prefer heavy office furniture—so that people cannot rearrange the chairs and possibly intrude on their personal space. In fact, Edward Hall (1966:137–38) reports that "a German newspaper editor who had moved to the United States had his visitor's chair bolted to the floor 'at the proper distance' because he couldn't tolerate the American habit of adjusting the chair to the situation." Regardless of whether we encounter a preference for open doors or closed doors, or flexible or inflexible office arrangements, these things are likely to have different meanings in different cultures, which can influence the nature of the international business relationship.

## BODILY CONTACT (TOUCHING)

Touching is perhaps the most personal form of nonverbal communication, and yet paradoxically it is one that most people are reluctant to discuss. For the first several months of life touching is by far the most intense channel of communication, particularly between mother and child. In fact, as Montagu (1972:93) has so dramatically pointed out, tactile communication is so important in infants that its deprivation can have devastating, even lethal, effects.

Humans touch in a variety of ways and for a variety of purposes. But of all the logical possibilities, each culture retains a limited number of forms of touching. For example, Argyle (1975:287) suggests that in Western cultures the following types of touching are commonly found:

| | |
|---|---|
| Patting (head, back) | Holding (hand, arm, knee) |
| Slapping (face, hand, bottom) | Guiding (hand, arm) |
| Punching (face, chest) | Embracing (shoulder, body) |
| Pinching (cheek) | Linking (arms) |
| Stroking (hair, face, upper body, knee) | Laying-on (hands) |
| Shaking (hands) | Kicking (bottom) |
| Kissing (mouth, cheek, breast, hand, foot) | Grooming (hair, face) |
| Licking (face) | Tickling (anywhere) |

Cultures outside of the West may use some or all of these forms of touch, and they may use others as well. Each culture has a well-defined system of meanings for different forms of touching for various parts of the body. Each culture also defines who can touch whom, on what parts of the body, and under what set of social circumstances. In the United States it is perfectly acceptable for two adult men to communicate friendliness and goodwill by shaking hands. But if these same two men held hands while walking down the street, they would be communicating a very different message—and one that is less congruent with conventional standards.

One of the most obvious cultural differences between Brazil and the United States involves physical contact—kissing, hugging, touching in general. Middle class Brazilian kids—both boys and girls—are taught to kiss (on the cheek, twice or three times, coming and going) every adult relative they ever see. Given the size of Brazilian extended families, this can mean hundreds of people. Girls continue kissing throughout their lives. Males go on kissing their female relatives and friends. Until they are adolescents, boys also kiss adult male relatives. Thereafter, Brazilian men greet each other with hearty handshakes and the traditional male hug (abraco). These embraces are tighter and last longer the closer the relationship. (Kottak, 1987:210)

While conducting anthropological field research in central Kenya during the 1970s I became particularly aware of how meanings conveyed through touch can vary across cultures. Even before going to Kenya I had known through ethnographic readings that Kikuyu men routinely held hands with their close personal friends. After several months of living and working with Kikuyu, I was walking through a village in Kiambu District with a local headman who had become a key informant and a close personal acquaintance. As we walked side by side my friend took my hand in his. Within less than 30 seconds my palm was perspiring all over his. Despite the fact that I knew cognitively that this was a perfectly legitimate Kikuyu gesture of friendship, my own cultural values (that is, that "real men" don't hold hands) were so ingrained that it was impossible for me not to communicate to my friend that I was very uncomfortable. This personal incident illustrates (1) how the meaning of touching can vary from one culture to another, (2) how our own cultures can socialize us so thoroughly that we have little or no control over our reactions (for example, perspiring), and (3) how such differences in touching behavior can lead to cross-cultural misunderstandings.

Some cultures are high-touch cultures and others are low-touch cultures. A number of studies (Montagu, 1972; Sheflen, 1972; Mehrabian, 1981) have suggested that Mediterranean cultures, Arabs, Jews, and eastern Europeans are high-touch cultures, whereas the English, Germans, northern Europeans, and many Asian cultures are low-touch cultures. Striking differences between high-touch and low-touch societies can be observed in certain public situations. For example, in crowded areas such as subways, white Londoners are likely to assume an overly rigid posture, studiously avoiding eye contact and in no way acknowledging the presence of other passengers. The same type of behavior is seen on subways in New York City, Washington, or San Francisco. The

*In some cultures this friendly gesture of touching another person's shoulder would be considered a grave insult.*

French, in contrast, have no apparent difficulty with touching total strangers in the Paris metro, as Montagu described:

> Here the passengers will lean and press against others, if not with complete abandon, at least without feeling the necessity either to ignore or apologize to the other against whom they may be leaning or pressing. Often the leaning and lurching will give rise to goodnatured laughter and joking, and there will be no attempt to avoid looking at the other passengers. (1972:304)

Some forms of touching routinely found in England or the United States are viewed as most inappropriate in other parts of the world. Take, for example, the practice of social (or ballroom) dancing as practiced in the United States, whereby two adults of the opposite sex move about the dance floor in time with the music while holding each other in a semiembrace. It is common in such dancing for the front of their bodies to be in constant contact—and they do this in public. In spite of the close physical touching involved in this type of dancing (a form of bodily contact not unlike that assumed in sexual intercourse), our society has defined it as almost totally asexual. Although ballroom dancing can involve high levels of intimacy, it is equally possible that there is no sexual content whatsoever. Many adult men in the United States have danced in this fashion with their mothers, their sisters, or the wives of their ministers at church socials without anyone raising an eyebrow. Yet many non-American cultures view this type of dancing as the height of promiscuity and bad taste. It is interesting to note that many of those non-Americans for whom our dancing is a source of embarrassment are the very people we consider to be promiscuous, sex-crazed savages because their women do not cover their breasts.

> The different meanings connected with certain types of touching can lead to serious mis-communications in international business. Sergey Frank cites one such case of a cross-cultural misunderstanding that occurred between a northern European businessman and a southern European businessman as they were walking to a restaurant to celebrate after reaching final agreement on the terms of a joint venture between their two companies. According to Frank:
>
> > When the Southern partner made an attempt to link arms as they set off to the restaurant, his Northern partner misread the signal and panicked. What's this man's problem? Touching in public? The gentleman from the North had visions of a scandal in the newspaper back home, even to the extent of homosexual implications, and rather clumsily spurned the gesture. His surprised partner immediately took offense, the once-positive climate deteriorated, and the meal went miserably. And even though the follow-up negotiations were eventually concluded, they were unnecessarily bogged down by the climatic misunderstandings that could easily have been avoided through a better mutual understanding of culture and etiquette. (1992:51)

Although it is generally valid to speak of high-touch versus low-touch cultures, one must be careful not to overgeneralize. One empirical study conducted by Shuter (1977), which examined touching behavior among Germans, Italians, and North Americans, found that some of these national stereotypes did not hold true for both males and females. For example, Shuter found that although German and U.S. men were less tactile than Italian men, they were more tactile than Italian women. These findings are important because they serve as an important reminder not to think in monolithic terms when trying to determine cultural characteristics. Touching behavior, in other words, can vary in any given culture according to a number of factors such as sex, age, or relative status, to mention only several key variables. Instead of relying solely on overly simplified stereotypes, it would be more advisable to sharpen one's skills of observation of what touching means in a wide variety of contexts.

## CONCLUSION

The United States is a highly literate society that tends to emphasize the verbal channel of expression. Most North Americans, if forced to think about it at all, see the word as the primary carrier of meaning. They are much less likely to give much credence to the nonverbal aspects of communication. As important as language is to facilitating inter-cultural communication within an international business setting, it is only a first step to intercultural understanding. Of equal importance is the nonverbal dimension, which we all rely on but which we only vaguely recognize. Now that we have examined six of the more common modes of nonverbal communication in some detail, it would be instructive to look at some of the more salient features of nonverbal communication in general.

1. Like its verbal counterpart, nonverbal communication is largely a learned, or culturally transmitted, phenomenon. Although there is some convincing evidence that certain limited aspects of nonverbal communication are universal (for example, the expression of emotions through smiles, frowns, or eyebrow flashes), the great majority of nonverbal cues, and the meanings attached to them, vary from culture to culture.

2. The comparatively new field of nonverbal communication studies, at least in its present state of the art, has not been able to describe comprehensive systems of nonverbal communication for a single speech community as linguists have done for language. That is, although linguists have demonstrated the logic and consistency of many linguistic structures through the careful descriptions of grammar and syntax, nonverbal communication studies have yet to reveal the systematic nature of any speech community's "silent language." In other words, we do not have, at least yet, a grammar specifying the rules for constructing nonverbal messages. Nor are nonverbal dictionaries available that might provide, in reference book fashion, the meaning of a particular nonverbal cue.

3. Unlike spoken language, many nonverbal cues are sent and received despite our best intentions to do otherwise. Whereas language is every bit as effective for masking our true feelings as it is for expressing them, much of nonverbal communication is beyond our purposeful control. We can smile when we are unhappy, and to that extent we can purposefully control some nonverbal cues, but we cannot control our blushing when embarrassed, perspiring when nervous, or pupil dilation when frightened.

4. Since some nonverbal communication is beyond the individual's control, it is not at all uncommon to find a noticeable lack of fit between a person's words and the nonverbal messages he or she might send. For example, in response to the question, "How are you?" a person might respond, "Fine," while at the same time sending a number of nonverbal messages (such as sullen tone of voice, downcast eyes, and a frown) that totally contradict the upbeat verbal response. Research (Burgoon et al., 1989:9–10) indicates that when there is a discrepancy between the verbal and the nonverbal, the observer will most likely believe the nonverbal.

5. To a much greater degree than with language, nonverbal behavior is, by and large, unconscious. We send nonverbal messages spontaneously without giving much, if any, thought about what hand gestures we are choosing to punctuate our words, how far we are from someone else's mouth in normal communication, or how long we maintain eye contact. Since so much of our nonverbal behavior is operating in the unconscious realm, it becomes quite impossible to seek clarification of a misunderstood nonverbal cue. Although we can ask someone to repeat a sentence, we would be quite unlikely to ask someone to explain what he or she meant by a half smile, a particular posture, or a sudden movement of the head.

6. Based on past research there is strong evidence that women are better able to read nonverbal cues than are men. J. A. Hall (1978), reviewing 52 gender-related studies, found that 75 percent of them showed a significant female advantage. More recently, Rosenthal (1979:80–84), using the PONS (Profile of Nonverbal Sensitivity) test, found an even greater female advantage than the earlier studies.

Although much has been made of the distinction between language on the one hand and nonverbal communication on the other, the two forms of communication are in fact inextricably interconnected. To learn just the spoken language and ignore the nonverbal behavior would be as inadequate a response to cross-cultural communication as doing just the opposite. An understanding of both modes is necessary to reveal the full meaning of an intercultural event. Being able to read facial expressions, postures, hand gestures, gaze, and space usage, among others, increases our sensitivity to the intricacies of cross-cultural communication so necessary for success in the international business arena. To really know another culture we must first learn the language, and then we must be able to hear the silent messages and read the invisible words.

### CROSS-CULTURAL SCENARIOS

Read the following cross-cultural scenarios. In each mini-case study there is a basic cultural conflict between the actors involved. Try to identify the source of the conflict and suggest how it could have been avoided or minimized. Then see how well your analyses compare to the explanations in the Appendix.

**4–1.**  After completing an MBA in international business and working for a Boston bank for several years, Don Bynum was assigned for several weeks as a troubleshooter in the Rome office. To facilitate his adjustment to the Italian banking system and to assist with translation, the branch manager had assigned Don to work with Maria Fellini, a bilingual employee of the bank. Maria, like Don, was single and in her early thirties, and she lived with her widowed mother. In response to a comment Don had made about the joys of Italian cuisine, Maria invited Don to her mother's home for dinner. The dinner went well and Don felt fortunate to have had a chance to be entertained in an Italian home. Several days later Don felt somewhat embarrassed because he had forgotten to bring Maria's mother a gift the evening he had gone to dinner. So several days before returning to the United States he made a special trip back to Maria's house to deliver personally a large bouquet of chrysanthemums to Maria's mother as a token of his appreciation for her hospitality. Maria answered the door, greeted Don, and took the flowers into the kitchen. But when she took Don into the living room to say goodbye to her mother, no mention was made of the flowers. Don felt that perhaps he had done something inappropriate.

WHAT WENT WRONG?

**4–2.**  Tom Bennett, a senior accountant with a major New York accounting firm, had just arrived in Bogota, Colombia, to assume a two-month assignment to set up an accounting procedure for a middle-sized local business. On his way to the office Tom stopped to cash a check at the main branch of the largest bank in the country where he had just opened an account a week earlier. Tom approached the least crowded teller's window, which had about eight people crowded around it. After about five minutes of jostling Tom worked his way in front of the teller's window and handed the teller his check. But while he was waiting for his money, several other people elbowed their way up to the window and handed the teller their checks. And the teller took them. Tom was getting increasingly annoyed with the rudeness of these people who kept interrupting his banking transaction. While Tom waited for his money a number of people kept trying to get in front of him, and what made things even more infuriating was that they seemed to be angry at him. And to think that people from the United States are always accused of being impatient. When his money finally arrived he couldn't wait to get out of that very unfriendly situation. As he walked on to his office he was already thinking about the letter of complaint he would send to the bank president.

HOW MIGHT YOU EXPLAIN TOM'S FRUSTRATION AT THE BANK?

**4–3.**  Aware of the enormous interest the Japanese have in the game of golf, a U.S. sports equipment manufacturer decided to explore the possibilities of a joint venture with a Japanese firm.

Three representatives from each firm met in San Francisco to work out the details of the proposed venture. After the six men were introduced to one another they were seated at opposite sides of a large conference table. In an attempt to show the Japanese their sincerity for getting down to the task at hand, the U.S. businesspersons took off their jackets and rolled up their sleeves. Then one of the U.S. representatives said to his counterpart across the table, "Since we are going to be working together for the next several days, we better get to know each other. My name is Harry. What's your name?" The joint venture never did take place.

WHAT WENT WRONG?

**4–4.** Randy Hightower, recently appointed to manage his firm's office in Singapore, was anxious to do well in his first overseas assignment. Shortly after his arrival he called his first staff meeting to outline the objectives for the coming fiscal year. He had already met with his staff individually and was feeling quite confident about the prospects for having a good first year. Toward the end of the staff meeting, Randy, in his characteristic upbeat fashion, told his employees that he looked forward to working with them and that he anticipated that this would be their best year ever. To emphasize his optimism for the coming year Randy punctuated his verbal remarks by slapping his fist against his palm. The reaction was instantaneous: Most people laughed, giggled, or looked embarrassed. Unfortunately, he felt that the point of his dramatic climax was lost amid the laughter.

HOW MIGHT YOU EXPLAIN THE CAUSE FOR THE HILARIOUS OUTBURST?

**4–5.** Fred Gardener, a 31-year-old sales manager for a small boat-building firm in Connecticut, decided to stop off in Lisbon to call on several potential clients after a skiing trip to Switzerland. Having set up three appointments in two days, he arrived for the first two scheduled meetings at the appointed times but was kept waiting for over a half hour in each instance. Based on these two experiences Fred assumed that the Portuguese, like other "Latin" types, must be *"mañana"* oriented and not particularly concerned with the precise reckoning of time. With this in mind, he was not particularly concerned about being on time for his third appointment. Instead, he extended his visit to the local museum and arrived at his third appointment more than 40 minutes late. However, Fred sensed that the Portuguese businesspeople was quite displeased with his tardiness.

HOW WOULD YOU EXPLAIN THIS REACTION?

# 5

# CONTRASTING
# CULTURAL VALUES

It is not at all uncommon for anthropologists to speak of people from different cultures as having different sets of assumptions or different value systems. A value system represents what is expected or hoped for in a society, not necessarily what actually occurs. Values deal with what is required or forbidden, what is judged to be good or bad or right or wrong. Thus, in any given society values represent the standards by which behavior is evaluated and not necessarily the actual behavior.

If communication between people from different cultures is to be successful, each party must understand the cultural assumptions—or cultural starting points—of the other. Unfortunately, our own values, the result of cultural conditioning, are so much a part of our consciousness that we frequently fail to acknowledge their existence and consequently fail to understand that they may not be shared by people from other cultures. When that occurs, cross-cultural cues can be missed, communication becomes short-circuited, and hostilities can be generated.

To maximize our chances for successfully understanding the cultural environment of international business, it is imperative that we examine cultural values—theirs as well as our own. It is necessary to recognize the cultural influences on our own thinking and how they conform to, or contrast with, those of culturally different people. Before we can conclude that the Calcutta street vendor is repulsively smelly, we must first realize how much emphasis U.S. culture places on eliminating odors of all types. Or before concluding that the Peruvian carpenter is either too lazy or too stupid to be on time, we must first come to grips with the importance North Americans place on the exact reckoning of time. In short, before we can begin to understand other cultures, we must first understand how our own culture influences our cognitive and behavioral assumptions.

However, any attempt to examine contrasting value systems is fraught with methodological pitfalls. Part of the difficulty stems from the inherent bias of analyzing one's own culture. Since no one is completely uninfluenced by the experiences of one's own culture, any description of it will inevitably be distorted. But equally troublesome is the magnitude of the task, for it presupposes that we are dealing with two unified, monolithic sociocultural systems, the U.S. value system and a contrastive (or logically opposite) system. In fact, we have no such neat and tidy categories. Many of the countries in which U.S. multinational corporations operate are linguistically and culturally heterogeneous. For example, in India there are no fewer than 13 major linguistic groups with populations in excess of 10 million people, each speaking mutually unintelligible languages. And it must be assumed that this level of linguistic heterogeneity brings with it an equal level of cultural variability as well.

By the same token, some might argue that it is not even possible to speak of "the" culture of the United States. Despite frequent descriptions of our nation as the "great melting pot," a number of subgroups have resisted homogenization by retaining much of their ethnic distinctiveness (for example, the Chicanos of Los Angeles; Italian-Americans in Boston, New York, and Philadelphia; the Amish of rural Pennsylvania; and the majority of people in Miami, who do not speak English as their first language).

Yet despite the difficulties inherent in making generalizations about values in such heterogeneous societies as India and the United States, some degree of contrasting value patterns certainly is possible, and indeed, is imperative if we are to enhance our understanding of other cultures as well as our own. Whether we live in Massachusetts or California, Oregon or Florida, in a small town or a large metropolis, there are some common U.S. value patterns that stop abruptly at the Rio Grande and somewhat less dramatically at the Canadian border.

When we speak of a "value pattern" of any specific cultural group, we must make some gross generalizations of a comparative nature. No statement that we make will be a perfect representation of reality, for as Perry has suggested,

> There is no indivisible Platonic essence of which America is the unique embodiment. There is no American characteristic which is not exemplified elsewhere, or which some Americans do not lack. All that one can possibly claim is that there is among the people of this half-continent taken as a whole, a characteristic blend of characteristics. (1949:5)

In other words, we cannot predict the exact values of any particular resident of the United States or any other country with absolute certainty. Rather the value patterns discussed should be viewed as statistical statements of probability—a broad heuristic framework to help us identify some basic value differences between ourselves and other cultures. If ignored, these value differences may affect in a negative way our attempts at communicating in an international business setting.

This chapter looks at nine critical dimensions of value contrasts between the United States and other cultures of the world. The U.S. culture places a relatively high value on (1) individualism, (2) a precise reckoning of time, (3) a future orientation, (4) work and achievement, (5) control over the natural environment, (6) youthfulness, (7) informality, (8) competition, and (9) relative equality of the sexes. In contrast, many of the cultures in which U.S. businesses are operating hold values that are quite different, and in many cases are the logical opposites.

The approach taken in discussing value differences is modeled after the "value orientations" suggested by Florence Kluckhohn and her associates at Harvard (Kluckhohn & Strodtbeck, 1961) and applied to a cross-cultural context by Hofstede (1980). This approach is predicated on the notion that people in all societies face certain universal problems, all of which have a limited number of solutions. To illustrate, all societies must somehow deal with the question of reckoning time. Some societies, like our own, take the precise reckoning of time very seriously by placing a high value on punctuality, deadlines, and not wasting time. Other societies have a much more loosely structured notion of reckoning time, whereby social relationships, not the arbitrary position of the hands of a clock, will determine when people should do something. However, all societies do not fall into two categories, those reckoning time precisely and those reckoning time loosely. In actual fact, these value orientations should be viewed more as relative points on a continuum rather than as two distinct and mutually exclusive categories.

## INDIVIDUALISM VERSUS COLLECTIVISM

The ideal of the individual is deeply rooted in American social, political, and economic institutions. Although historians, philosophers, and social scientists don't always agree on its origins or its more recent forms, there is a general understanding that the value of the individual is supreme and it is the individual who has the capacity to shape his or her own destiny. The individual is the source of moral power, totally competent to assess the effects of his or her own actions as well as to be responsible for those actions. Since society is seen as an instrument for satisfying the needs of the individual, a political philosophy has developed that calls for freedom from coercion by church, state, or traditional authority.

Since individualism has been a recurring theme in American culture, family ties tend to be *relatively* unimportant. That is not to say that in the United States the family is unimportant in any absolute sense, for the family remains the primary group to which most Americans have their strongest loyalties. It is the group within which our relationships are the most intimate and the most long-lasting. Nevertheless, when compared to other cultures, Americans divide their time and emotional energy between family and a wider variety of social groupings, including churches, schools, labor unions, places of employment, and a host of voluntary organizations. Moreover, the constant preoccupation with self has resulted in the truncation of extended family ties. We have, in effect, reduced the notion of family to its smallest possible unit, the nuclear family.

The physical layout of the typical North American house clearly reflects the emphasis placed on individualism and personal privacy. Houses are designed to maximize individual space. There are doors on bathrooms and bedrooms. Parents are expected to acknowledge the private space and possessions of their children's rooms, and children are usually restricted in their use of space that is considered the domain of the parents. In other cultures, particularly third world cultures, there is considerably less privacy. Children, even in those homes with ample room, frequently share the same sleeping areas with their parents and siblings until well into adolescence. Although not always realized, a separate room for each member of the family remains the ideal in the United States. A child is considered disadvantaged if he or she must share a room with another member of the family.

The concept of individualism is instilled from an early age in the United States by

*The sense of individualism is so well developed in the United States that most people aspire to have their own cars.*

constant encouragement of children to become self-sufficient. Children are taught to make their own decisions, clarify their own values, form their own opinions, and solve their own problems. Children are encouraged to search out answers for themselves, rather than relying on the teacher or adult. How often do we tell children, "Go look it up for yourself," a statement that most often reflects our desire to instill the personal qualities of individualism and self-reliance. In fact, the effective teacher in the United States is not the articulate lecturer but rather the one who can help the student develop to the fullest his or her capabilities to be an autonomous and fully functioning *individual* in a society that presents a limitless number of choices. In short, the aim of education in the United States is not to serve God or country but to enable the individual to maximize his or her human potential—or in the words of the U.S. Army recruiting campaign, "Be all that you can be!"

Individualism as a highly valued ideal finds strong expression in a number of areas of contemporary American life. It runs through American literature, social history, theater, advertising copy, and many aspects of popular culture such as television, radio, motion pictures, popular song lyrics, and the comics. For instance, most bookstores today have entire sections devoted to literature popularly known as "self-help" books, designed to help the *individual* improve and get ahead. This self-help genre, dating back to Benjamin Franklin's *Poor Richard's Almanac* of 1759, includes books with such cryptic titles as *How to Take Charge of Your Life, How to Start and Manage Your Own Business, Creative Divorce, Successful Deer Hunting, Helping Yourself with Hypnosis, Looking Out for Number One,* or simply and directly, *How to Be Rich.* Even though many of these books focus on different areas of self-improvement and many of the writers offer different formulas for success, the basic theme of individuality is unmistakable: Personal success depends on activating the forces that lie within the individual.

Many cultures in Africa, Asia, and South America stand in marked contrast to the American ideal of individualism. These societies simply start from a different set of cultural assumptions. Whereas Americans assume the primacy of the individual, many third world peoples traditionally, and to a large extent today, assume that the highest goal is conformity to and identity with the extended family group. And just as individualism can be traced through many everyday aspects of American culture, so too does this collective consciousness run through the thoughts and actions of many non-Western peoples.

To illustrate, a person's very identity in Kenya is still much influenced by group membership. In answer to the question "Who are you?" the typical American would respond by giving her name (Jane Smith), followed most likely by what she does for a living (architect) and where she comes from (Philadelphia). The typical Kenyan, on the other hand, most likely would give his name, followed by his father's name and then his lineage affiliation.

Group orientation, as compared to an individual orientation, is evident also when we look at how many traditional third world people deal with property. With the exception of property held by either corporations or government, most property in the United States is privately owned by individuals. Large property items such as houses and cars are title-deeded to individuals. Most items of clothing found in American homes are the individual property of specific members of the household, and by and large, the people to whom those articles of clothing belong are at liberty to dispose of them in any way they see fit. Even small children in America retain strong individual property rights over certain objects ("Elizabeth, that bicycle belongs to your brother!"). Thus, in America individuals have total rights and obligations over many pieces of property; that is, they *own* them. In many parts of Kenya, however, property rights for individuals tend to be much more limited and shared with other members of the group. To illustrate, in Swahili, the lingua franca of East Africa, there is no equivalent to the English verb *to own*. If you want to express in Swahili that "Njoroge has a brown cow," you would have to use the expression "Njoroge ana ngombe," which means literally "Njoroge *is with* the brown cow." That is, he has the right to milk that brown cow at present, but tomorrow his father's brother's son may have milking rights. And next month that cow may be transferred to an entirely different extended family group as part of a marriage payment for one of Njoroge's male relatives. The decision as to who has these limited rights and obligations to any particular cow is made by the group, thereby making the disposition of property a collective decision rather than an individual one.

Also, marriage reflects the corporate consciousness found among other cultures of the world. Marriage in Western societies is viewed as a very personal contract between two consenting adults. By and large the prospective bride and groom decide for themselves if they will marry, when they will marry, the type of ceremony that will take place, and all other details governing the contract. It is possible for a marriage in the United States to be entered into and legitimized in a matter of days or even hours, because all that is required are two consenting adults, a blood test, and a valid marriage license.

The marital process widely practiced in a number of third world countries is far more complicated and time-consuming, primarily because of its corporate nature. Large numbers of relatives of both the bride and groom become personally involved in legitimizing the union.

---

The individual versus collective value orientation is well illustrated by Anderson, who tells of a U.S. businessperson who rewards the most outstanding member of a Japanese marketing team by promoting him to head up the group. But, as Anderson relates:

> Instead of feeling proud, the rewarded man seems deeply ashamed, the others uncomfortable and demoralized. Performance rapidly deteriorates.

> What was wrong? One of the group finally explains that the Japanese had felt most comfortable working as a team, with all sharing equally in decisions. The attempt at motivation, American-style, destroyed a sense of harmonious cooperation the Japanese workers had cherished. (1985:54–55)

---

Personal identity, control over property, and marriage are only three aspects of certain cultural differences between some non-American societies and U.S. society. These contrasts are not made to suggest that Americans are incapable of collective action or have no loyalties to groups. Nor should we conclude that the non-Americans totally fail to recognize individual achievement. But for many peoples of the world the recognition of achievement is not defined in terms of how well the individual distinguishes himself or herself from the rest of the group, but rather in terms of how many contributions he or she makes to the general welfare of the group.

In terms of business behavior, people in individualistic societies tend to be self-motivated and their business relationships are based on self-interest. They are comfortable working alone, they tend to be task oriented, and they seek personal recognition. By way of contrast, businesspersons from a more collective society base their work relationships on mutual self-interest, seek to advance the interests of the group, and seek group rewards. According to Hofstede's findings (1980:222), the United States has the most individualistic set of business values and Venezuela has the least.

## THE TEMPORAL DIMENSION

A major component in any constellation of values is how a particular culture deals with time. To the North American, time is seen as being fixed in nature, just another part of our environment, and as such is treated like a tangible commodity. Much like money, we speak of spending time, saving time, earning time, and wasting time. Indeed, the relationship between time and money is expressed in the American idiom "time is money." To ensure that we use our time wisely, we schedule it in advance, establish timetables, and set deadlines for ourselves. Involved in the process of scheduling is the compartmentalizing of time into discrete segments; that is, we generally schedule one thing at a time.

Thus, time becomes a major concern, and in fact, plays a central role in the everyday life of the typical North American. The majority of adults in the United States have strapped to their wrist a device that divides hours into minutes and minutes into seconds, so that no matter where we are we will always know the correct time. We punch timeclocks to determine the quantity of our work. We measure how long it takes a sprinter to run 100 meters in hundredths of a second. Even the biological function of eating is done in response to the clock, for we often eat because it is lunchtime or dinnertime. Several years ago a major U.S. watch company spent millions of dollars on an advertising campaign that claimed that their watches were guaranteed to lose less than two seconds per month. Clearly, the company would not have spent that much money to convey that particular message if it was not what the American consumer wanted to hear.

Since we divide units of time so precisely, promptness in U.S. society is highly valued. To be kept waiting is frequently taken as an insult or a sign of irresponsibility. If, for whatever reason, we are late for a prearranged meeting, we would expect to offer an apology. Most North Americans fail to appreciate the high value they place on punctuality until they are forced to cope with a lack of promptness in other cultures. To be kept waiting 45 minutes for an appointment may be unthinkably rude for the North American, whereas for many South Americans a 45-minute delay would be well within the acceptable limits.

In some of the less industrialized parts of the world people do not highly value the precise reckoning of time so commonly found in the United States. Whereas the typical North American reacts to absolute measures of time (that is, since it is noon, it is lunchtime, and therefore it is time to eat), the Southeast Asian tends to act in response to social events (that is, one eats food because there is someone with whom to share it.)

Thus, the more technologically simple peoples of the world see no particular merit in punctuality for its own sake. Rather than doing something or not doing something because of a clock, their actions are prompted by social events, such as meeting one's kinship obligations, or natural occurrences, such as the setting of the sun. In fact, many traditional peoples frequently interpret the Western preoccupation with time as a direct affront to meaningful interpersonal relations. Westerners in general, and North Americans particularly, are seen as wanting to rush through their personal encounters so they can get on with their next appointment. Such an emphasis on rigid schedules and punctuality is viewed as a most undignified form of behavior as well as a dehumanizing way of interacting with others.

This basic difference in the way culture defines time has been elaborated by Edward Hall (1976:14–18) in his distinction between monochronic time (M-time) and polychronic time (P-time). M-time cultures, which are best represented by the United States, Germany, and Switzerland, emphasize schedules, a precise reckoning of time, and promptness. They view time as a discrete commodity that can be saved, wasted, borrowed, or killed. In contrast, P-time cultures emphasize the completion of transactions and the involvement of people rather than a rigid adherence to the clock. Being "on time" is of less importance to P-time people than it is to M-time people. When two people from a P-time culture are interacting, they are more likely to continue what they are doing until they have finished rather than end it and move on to the next scheduled activity, as would be the case with two M-time people.

A major obstacle to adjustment for many Americans abroad (perhaps second only to language) is the problem of time or "pace of life." Even though most cultures understand the meaning of clock time (hours and minutes), each culture has its own vocabulary of time. In one cross-cultural study of social time Levine and Wolff (1985) compare the temporal pace in six cultures (England, Indonesia, Italy, Japan, Taiwan, and the United States) by using some creative unobtrusive measures: (1) the accuracy of bank clocks, (2) the average length of time it took pedestrians on a clear day to walk 100 feet on a city street during business hours, and (3) the average length of time it took to buy a single stamp from a postal clerk. The findings suggest considerable cross-cultural differences on these three time indicators. A quick pace of life and concern for speed and accuracy were most noticeable in Japan, followed closely by the United States, whereas Indonesia scored consistently at the other extreme.

---

Telberg shows us how different time perspectives among the various delegates at a UNESCO meeting can lead to cross-cultural misunderstandings:

"Gentlemen, it is time for lunch, we must adjourn," announces the Anglo-Saxon chairman, in the unabashed belief that having three meals a day at regular hours is the proper way for mankind to exist.

"But why? We haven't finished what we were doing," replies—in a puzzled manner that grows rapidly more impatient—an Eastern European delegate, in whose country people eat when the inclination moves them and every family follows its own individual timetable.

"Why, indeed?" placidly inquires the Far Eastern representative, hailing from a country where life and time are conceived as a continuous stream, with no man being indispensable, with no life-process needing to be interrupted for any human being, and where members of electoral bodies walk in and out of the room quietly, getting a bite to eat when necessary, talking to a friend when pleasant; but where meetings, theatre performances, and other arranged affairs last without interruption for hours on end, while individuals come and go, are replaced by others, meditate or participate as the occasion requires, without undue strain, stress or nervous tension. (1950:6)

---

In addition to their precise reckoning of time and all it implies (that is, punctuality, scheduling, and compartmentalizing), people in the United States tend to be future oriented rather than past or present oriented. It is generally thought that with this view of the future—coupled with a high value placed on action—it is not only possible, but mandatory, for people to improve on the present.

That North Americans tend to be future oriented—that is, looking toward the future as a guide to present action—can be seen in a number of aspects of American life. To illustrate, Western psychology has as one of its fundamental assumptions the notion that the capacity to defer gratification (doing something that is not particularly pleasant

*People in M-time cultures emphasize a precise reckoning of time.*

today to maximize future pleasure) is an indication of both maturity and good mental health. That is, rather than buying a new car today, one should leave the money in a high-interest bank account to be able to buy an even better car several years later. By paying life insurance premiums now Americans can protect their families in the event they should die prematurely sometime in the future. Municipal governments are purchasing land today that will be used for new road construction two decades in the future, when automobile traffic will be greatly increased. North Americans make best-sellers out of such futuristic books as *Megatrends* (Naisbitt, 1982) and *The Third Wave* (Toffler, 1981), which make predictions about where our society is heading. The recent popularity of IRAs and other forms of long-term investments enable North Americans to put away a nest egg for their retirement years. Even the Christian concept of heaven and hell implies that it is one's present thoughts and actions that are believed to determine one's place in the future. Although there is certainly no consensus on what the future will bring, few North Americans would disagree with the idea that people should plan and work today in order to make the future a better place in which to live.

In many other traditional cultures there appears to be a rather different view of time. Dr. John Mbiti has put forth the thesis that " . . . according to traditional [African] concepts, time is a two-dimensional phenomenon, with a long past, a present, and virtually no future" (1969:17). According to Mbiti, since African time is composed of a series of events that are experienced, the future must be of little meaning because future events have not yet occurred. Mbiti supports his argument with linguistic data from the Gikuyu and Kikamba languages. There are three future verb tenses, which cover a period not exceeding two years from the present. If coming events do not fall within this limited range (which he interprets simply as a projection of the present), there are virtually no linguistic mechanisms to conceive or express them. Mbiti concludes that given these linguistic structures, Africans have little or no interest in events that lie in the distant future.

Although some have argued that Mbiti has overstated his case, few would deny that traditional African societies are more oriented toward the past than toward the future. Whereas the Westerner is constantly looking toward improving upon the past (that is, continual progress), the African tends to look to the past as a guide to present behavior. That is, history provides a chronicle of past events but also a set of normative guidelines for the present. In traditional African cultures people look back with fondness to the good old days of the founding ancestors. History points to the roots of their existence. That which is older is generally viewed more positively than that which is more recent.

Given this traditional African concept of time, it follows, as Horton has suggested, that " . . . the passage of time is seen as something deleterious or at best neutral" (1967:177). Whereas Westerners, with their scientific orientation, are attempting to speed up their arrival into the future, traditional Africans try to forestall the passage of time. Africans traditionally have engaged in a variety of ceremonial activities designed to negate the passage of time. These activities, such as rebirth ceremonies, are intended to re-create symbolically a past event, thereby obliterating "the passage of time which has elapsed since its original occurrence" (Horton, 1967:177).

## WORK AND ACHIEVEMENT

Another element in America's lexicon of values is the emphasis placed on work, activity, and achievement. Throughout our history as a nation, the United States has been known for its high levels of human energy, its aversion to idleness, and its preference for the person of action over the person of ideas. To be certain, constant toiling was the price that the colonial farmers had to pay for surviving and taming the wilderness. Yet it would be misleading to suggest that the harshness of the frontier alone gave rise to the strong work ethic in the United States; most of the early colonists were already imbued with the value of work per se, an idea arising from the Protestant Reformation, which viewed work as a means to salvation. Martin Luther held that a person's highest duty was the conscientious discharge of his labor. Subsequent interpretations of Calvinism gave positive sanctions to work, achievement, and activity. Thus, the notion that hard work is the only way to serve God, when coupled with the nineteenth-century philosophies of social Darwinism and free enterprise economics, gave rise to the well-known concept of the Protestant ethic.

The Protestant ethic holds that people do not work for themselves alone. A person's work—or "calling"—comes from God, and it is through their work that people demonstrate their worth to both God and themselves. This notion—so much a part of

American culture—that work is not only respectable but actually virtuous, finds expression in such proverbs as these:

> Blessed are the horny hands of toil.
> Blessed is he who has found his work.
> To work is to pray.
> Satan finds some mischief still for idle hands to do.

The early American settlers, having arrived in the New World with a strong sense of the Protestant ethic, gave it new meaning as they worked to create a new nation. Work for its own sake was as heartily revered in the United States as anywhere else in the world. It has even been suggested that one of the major sources of conflict between Northerners and Southerners in the Civil War revolved around different interpretations of the work ethic. Many Northerners viewed slavery as wrong not only because it held blacks in servitude against their will but also because Southern whites were seen as losing their virtue by insisting that others do their work for them. According to historian Arthur M. Schlesinger, "after the Civil War, General W. T. Sherman found public occasion to thank God that now at long last Southern whites would have 'to earn an honest living'" (1970:107).

Although social scientists throughout the twentieth century have not always agreed on the precise impact of the so-called Protestant ethic on American capitalism, few would disagree that when contrasted with many other cultures of the world, Americans have had a long tradition of valuing hard work sui generis. Many Americans have surnames that reflect, if not their own profession, that of an ancestor, such as Carpenter, Clark, Cook, Miller, Baker, and Smith.

And even if one's work is not reflected by one's surname, one's occupation in American society plays a powerful force in shaping an individual's personal identity. For example, when meeting someone for the first time, most often the second piece of information we receive (after the name) is what the person *does:* "I am a chemistry professor at MIT" or "I work as a lineman for the telephone company." And of course, that is important information in American society, for it tells you how that person spends at least eight hours per day, can provide certain clues to a person's interests and values, and may even determine the nature of the subsequent conversation. To hold that in the United States "you are what you do" would be to overstate the case, but personal identity is, to a significant degree, influenced by our work or occupation.

Most Americans are not aware of the degree to which their identities are intertwined with their work activity until their jobs or occupations are threatened. Studies of unemployed workers have shown on numerous occasions the disorienting consequences of losing one's job. Those who are forced to stand in line for their unemployment checks demonstrate dramatic losses in self-esteem; they view themselves as "nobodies," or worse, as social freeloaders; frequently this loss of identity is followed by a deterioration of their social relationships. This same work-related identification emerges unequivocally from the sociological and psychological literature on retirement and aging. People who have worked at a particular job all their lives suffer significant losses of identity when they are forced to retire. In an effort to help the retired adjust to their loss of work and maintain a positive identity of "worth through work," retirement homes or planned communities attempt to build meaningful activities into their programming. Rather than engaging in purely recreational pursuits (for example, golf or bridge), many retired Americans choose to collect clothing for the needy, transcribe books into Braille for the blind, and serve as volunteers in local hospitals. This can be viewed as an attempt by retirees to legitimize their leisure activities by infusing into them aspects of work. Even those who leave their conventional jobs voluntarily for self-employment often experience identity crises, as Paul Dickson relates:

> These identity crises and situations usually come packaged in little episodes which occur when others find that they have encountered a bona fide wierdo without a boss. . . . You are stopped by a traffic policeman to be given a ticket and he asks for the name of your employer and you say that you work for yourself. Next he asks, "Come on, where do you work? Are you employed or not?" You say, "Self-employed," with the pride of a robber baron but you know that he thinks you are an able bodied welfare loafer. . . . He, among others you meet, knows that self-employed is a tired euphemism for being out of work. . . . (1971:52)

Thus, to be denied work—or to work at low-status or nonconventional jobs—involves more than the denial of those things that wages can buy. In the United States at least, it can be viewed as the denial of one's self-esteem and personal identity.

In contrast, work—particularly physical labor—is not highly valued *in and of itself* among some cultures of the world. This is hardly to imply that these people are not industrious, for in fact they may engage in more hard work per day than does the typical North American. But they work because it is necessary to survive, not because they derive dignity or self-worth from the process. In fact, if given the choice, people from a number of non-American cultures would prefer that others work rather than themselves. According to Lystad, far preferable to work for most sub-Saharan Africans

> are the hours which can be spent in visiting, in argument and discussion, in contemplation, in the enjoyment of and the direct participation in the arts, in music and the dance and the story, in play and the enjoyment of the body, in the numerous group activities which provide, as does the funeral, legitimate relief from the tensions of work in addition to other social benefits. (1962:19)

United States culture, with its emphasis on "doing," demands of its members the kind of activity that results in measurable accomplishment. Some other cultures, however, tend to emphasize as important those traits thought to be "given" in the human personality. That is, most frequently it is the intellectual, the contemplative person, the wise or just person who is held in the highest esteem rather than the person who performs visible deeds.

## RELATIONSHIP TO NATURE

A basic assumption of U.S. culture is that nature and the physical environment not only can be, but should be, controlled for human convenience. If a river overflows its banks and destroys homes and crops, dam it up or change its course; if a mountain stands in the way of convenient travel between two points, slice off the top of the mountain or tunnel through it; if gravity is a barrier to walking on the moon, simply build a sufficiently large enough engine to propel past the earth's gravitational pull. To most North Americans the expression "to move a mountain" is not a metaphor symbolizing the impossible but rather an optimistic challenge based on past experience. As Condon and Yousef remind us, we speak glibly of "conquering space," "harnessing the power of the river," and "taming the wilderness" (1975:103). We attempt to control the natural process of birth by a wide variety of methods (that is, chemical substances, mechanical devices, and surgical procedures), and in fact, we now have the technology to create human life outside of the human body. Moreover, we can intervene (technologically) into the natural process of death by organ transplants and the implantation of mechanical organs. In short, North Americans assume that given enough time, effort, and money, there is no aspect of the natural environment that cannot be subjugated eventually to the human will.

In contrast to this basic U.S. cultural assumption, alternate assumptions are found in other parts of the world regarding the proper relationship between people and the natural environment. For example, Japanese culture emphasizes the integration of people with the natural world, whereby the natural environment shapes people and, in turn, is shaped by people. Or there are those cultures (for example, India) that, in stark contrast to North American culture, see people as dominated by nature. This highly fatalistic position sees nature as exerting potentially harmful powers over people, and to try to understand or counteract these harmful powers would be hopeless. The human-nature relationship most commonly found in the world would be some combination of those found in Japan and India. To many people the natural world is closely associated with supernatural forces, and although natural phenomena are not envisioned in such malevolent terms as in India, the world of nature is seen as a manifestation of God, and as such, is not able to be influenced, much less transformed, by the human hand.

In an appreciable number of cultures outside of the United States God is closely

*In the United States people value having control over the natural environment.*

associated with the natural world. The sky, or heaven, for example, is thought to be where God lives and reigns. Some cultures, such as the Luo and Nandi of western Kenya, use the same or similar word for both God and the sun. Moreover, rain is a manifestation of God, and some languages use a single word to designate both God and rain. Among some cultures mountains are seen as physical evidence of God's presence. Many people believe that certain mountains are the dwelling place of God, and it is for this reason that they face these mountains when offering their prayers. God is seen as being "in" these natural phenomena. They are God's creation, they manifest God, and they symbolize God's being and presence. Given this world view, it is little wonder that many non-Americans do not share our cultural desire to transform the natural environment for our own purposes. For them the world of nature is to be respected and revered. If in fact such natural phenomena as rain, rivers, and mountains are conceived of as God's creations and symbols of God's presence, it would be grossly presumptuous—indeed blasphemous—for people to want to alter, control, or dominate nature. Rather, people are expected to establish the proper relationship with God, which among other things, involves respecting and living in harmony with the world of nature.

## YOUTH ORIENTATION

The United States is a youth-oriented society, extolling the virtues of the young while devaluing, or at least ignoring, the old. We tend to emphasize what is new and young by keeping up with new trends and maintaining a youthful spirit. The U.S. free enterprise system has encouraged this love affair with all things new. As a way of increasing sales, U.S. clothing manufacturers have convinced us to discard perfectly functional clothing on the grounds that it is old-fashioned or out of style. We have become a "throwaway" society, willing to discard what we have in favor of next year's "new and improved" model. This disposable mentality carries over into the area of human relations, for our homes for the aged are filled with the discarded faces from previous years.

However, U.S. culture has not always exalted youthfulness. According to Harris and Cole (1980:67), until the latter part of the eighteenth century elders were treated with great deference, respect, and veneration. Nowhere was this better illustrated than by the Puritan ancestors, who held that long life was not fortuitous but rather a gift of God's pleasure. Thus, the highest political offices were held by old men, and the elderly wielded unquestioned authority within the family structure. However, the far-reaching social, political, and economic changes that swept the country following the American Revolution included a revolution in how we viewed the aged. For a new democratic society to emerge, traditional hierarchies had to be replaced. And since older people had been in control in pre-Revolutionary America, they became logical targets of attack. Spurred on by urbanization and industrialization, the nineteenth century witnessed an unmistakable reversal of the earlier cult of old age. As Fischer put it, "veneration of the old had been an idea at the center of American society in the 17th century; in the 19th century old age existed increasingly on the margins of society" (1977:122).

Since old age has become devalued to such a significant degree, it is not surprising that people in the United States fear the prospects of aging and take considerable measures to postpone some of its more obvious telltale signs. North Americans spend hundreds of millions of dollars each year on a variety of products designed to keep us looking as young as possible. A wide variety of hair coloring products are purchased each year to help prevent the graying process. We try to hide our loss of hair with chemical preparations, hair transplants, and wigs and toupees. We purchase specific brands of dish detergent that promise to keep hands looking young and many forms of skin creams that claim to prevent wrinkling. Plastic surgeons can now make us appear years younger by taking tucks in our skin or rearranging our anatomy. And of course, we purchase running shoes, exercise machines, and health spa memberships in an effort to keep our bodies looking slim, trim, and youthful.

The cult of youth, which has grown steadily since the early nineteenth century, can be seen in a number of areas of contemporary U.S. culture. Such commonly used proverbs as "Age before beauty" (implying that youth is beautiful and old age is ugly) and "You can't teach an old dog new tricks" (denying the educability of older people) tend to reinforce our preoccupation with youth. Moreover, much of our humor reflects our generally negative attitudes toward the aged. Nowhere is this bias more evident than in the mass media, particularly television. Rarely has television shown elderly people in anything other than peripheral roles as grandparents, crotchety old fools, or ancients willing to dispense pithy sayings or pieces of advice from bygone days. With very few exceptions, old people rarely appear on television as central figures coping with everyday human problems and emotions, much less as heroes. And of course, TV advertising reflects this lopsided fascination with the young. Most ads revolve around young, long-legged blondes, shaggy-haired surfers, or yuppielike professionals. Television commercial jobs for older actors seem to be limited to ads for laxatives or dental adhesives.

In recent years the avoidance of old age has brought on some bizarre forms of behavior. Frequently, middle-aged or older people in the United States will adopt the fashions in clothing, hairstyles, and music set by their children's generation. One social commentator spoke of

> . . . a Boston matron on the far side of fifty, who might have worn a graceful palla in ancient Rome, dressed in a miniskirt and leather boots . . . a man in his sixties, who might have draped himself in the dignity of a toga, wearing "hiphugger" jeans and a tie-dyed T-shirt . . . a conservative businessman, who in an earlier generation might have hesitated each morning, wondering whether to wear black or charcoal gray, going to the office in white plastic shoes, chartreuse trousers and cerise shirt, purple aviator glasses, and a Prince Valiant haircut. Most astonishing were college professors who put aside their Harris tweeds and adopted every passing adolescent fad with an enthusiasm out of all proportion to their years. One season it was the Nehru jacket; another dashikis; the next, railroad overalls. In the early 1970's it was love beads and leather jackets. Every twist and turn of teen-age fashion revolutionized their costumes. But always, old was out and young was in. (Fischer, 1977:132–33)

It follows logically that in a future-oriented society like the United States those persons who are least valued—the old—are those with the least amount of future ahead of them. Youth are thought to be energetic, enthusiastic, resourceful, and resilient, all characteristics needed for becoming an achieving, productive member of society. It is all too generally accepted in the United States that all worthwhile things in life stop (or at least drastically diminish) after one reaches a certain age. Physical attractiveness, creative thought, continued personal growth, and even sexual activity tend to be thought of as being the primary, if not exclusive, domain of the young. Once we reach the age of 65 our society forces us to stop our life's work, gives us a gold watch, and tells us in a number of not so subtle ways that the best thing we can do is to get out of the way.

In contrast, in many non-Western societies aging brings respect and honor. Older people are looked to as advisors whose opinions are highly valued because of their vast experience. In these predominantly nonindustrialized areas of the world, where relatively few survive past middle age, the mere fact that one arrives at old age is in itself worthy of respect. Moreover, since change in many of these cultures is slow, the knowledge and skills of the aged remain useful. Thus, older people are viewed as being wise, thoughtful, and trustworthy. For example, Samoan society, which draws its leaders from among the oldest family members, places high value on the aged; the Sidamo of southwest Ethiopia considers the promotion to "elder" (usually reached in one's fifties) to be the most important transition in life. And in North Burma older people are held in particularly high esteem since it is believed that longevity is the reward for living virtuously in a previous life. Similar examples of respect for age have been reported from Thailand to rural Mexico. Even in such highly industrialized societies as Japan, the traditionally high value placed on aging has not disappeared:

> Most Japanese over 60 do not try to hide their age. In fact, they are usually proud of it. It is considered polite and proper to ask an older Japanese his age and to congratulate him on it. Most Americans know it is impolite to ask an older American his age. . . . The popularity of hair dyes and cosmetics to conceal wrinkles attests to the prevalence of age concealment among older Americans. Some middle-aged Japanese also dye their greying hair, but most older Japanese do not. It is probably not an exaggeration to say that most Japanese believe "grey is beautiful" and that most Americans do not. (Palmore, 1975:104–105)

## INFORMALITY

Informality, another important theme running through the U.S. value system, dates back to our nation's early history. By moving onto the great American frontier, the early settlers gave up much of the formality found in the East Coast cities. The hard work required for survival on the frontier was hardly conducive to the preservation of pomp and circumstance. Consequently, there developed much more informal customs of dress, speaking, etiquette, and interpersonal relationships, which to a large extent have persisted to the present time.

North Americans, a diligently casual people, frequently assume that informality is a prerequisite for sincerity. They seem to become uncomfortable when faced with the type of ceremony, tradition, and formalized social rules found more widely throughout Europe. They are likely to feel uneasy with titles, which partially explains our view of the British (with their dukes, duchesses, and viscounts) as oppressively pompous and socially rigid. Our fondness for informality is well illustrated by the anecdote about former Chicago Mayor Richard Daley, who in a farewell speech to Queen Elizabeth and

Prince Philip, is reported to have said, "Next time you come, bring the kids" (Condon & Yousef, 1975:87).

This general aversion to social rank is so pervasive that most North Americans make a conscious effort to resist showing deference to age, birth, or any other status based on ascribed characteristics. Moreover, this tendency for informality and social leveling is not infrequently extended to those whose position has been achieved. For example, we are quite reassured when we see Ronald Reagan chopping wood in his Levi's or Jimmy Carter playing softball in Plains, Georgia. Many people in the United States tend to increase their respect for the company president who mows his own lawn or is seen rolling up his sleeves and working alongside his employees. Also, the United States is one of the few countries in the world where it is not considered inappropriate for students to address their college teachers by their first names. As one U.S. college professor remarked, only half jokingly, "My mother is the only person who calls me 'Dr.'"

Since language and culture are so intimately interconnected, the U.S. cultural propensity for informality is reflected in the structure of our language. Whereas such European languages as French and German have retained the structural distinctions between the formal *you* and the intimate *you,* the English language makes no such distinctions. When considering some oriental languages, one can observe a fairly complex system of pronouns used to express different levels of formality and respect. Moreover, in addition to language, even such nonverbal forms of communication as dress, the use of bright colors, posture, and seating behavior reveal the relatively low level of formality found widely in the United States.

To be certain, North Americans seem to go out of their way to play down the importance of rank and status. But informality is also evident from the strong desire in the United States to establish friendships quickly by getting on a first-name basis as soon as possible. Nor are most North Americans reticent to ask relatively personal questions of a new acquaintance. It is not at all unlikely that after being introduced to a total stranger a North American would ask such questions as "Where do you work?" or "How many children do you have?" or "What is your golf handicap?" Since we are a mobile population, it is important that we establish friendships quickly before moving on to a new location. Such "personal" questions are a convenient way of telescoping the process of getting acquainted by enabling people to find a common interest. As friendly a social mode as this may appear to be to most North Americans, people from more formal cultures see this barrage of questions as brash, impudent, and an invasion of privacy, for it imposes a degree of intimacy that has not yet been developed.

Closely related to this value of informality is the type of kidding or joking so prevalent in U.S. society. Kidding behavior plays an important social function in that it serves as a social equalizer, a way of bringing a person "down off his high horse." Kidding, in other words, gives us a socially legitimate way of telling people exactly what we think without worrying about hurting them. However, it is important to remember that people from other cultures not familiar with our kidding customs may well take offense. In such countries as Japan, for example, where formality, courtesy, saving face, and indirectness are all highly valued, the custom of kidding may be totally inappropriate and lead to serious cross-cultural misunderstanding.

*In the United States the value of informality extends even to our heads of state.*

In his monumental study, *Culture's Consequences,* Hofstede (1980) examines this formal-informal dimension by introducing the somewhat broader notion of *power distance,* a term used to measure how individuals from different cultures relate to authority in the workplace. Hofstede found that in some cultures there is great social distance between those who hold power and those who are affected by that power (high power distance). In such societies, subordinates and superordinates adhere to a rigid hierarchy, status is often ascribed (that is, based on age or gender), and social relations are highly formal. By contrast, some cultures characterized by low power distance tend to play down status distinctions while emphasizing less formal forms of communication and interaction. According to Hofstede's findings, the United States, New Zealand, Australia, and the Nordic countries have low power distance ratings, whereas most Latin American and Southeast Asian countries have higher power distance ratings.

## COMPETITION

Closely associated with the U.S. preference for individualism and achievement is the emphasis placed on competition. Most North Americans, particularly men, share with one another a strong desire to experience the "thrill of victory," to be the best at what they do. From a very early age we point out to our children the qualities of a winner and communicate in many ways our desire for them to be the same. Former Green Bay

*The game of Monopoly is the best-selling game in the history of the United States because it is a microcosm of our highly competitive society.*

Packer coach Vince Lombardi epitomized this U.S. love affair with competition when he said "Winning isn't everything; it's the only thing."

To be winners, people in the United States must compete, and there are many opportunities to practice honing our competitive skills from a very early age. Children in the United States compete for grades, engage in competitive sports, play competitive board games, play cops and robbers and cowboys and Indians, and engage in arguing and fighting. Of all these types of competition, only fighting is considered to be objectionable, but even here, according to Beals, Hoijer, and Beals, "it is assumed that fighting among children is inevitable and must be tolerated so long as the degree of violence involved is kept within carefully defined limits . . . " (1977:451).

So from their earliest days in school, as a way of preparing children for adult life, they are expected to compete, the winners being rewarded with gold stars, good grades, and positive nods and smiles from teachers and parents. Competition is as much a part of the extracurricular activities of school life as it is of the academic component. Students are encouraged to compete for election to student government offices; on projects in such organizations as scouting, 4-H, and Junior Achievement; and of course, on the athletic fields. Children in the United States who might enjoy hitting or throwing a baseball just for the fun of it are usually put on a team, outfitted in a uniform, and encouraged to be "number one." Perhaps the most blatant form of competition in the U.S. classroom is the spelling bee, in which two teams are pitted against one another as a very deliberate educational strategy for teaching children how to spell.

Bringing up children in an environment where competition per se is viewed as a force for good inevitably leads to an overall competitive society. There certainly is no derth of evidence of the high value placed on competition, winning, and getting ahead in the wider U.S. society. Our laissez-faire economic system is on the principle of competition. That is, it is assumed that prices will be kept low while the quality of goods and services will remain high as long as competition exists. To prevent the restraint of competition in the U.S. marketplace, the U.S. Department of Justice, through its Anti-Trust Division, is empowered to act as a watchdog against the development of monopolies. The legal system in the United States, based on an adversarial process, relies on competition for the administration of justice. Such a system is predicated on the assumption that justice will result when plaintiff and defendant compete with one another to marshal the most and best legal arguments, facts, and precedents. Even adult recreation in the United States, to a large extent, tends to be based on competition. As spectators we follow our favorite players and teams as they compete for the best batting averages, field goal percentages, or win-loss records. Much of our own leisure time is used for playing games (which, of course, have winners and losers) such as bridge, golf, tennis, or Trivial Pursuit. It is hardly a coincidence that the board game of Monopoly (the purpose of which is to wipe everyone else off the board by getting everything for yourself) has been played by generations of North Americans and remains the most popular board game of all time in the United States.

The stress on individual competition is evident throughout U.S. society. Although the spirit of competition is economically based, it extends to all domains of cultural life, including our most intimate social relationships. It has even been suggested (Potter, 1954:59) that the attainment of competitive goals in the United States frequently takes precedence over the attainment of personal satisfaction. But like so many other aspects of culture, not all societies of the world share our proclivity for the competitive mode. People for whom saving face, cooperation, and group obligations are important will not respond to competitive stimuli as enthusiastically as middle-class North Americans. People who are group oriented are not likely to want to excel over others. A U.S. military advisor expressed his incredulity over the conspicuous lack of competitiveness he observed in Laos:

> Watching them play a game—volleyball. To us, it's a game. I know when our teams compete, whether it's baseball or basketball—anything, we'd be serious, playing it because we like to win. With them, they wouldn't be; they would team up and have teams going, but they just didn't give a hoot whether they won or not. (Stewart, 1971:38)

This same lack of competitiveness—in stark contrast to what might be anticipated in the United States—was related by Otto Klineberg in his description of how performance on IQ tests varied cross culturally because some cultures stressed cooperation and group problem solving rather than competition. Klineberg (1969:66) relates the experience of a social scientist administering an IQ test to a group of Australian aborigines. Although each subject was expected to solve each task individually, it proved to be a most uncomfortable situation for the test takers, who were accustomed to solving problems in groups through a consensus process. The subjects could not understand why the examiner, whom they considered their friend, would not help them solve the problems. The aborigines, accustomed as they were to group deliberation and problem solving, remained perplexed throughout the examination, as they would continually pause for approval and assistance from the examiner. It should come as no surprise that the test scores were not high because of this near total absence of cultural familiarity with the competitive mode.

## RELATIVE STATUS OF WOMEN

All cultures define masculinity and femininity in their own terms and place different values on gender-related traits. In some cultures masculinity is defined in terms of self-assertion and task orientation, and femininity is associated with such qualities as nurturing, an inherent interest in interpersonal relationships, and the enhancement of the quality of life. Some cultures—which tend to value masculine traits highly—expect men to be assertive and women nurturing, with little or no possibility for role reversals. In more feminine cultures, which tend to emphasize nurturing, quality of life values, and interpersonal relationships, these traits are, to a much greater extent, shared among both men and women. Masculine cultures are more competitive, advancement oriented, and driven; feminine cultures are more cooperative, nurturing, and accepting of the status quo.

In measuring this masculine-feminine dimension, Hofstede (1980:279) found that Japan scored the highest on the Masculinity Index, followed by certain German-speaking countries (Germany, Austria, and Switzerland) and certain Latin American countries (such as Venezuela and Mexico). Interestingly, although the United States ranked above average on the Masculinity Index, it was not overwhelmingly masculine. At the other extreme, the most feminine cultures are the four Scandinavian countries of Sweden, Norway, Denmark, and Finland, as well as the Netherlands. In these feminine cultures—known for their high degree of social concern and nurturing—both sexes are concerned with such quality of life issues as day care, old age security, and the environment.

Difficulties can arise when people from masculine and feminine cultures attempt to conduct business together. To illustrate, a salesman for a U.S. chemical manufacturer may be required to supply his Swedish customer with documentary evidence that the production of the chemicals has not contributed to the destruction of the environment. Such a requirement can be a significant obstacle to the sales negotiation because the U.S. chemical salesman (who comes from a relatively masculine culture) does not necessarily share the Swede's intense concern for the environment. Or another possible scenario could involve the notion of paternity leave, which is widely practiced in Sweden but virtually unheard of in the United States until recently. For example, negotiations between the U.S. chemical salesman and his Swedish male customer might be temporarily interrupted for a number of months while the Swede becomes a house husband.

The status of women and the relationships between the sexes vary appreciably from one society to another. Although a number of countries could be cited as having a greater degree of equality between the sexes than the United States, when viewed from a broad cross-cultural perspective, the United States affords women a relatively high degree of status in terms of legal, economic, political, and social prerogatives at their disposal. In contrast, women from other cultures—particularly from the third world—come from traditions that afford them few of the freedoms Western women take for granted. The appreciable contrast between traditional views of women found among the labor force of certain third world nations, on the one hand, and those that guide the American-operated, multinational corporation, on the other, can create special problems for the organizational efficiency of the corporation.

To suggest that women enjoy a higher status in the United States than they do in certain third world countries is hardly to suggest that U.S. women have parity with men. Even though women in the United States have made dramatic gains in capturing a larger percentage of the labor force, from approximately 30 percent in 1950 to 45 percent in 1990, women are more likely to serve in jobs that are subordinate to those of men, such as secretaries rather than bosses, teachers rather than principals, and nurses rather than doctors. And in the political arena U.S. women, despite some modest gains, remain embarrassingly underrepresented in our legislative, judicial, and administrative bodies. Nevertheless, the status of women in the United States—when contrasted to most other cultures in the world—is *relatively* high in terms of access to economic, political, and legal prerogatives.

One such third world nation that can serve as a useful contrast to the United States is Kenya, a country whose capitol of Nairobi houses the branch operations of some 97 U.S. firms, including such corporate giants as Chase Manhattan, General Motors, Ford, Firestone, Exxon, Union Carbide, Mobile, Xerox, and 3M.

When examining the subject of sex roles of those ethnic groups that make up the Nairobi work force, the picture that emerges unquestionably shows women to be subordinate to men. For example, among the Luo, Kenya's third-largest ethnic group, women do not hold property, play no part in the major ceremonies or rituals, and have little or no political authority. Parkin describes Luo men as giving an "open and unambiguous definition of women's status as producers of men's children . . . confined to domestic activities," whereas they define themselves as "political leaders and wage earners" (1978:168). Wilson describes the relatively low status of women in Luo society by speaking of them as "the property of their father and his lineage or, on marriage, the property of their husband and his clan" (1960:180). And as an effective mechanism for keeping the Luo women in their humble place, even the Luo creation myth (no doubt originated and perpetuated by men) blames women for bringing the curse of work to men.

International business expert Sondra Snowdon relates how she learned a valuable lesson in protocol while heading international protocol services for an international bank:

I was given the responsibility to meet a plane on which a very important sheik, a client of the bank, was arriving. I was to greet him officially. We at the bank were unaware that by sending a woman to the airport, we were, in keeping with his custom, offering the company of the woman to him during his stay. We had a very unhappy customer to contend with when he learned this was not the case. (1986:25)

Despite Kenya's reputation among African nations as being one of the most Westernized and progressive, the role and status of women have not changed appreciably in recent decades. The lives of the overwhelming majority of Kenyan women are dominated by hard work as both homemakers and farmers. A frequent sight in rural Kenya is a woman carrying a heavy load of firewood on her back or a debe of water on her head and working long hours in the sun tending her crops. Typically she marries in her mid- to late teens, takes up residence with her husband's relatives, and produces children for as long as her health permits. She may earn a little money by selling some surplus crops, brewing homemade beer, or joining a self-help cooperative, but these activities are usually done *in addition* to the gardening, cleaning, cooking, water fetching, firewood collecting, and child care.

That women in Nairobi are generally viewed more negatively than men has important implications for hiring practices and overall team building within the organization. The American multinational corporation is faced with a Hobson's choice in this respect, for accommodation to traditional African views of women will invariably lead to sex discrimination, whereas a policy that aims at treating the sexes with relative equality is likely to lead to personnel problems and a reduction in organizational efficiency. Although neither option is particularly desirable, it is important for corporate managers to be aware of the cultural realities so they will be able to make the most informed decision.

Urban anthropologists have provided other information on social differences between men and women that have important consequences for personnel and managerial issues of corporations operating in Nairobi. For example, Ross (1975:104) reports that men in Nairobi have more elaborate social networks than women, to the extent that they have larger ranges of interactions, come into contact with more people, and remain in the city for longer periods of time. On the basis of these behavioral differences between the sexes, Ross (1975:104, 141) concludes that men are more likely to be members of labor unions. Thadani (1976:96) also mentions sex differences in terms of contact with rural homelands, for she claims that men are more frequent sojourners to their rural homes and spend more time at home when they do go. If, in fact, it is normative for men to be responsible for maintaining contact with rural kin and traveling home for funerals and other ritual occasions, it is likely that male workers are more likely to request leaves of absence (and may have higher rates of absenteeism and job turnover than women) in order to maintain these long-distance kinship obligations.

## CONCLUSION

This chapter has explored some basic value contrasts between the United States and other cultures with two objectives in mind. First, in keeping with the traditional role of cultural anthropology, the preceding discussion was designed to demonstrate that different cultures have not only different practices, behaviors, and rituals but also very different philosophical assumptions, which represent what transformational grammarians refer to as the "deep structure" of the culture. And second, the discussion should facilitate for the U.S. businessperson an increase in cultural self-awareness. Once equipped with an understanding of (1) how their own cultural values affect their thinking and behaving and (2) how their own values differ from those in other cultures, American businesspersons will be in the best position to avoid, or at least minimize, breakdowns in cross-cultural communication.

Based on the preceding discussion of U.S. values, it is possible to summarize the comparative value orientations as follows. It should be remembered, however, that these nine dimensions of values hardly exhaust all the possibilities, but they do suggest some of the more germane dimensions of value structures that can influence the conduct of business in a cross-cultural setting.

### Comparative Value Orientations

| *U.S. Culture* | *Contrastive Cultures* |
|---|---|
| Individualism | Collectivism |
| Precise time reckoning | Loose time reckoning |
| Future oriented | Past oriented |
| Doing (working, achievement) | Being (personal qualities) |
| People controlling nature | Nature controlling people |
| Youthfulness | Old age |
| Informality | Formality |
| Competition | Cooperation |
| Relative equality of sexes | Relative inequality of sexes |

In conclusion, it cannot be overstated that our search for U.S. values, and how they compare to those found in other cultures, must be tempered with considerable caution. As mentioned earlier, the United States has long been a multicultural society, and this very real cultural and linguistic diversity makes generalizations risky. The problem of contrasting U.S. with non-U.S. values is made all the more difficult by the fact that all cultures—and their value systems—are constantly in a state of flux (Williams, 1970). This fact holds true for U.S. culture as well as the numerous non-U.S. cultures with whom U.S. businesspersons are expected to interact. When we state that people from the United States tend to place a high value on individualism whereas laborers in Djakarta tend to emphasize a more collective or group-oriented mentality, we are making generalizations at a relatively high level of abstraction. However, this should not deter us from the task of discovering basic value differences and how they can affect communication across cultures. Only after this understanding can the international businessperson begin to make the adjustments necessary for meaningful cross-cultural communication.

### *CROSS-CULTURAL SCENARIOS*

Read the following cross-cultural scenarios. In each mini-case study there is a basic cultural conflict between the actors involved. Try to identify the source of the conflict and suggest how it could have been avoided or minimized. Then see how well your analyses compare to the explanations in the Appendix.

**5–1.** Howard Duvall, an up-and-coming accountant with a New York–based firm, was on contract in Mombasa, Kenya, for three months setting up an accounting system for a local corporation. Since he had never been out of the United States before, he was interested in learning as much as possible about the people and their culture. He was fascinated by the contrasts he saw between the traditional and the modern, relations between Africans and Europeans, and the influence of the Arabic language and the Muslim religion. Every spare moment he had the company's driver take him to see the interesting sites both in town and in the rural villages. To document the sites for friends back home he brought his 35 mm camera wherever he went. Although Howard was able to get a number of good pictures of game animals and buildings, he became increasingly frustrated because people turned their backs on him when he tried to take their picture. Several people actually became quite angry.

WHAT ADVICE COULD YOU GIVE HOWARD?

**5–2.** George Burgess was a chief engineer for a machinery manufacturer based in St. Louis. His company had recently signed a contract with one of its largest customers in Japan to upgrade the equipment and retrain mechanics to maintain the equipment more effectively. As part of the contract, the Japanese company sent all ten of their mechanics to St. Louis for a three-month retraining course under George's supervision. Although George had never lived or worked abroad, he was looking forward to the challenge of working with the group of Japanese mechanics, for he had been told that they were all fluent in English and tireless workers. The first several weeks of the training went along quite smoothly, but soon George became increasingly annoyed with the constant demands they were making on his personal time. They would seek him out after the regularly scheduled sessions were over for additional information. They sought his advice on how to occupy their leisure time. Several even asked him to help settle a disagreement that developed between them. Feeling frustrated by all these demands on his time, George told his Japanese trainees that he preferred not to mix business with pleasure. Within a matter of days the group requested another instructor.

WHAT WAS THE CRITICAL ISSUE OPERATING HERE?

**5–3.** Martha and Ted Harding, owners of the largest travel agency in Salt Lake City, were invited on a "familiarization" tour of Australia by that country's Ministry of Tourism. They were part of a group of eight U.S. travel agents who were being wined and dined and shown all the major tourist attractions by the ministry in hopes that they would recommend Australia as a vacation spot to their clients. Shortly after their arrival they attended a lavish cocktail party sponsored by the Association of Hotels and Restaurants in Sidney. Everyone seemed to be very cordial and good-spirited. Yet Martha noticed that she got some cool glances from some of their Australian hosts when she declined a drink. Moreover, Martha noticed that the party was segregated sexually, the men talking at one end of the room and the women talking among themselves at the other end. Martha was beginning to feel increasingly uncomfortable at the cocktail party.

WHAT COULD YOU TELL MARTHA THAT MIGHT HAVE MADE HER FEEL A BIT
MORE AT HOME?

**5–4.** Andy Ross, an electrical engineer for a Chicago firm on a contract with the Turkish government, had been living with his wife in Istanbul for several months. When Andy had to spend several weeks in Ankara he thought it was a good opportunity to combine business with pleasure. Since he was entitled to some vacation time, he decided to travel leisurely to Ankara by car with his wife in order to spend some time in rural Turkey and get a better feel for village life. Living in Istanbul had been very enjoyable, for both Andy and his wife had found it to be a sophisticated and interesting European city. But when traveling in the outlying regions they began to feel uneasy for the first time since coming to Turkey because the local people seemed hostile. On their second day out of Istanbul they stopped in a small coffeehouse that they had heard was a focal point of social activity in rural Turkey. But shortly after arriving they sensed that they were not welcome. People stared and stopped talking to one another. They could not understand why people were so hostile, particularly since people seemed so friendly in Istanbul.

WHAT EXPLANATION MIGHT YOU OFFER ANDY AND HIS WIFE?

**5–5.** Stefan Phillips, a manager for a large U.S. airline, was transferred to Dhahran, Saudi Arabia, to set up a new office. Although Stefan had had several other extended overseas assignments in Paris and Brussels, he was not well prepared for working in the Arab world. At the end of his first week Stefan came home in a state of near total frustration. As he sat at the dinner table that night he told his wife how exasperating it had been to work with the local employees, who, he claimed, seemed to take no responsibility for anything. Whenever something went wrong they would simply say *"Inshallah"* ("If God wills it"). Coming from a culture which sees no problem as insoluable, Stefan could not understand how the local employees could be so passive about job-related problems. "If I hear one more *inshallah*," he told his wife, "I'll go crazy."

WHAT MIGHT YOU TELL STEFAN TO HELP HIM BETTER UNDERSTAND
THE CULTURAL REALITIES OF SAUDI ARABIA?

# LOCATING RELEVANT
# CULTURAL INFORMATION

In recent years there has been an increased awareness in the international business literature regarding the need for a fuller understanding of the cultural environment of international business. Whether one is managing a firm's overseas operations, directing an international sales force, or helping expatriate employees and their families adjust to living and working in a foreign culture, the need for understanding the cultural environment has never been greater than it is today.

The difficulty lies not with identifying the problem but rather with knowing how to solve it. Much of the literature from international business tends to be anecdotal, illustrating by endless examples how well-meaning but short-sighted businesspersons can run amok because of their imperfect understanding of the cultural realities of the people with whom they are attempting to do business. Or the literature deals with general pleas for cross-cultural understanding. This approach is of little assistance to the international businessperson who must deal with culturally specific problems as they apply to the immediate international situation. Clearly, international businesspeople need to be able to acquire culture-specific data that are accessible, relevant, and applicable to their immediate business situations.

## THE TRADITIONAL ANTHROPOLOGICAL APPROACH

Although the discipline of anthropology, with its central focus on the concept of culture, is the logical place to turn for culture-specific information, most international businesspersons contend that the conventional anthropological approach to research is not particularly well suited to meeting their informational needs. Traditionally, and to a large extent today, cultural anthropologists spend many months collecting data in a particular culture by means of the time-consuming technique known as participant observation. The field anthropologist must master the language, gain acceptance into the foreign culture, and develop networks of relationships before the formal data gathering can even begin. Thus, it appears to most international businesspersons that the traditional data-gathering process used by anthropologists is so cumbersome and snail-like in pace that it is virtually useless for their more immediate needs.

As time consuming a process as traditional cultural anthropological research is, there may well be international business situations that would require such an approach. For example, a U.S. multinational corporation about to invest millions of dollars in a manufacturing facility in Colombo, Sri Lanka, will not be acting extravagantly by hiring one or more anthropologists to conduct a cultural study of the local people, who would eventually make up its work force. Such a study might include traditional techniques such as participant observation and interviewing as well as drawing on the already existing ethnographic and social science literature on the region. Although conducting such first-hand research would cost thousands of dollars, it nevertheless provides the best assurances that the corporate values and assumptions will be integrated into those of the local work force. To do anything less would be to invite serious long-term managerial problems. Marietta Baba, in a publication on business and industrial anthropology illustrates how Richard Reeves-Ellington, a professionally trained anthropologist, made a significant contribution when his firm (Upjohn Corporation) was establishing operations abroad:

> When Reeves-Ellington joined Upjohn, the company was planning to expand its international operations by marketing products in Indonesia. No one in the firm at the time (including Reeves-Ellington) had experience in Indonesia, but Reeves- Ellington had enjoyed doing fieldwork in Mexico as well as living in Europe, and he felt that his anthropological training would permit him to function effectively in another culture. The company concurred, and Reeves-Ellington was sent abroad to set up operations in Indonesia, where he stayed for 10 years. While in Southeast Asia, Reeves-Ellington says he "did a lot of applied anthropology." An ability to analyze social systems from the native's point of view and to determine the interconnections among and reasons for human behavior enabled Upjohn's anthropologist to establish good working relationships with local officials and thus to move the company's products effectively into local marketing and distribution channels—a process that could have taken many times longer or failed altogether without an appreciation for local logic and custom. (1986:20–21)

This is only one example of how applied cultural anthropologists could be used to generate an accurate picture of the cultural realities of the international operation. However, a myriad of other international business situations might not require such long-term, intensive cultural research but rather could draw on previously collected anthropological findings.

Like any science, cultural anthropology involves more than the mere collection of an endless laundry list of facts about the various exotic and not-so-exotic cultures of the world. From its beginnings in the mid-nineteenth century, anthropology has been primarily concerned with the comparative study of human behavior, culture, and society. The conduct of cross-cultural studies—whether we are talking about large-scale, worldwide comparisons or more limited comparisons of two cultures—requires in most cases accessibility to secondary sources (that is, findings from previously conducted cultural studies). Even though professional anthropologists continually use secondary data in their comparative studies, these sources have not always been accessible to or usable for the international businessperson. To use already existing anthropological data successfully, the international businessperson must first assess the ethnic-linguistic composition of the specific business environment and then search out the relevant literature for the appropriate groups. Even after the relevant cultural groups have been identified, there remains the additional problem of having to locate and then sort through, in some cases, reams of literature, much of it dated, unintelligible, or not directly related to the problems of management in an international context. Given the relative inaccessibility of cross-cultural data, it is little wonder that international businesspeople tend to deemphasize the impact that cultural variables have on their operations and instead focus on such problem areas as international finance or the political environment, which they perceive to be more manageable.

However, there are several important ways of addressing the problem. One approach is for international businesses to employ cultural anthropologists—either on a contractual basis or as full-time staff members, depending on the nature and extent of the international involvement—to develop cultural profiles and generally transform the relevant cultural data into a form usable by the corporation. There is a small but growing number of professionally trained anthropologists who are specializing in various aspects of international business. These applied anthropologists can serve as "cultural brokers," making important connections between the enterprise and its immediate cultural environment.

## HRAF: AN UNDERUTILIZED CULTURAL DATA BANK

Short of hiring cultural anthropologists to work within the corporation, there are sources of culture-specific information that are accessible to corporate planners and decision makers with a little digging in the right direction. It would indeed be convenient if all the cultural data on all peoples of the world were systematically computerized so that information about a particular custom or practice could be retrieved almost instantaneously by pressing a button.

Although we have not as yet applied our computer technology to such a purpose, there has existed for the past 40 years a retrieval system for anthropological data that can greatly facilitate research on various aspects of particular cultures. It was not until the late 1940s that the Human Relations Area Files (HRAF), the largest and most sophisticated cultural data bank ever devised, was made available for comparative cultural studies. Unfortunately, this cultural data bank has gone largely unnoticed and unused by most people outside the field of anthropology, particularly in the area of international business.

Developed largely by George Peter Murdock at Yale University's Institute for Human Relations, HRAF is a vast ethnographic archive structured according to two basic principles. First, the materials are divided into over 310 separate cultural files, each representing descriptive information on a single culture (or a closely related group of cultures) such as the Yoruba of Nigeria, the Navajo Indians, or the Koreans. A full listing and description of all 310-plus cultural groups (each with its own alphanumeric code) are found in the manual entitled *The Outline of World Cultures* (*OWC*) (Murdock, 1972).

The second basic organizational principle is a highly detailed subject classification system composed of more than 700 categories grouped into 79 major topical sections. The concepts covered include such topics as food consumption, property systems, labor and leisure, age stratification, gestures, theories of disease, and in-group antagonisms. An explanation of these and other topics, along with cross-references to other categories, is presented in a second manual (Murdock, 1971), entitled *The Outline of Cultural Materials (OCM)*.

When these two guides (*OWC* and *OCM*) are used together it is possible to have before you within a matter of minutes most of the information on a given subject for a particular cultural group. The HRAF files are well designed for the rapid and accurate retrieval of data on specific cultures and subjects so that the time of the international business analyst can be devoted to the search for structural similarities and differences between the corporate and the local culture rather than to the search for the information itself. In addition to being easy to use and enormously efficient, the HRAF files contain approximately 90 percent of all the cultural data on any given topic and for any given culture. The files even include exclusive English translations of cultural materials from 15 different foreign languages.

Physically HRAF have two formats, the original 5 × 8 inch paper files (started in 1949) and the more recent 4 × 6 inch microfiche version (developed in 1958). Representing a cost of approximately $65,000, the HRAF files are located in approximately 250 participating member institutions—universities, museums, libraries, and educational/research organizations—in the United States and some two dozen other countries. The HRAF are located in most of the major universities in the United States, particularly those universities found in the major urban areas where most of the headquarters of international corporations are found.

In recent decades cultural anthropologists have glutted conventional libraries with a vast and largely indigestible number of books, articles, and field reports on specific

*The Human Relations Area File (HRAF) is a valuable, easy-to-use data bank for cultural information.*

world cultures. The major significance of HRAF is that they organize this unwieldy quantity of cultural data into a form usable by nonanthropologists.

To be certain, the HRAF files are not without their limitations. For example, they are an organized collection of data, and as such, require the user to see connections between the data, develop his or her own theory, and eventually relate these generalizations to the structure and operations of the organization. Moreover, some of the information contained in the files is outdated and no longer accurate. The mere age of the data, however, is not always an appropriate measure of their present validity, for various cultural features change at differential rates. We must bear in mind that no specific piece of information gleaned from the HRAF files can be used by itself as a precise representation of present reality. Rather it should be viewed as a starting point—a type of traditional ethnographic baseline—for asking the proper questions in one's search for contemporary cultural realities.

## NONANTHROPOLOGICAL SOURCES USEFUL
## IN DEVELOPING A CULTURAL PROFILE

A particularly effective way to access culture-specific information is by contacting the many associations, both at home and abroad, that focus on a particular country or culture. A primary reference book that can be found in the reference department of any good research library is the three-volume *Encyclopedia of Associations* edited by Burek (1992). Let us assume one is interested in obtaining culture-specific information on Japan. By consulting the Keyword Index (part 3) of this encyclopedia under "Japan," one will find entries for approximately 150 associations based in the United States having to do with Japan, including the Japan-American Society, the Japan Foundation, the Japan National Tourist Organization, the Japanese American Citizens' League, and the Japanese-American Curriculum Project. Parts 1 and 2 of the encyclopedia provide pertinent descriptive data on these culture-specific associations, including address, telephone number, contact person, membership, and publications.

In addition to cultural data generated by professionally trained anthropologists, there is an appreciable amount of published information that can be helpful to the international businessperson in constructing cultural profiles. Since this literature is quite diverse, it is likely to be spread throughout a number of different locations in any good research library. Some of this material is cultural in the narrowest sense of the term, in that it specifically addresses how people think and behave in different parts of the world. Other sources provide surveys of a nation's population, geography, economy, government, and foreign policy pursuits. Other sources address such everyday practical concerns as health regulations, national holidays, data on gift giving, and tips on how to use the local telephone system. There are also a number of country-specific periodicals of current events that can help the international businessperson keep abreast of the latest happenings in any particular country or region of the world. Although some of this literature is published commercially, a good deal of it is published through the U.S. Government Printing Office at very reasonable prices by various branches of the federal government. Regardless of the source, all these types of materials can help the international businessperson develop more complete cultural profiles, minimizing surprises and consequently reducing the chances of serious culture shock. It would be helpful to look at some of these varied sources in more detail.

### Some Country-Specific Series

Perhaps the best single series of culture-specific data for the international businessperson has been prepared by Alison Lanier under the general title of *Updates*. Each of the 15 volumes, approximately 100 pages in length, deals with a different foreign country and is periodically revised. Lanier, who has had considerable experience in preparing U.S. businesspeople to live and work abroad, has provided valuable insights into the cultural factors that affect everyday life as well as some very practical information on coping with the new environment. Each volume in the series includes sections on the country's background, tips before leaving home, the language, getting around, business culture, everyday customs and courtesies, health and medical advice, leisure activities, household pointers, schooling for the children, and so on. Each volume includes a reading list and a guide to other sources of information. The *Update* series is available through Intercultural Press, Inc., Yarmouth, Maine, a publisher specializing in international and cross-cultural subjects.

The *Interact* series, edited by George Renwick and also published by Intercultural Press, is designed to explore the bases of cross-cultural conflict in various countries. Each of the five books in this series (dealing with Mexico, Australia, Thailand, Japan, and the Arab world) analyzes how nationals from these countries perceive the world, how their actions differ from those of middle-class North Americans, and how these differences influence their relationships. It is hoped that there will soon be more volumes in this excellent, but small, series.

The David M. Kennedy Center for International Studies at Brigham Young University produces a series entitled *Culturgrams*, four-page cultural orientations covering the customs, courtesies, and lifestyles in 90 different countries. Each *Culturgram*, which represents a condensation of a wide variety of data sources, is designed for those with more interest in cross-cultural communication than with time. Although these mini-cultural briefings are, by design, not in-depth cultural profiles, they do provide some valuable information on a wide variety of contemporary cultures.

Similar in format and content to the *Culturgrams* is a monthly newsletter for international business protocol and etiquette called *The Diplomat*. Each month is devoted to a different country profile and includes information on travel hints, social and business customs, dining, gift giving, holidays, and important addresses. *The Diplomat*, which runs about five pages and folds into a convenient size, can be ordered on a yearly subscription basis or by individual issues.

### Basic Descriptive Profiles

Any good reference librarian will be able to suggest a wide variety of reference works that provide useful introductory survey data from various countries of the world. For example, *The Europa Year Book* (1992) provides a narrative description of most of the countries of the world accompanied by detailed statistical data and current lists of government officials. *The Encyclopedia of the Third World* (1991) includes compact and balanced descriptions of the political, economic, and social systems of 122 countries. Further, the encyclopedic *Cities of the World* (1992) is a four-volume compilation of the current cultural, geographic, and political conditions in more than 2,000 cities in 131 countries.

In addition, the U.S. government (with its intelligence network made up of perhaps the largest research organization in the world) makes available through the U.S. Government Printing Office a number of current, thoroughly researched, and relatively inexpensive country-specific publications. By far the most comprehensive are those found in the *Country Studies* series developed by the Foreign Area Studies Group at American University for the Department of Defense and other government agencies. Formerly called *Area Handbooks*, each of the 110 books in the series, dealing with a particular foreign country, describes and analyzes how the economic, national security, political, and social systems and institutions are influenced by the cultural factors. Researched and written by interdisciplinary teams of scholars, each volume attempts to describe a whole society as a coherent, dynamic system. All the books, ranging from 300 to 500 pages in length, are updated on a fairly regular basis.

For a less encyclopedic approach to country profiles, the U.S. Department of State publishes periodically a series entitled *Background Notes*, short pamphlets (four to eight pages in length) on approximately 160 countries. Each pamphlet in the series includes information on the demography, geography, government, economy, history, and foreign relations of the country. Included also are a statistical profile, brief travel notes, a map, a listing of government officials, and a brief reading list. Single issues or annual subscriptions of *Background Notes* can be obtained from the U.S. Government Printing Office. Also, *Background Notes* for all 160 countries have been compiled by the Gale Research Company in a commercially bound, two-volume book entitled *Countries of the World and Their Leaders Yearbook* (1992).

A less well known, yet very helpful, country-specific series of publications is the U.S. Department of State's *Post Reports*. Written for virtually every country where there is a U.S. embassy, each of these periodically issued *Post Reports* (approximately 16 to 20 pages in length) provides valuable background information on such topics as the telephone system, in-country transportation facilities, newspapers, medical facilities, housing availability, food, clothing, domestic help, and leisure activities. Although the information in *Post Reports* is directed to U.S. government employees and their families, most of it is also relevant to U.S. businesspeople living and working in the specific countries.

### General Reference Works for the Business Traveler

A number of commercial publishers have developed country- and city-specific compendia. Perhaps the most comprehensive such handbook that has appeared in recent years is the *International Business Travel and Relocation Directory* (1987), published by the Gale Research Company. Nearly 1,000 pages in length, this directory provides valuable information for those on either long-term or short-term assignment. The volume is divided into two parts: first, a general discussion for both personnel officers and employees of some of the issues to be considered when making an international transfer; and second, a country-by-country profile of just about everything one should know in order to make a successful adjustment in the 50 most-traveled-to countries. To illustrate, each section includes current information on the country's characteristics, currency, transportation, hotels, useful phrases, telephone service, housing availability, schooling, and medical facilities, among many other topics. Two other compendia are Cummings' *Business Travel Survival Guide* (1991) and Fodor's *Wall Street Journal Guide to Business Travel—International Cities* (1991).

### Sources of Country-Specific News and Current Events

It would be hard to find any successful U.S. businessperson in Chicago, New York, or Atlanta who was not in the habit of keeping abreast of local, national, and international news through newspapers, periodicals, and the electronic media. Hardly a day passes without something being reported that affects one's business or personal life. The same holds true for those conducting business abroad. In addition to knowing the language, history, and culture of the host country, the international businessperson must also be well aware of current happenings. When living and working in any of the major cities of the world it will not be difficult to procure local English-language newspapers or news magazines. However, if the U.S. international businessperson is in the United States or wants to supplement the in-country news coverage, there are a number of very adequate alternatives.

Perhaps the most complete news reporting system available is the *FBIS Daily Report* compiled by the Foreign Broadcast Information Service. This report is published Monday through Friday in eight volumes: (1) *China*, (2) *Eastern Europe*, (3) *Soviet Union*, (4) *Asia and the Pacific*, (5) *Middle East and Africa*, (6) *Latin America*, (7) *Western Europe*, and (8) *South Asia*. Each daily volume of approximately 64 pages contains news and commentary monitored from foreign broadcasts, news agency transmissions, newspapers, and periodicals. Foreign-language items are translated into English by FBIS. Private businesses may subscribe to either hard copy or microfiche versions of the *FBIS Daily Report* through the National Technical Information Service (NTIS) of the U.S. Department of Commerce.

In addition to the prodigious FBIS, which produces more than 500 pages of country-specific news each day, there are other, less voluminous news reporting services that are devoted to smaller segments of the world. For example, the *Information Services on Latin America (ISLA)* compiles each month country-by-country news reports on 27 Latin American and Caribbean countries gleaned from nine major English-language newspapers. *The Asian Recorder* is a weekly digest of current events dealing with country-specific news from the Middle East to Japan. Following a similar format, *The African Recorder*, published by the same company in New Delhi, is a fortnightly record of news for all African countries. International businesspersons interested in keeping informed of current developments in mainland China can subscribe to *Inside China Mainland*, published monthly by the Institute of Current China Studies.

Another important source of information on current developments are the many periodic news reviews published by various foreign governments. *The Week in Germany*, an eight-page weekly news summary, is available through the German Information Center in New York City. *News from France, Indonesia: News and Views*, and *Pakistan Affairs* are examples of biweekly news publications for these countries put out by their embassies in Washington, D.C. Since these periodicals are compiled by governments with a strong interest in putting their best foot forward, they do not always represent the most balanced coverage of in-country news. Nevertheless, they are easily accessible, usually free of charge, and should be used to supplement other sources. In fact, what a government's information services chooses not to report can be valuable to the international businessperson in his or her attempt to develop an accurate and realistic cultural profile.

### Sources on Business Customs and Protocols

The most specific form of country-by-country information relates to business cultures, the do's and don't's of conducting business in a specific country. For the overwhelming majority of the post–World War II era there was a near total absence of descriptions of foreign business customs in the international business literature published in the United States. This lack reflected the very strong position of U.S. business in the world marketplace during the 1950s and 1960s. If the rest of the world wanted our goods and services, it was thought, they would come to us and play the game of business according to our set of rules. Since U.S. products and services are no longer the only or best around—our corner on so many markets simply no longer exists—the U.S. international business community is becoming painfully aware that if we want to sell to other parts of the world we will have to go to them and play according to their rules. In short, to be successful in today's highly competitive international marketplace, it is absolutely imperative that we understand the business customs, practices, and protocols of those with whom we are trying to conduct business.

Although there has been an appreciable amount of literature on different business customs in the last decade, it remains relatively small and uneven in terms of both quality and countries covered. Nevertheless, a number of useful sources deserve mention. First, there is a fairly wide, and growing, number of individually written books that deal with how to avoid shooting oneself in the foot when trying to navigate through a foreign business culture. The best way to find these works is to search the card catalogue (and other reference tools) of the local library. To illustrate, a spate of full-length books have appeared recently on how to understand the often enigmatic (at least to Westerners) business customs of the Japanese. Such titles as *The Intelligent Businessman's Guide to Japan* (Alston, 1990), *Business Guide to Japan: Opening Doors and Closing Deals* (De Mente, 1989), *The Rising Sun on Main Street: Working with the Japanese* (Lanier, 1990), and *How to Do Business with the Japanese: A Strategy for Success* (Zimmerman, 1985) all sound suspiciously similar, yet they do provide a wide variety of excellent information on the Japanese business culture. The recent interest in Japan and its strategic importance to the U.S. economy has spawned this plethora of literature. Unfortunately, the literature on the business customs of Indonesia, Kuwait, or Argentina is considerably more modest, and the literature on the business customs of some of the more obscure parts of the world is either nonexistent or so superficial or inaccessible that it is virtually useless.

In addition to single volumes on one country, several excellent books dealing with the foreign business cultural milieu in general also include helpful country-specific data. For example, Harris and Moran in their 1989 publication entitled *Managing Cultural Differences* discuss key insights into the business cultures of the major regions of the world, including Africa, Europe, South America, the Middle East, and Asia. As with so much of this literature, the treatment is uneven, with some 25 pages devoted to the People's Republic of China and only six pages to all of sub-Saharan Africa. Moreover, there is little consistency in the level of specificity or categories of culture discussed. A more uniform approach is provided by Chesanow (1985) in *The World Class Executive*. In fact, the final three-fourths (220 pages) of this volume is devoted to strategies and tactics for coping with the business cultures in Europe, the Arab world, Japan, China, South Korea, and Latin America. Very concise descriptions of the business cultures of 30 countries are included in Copeland and Griggs (1985), *Going International*. Each of the one-page "country at a glance" summaries includes such topics as sensitivities, forms of address, courtesies, business do's and don't's, negotiations, and entertainment. Even though these brief cultural summaries are not in-depth studies, they do focus on the 30 specific countries with whom the United States conducts most of its business rather than broad regions of the world. In other words, although not definitive, they do provide what the name implies—that is, the business culture "at a glance"—and consequently are a good place to start one's search for an accurate profile of a foreign business culture.

Perhaps the greatest need is a periodically updated series, under a single editor, using consistent categories of analysis and covering a large number of countries. At the present time there are only two series that meet some, but certainly not all, of these requirements. The previously mentioned *Update* series published by Alison Lanier, although providing an excellent general cultural orientation to 15 countries, only devotes a fraction of its attention to the business culture. One series, entitled *Business Customs and Protocol Guides*, is aimed exclusively at providing country-specific descriptions of business customs and is published by the Business Intelligence Program of the Stanford Research Institute. Each of the 14 short volumes in the series (approximately 25 pages in length) covers a uniform set of topics, including making initial contacts, setting appointments, negotiations, the meaning of time, decision making, and connections, as well as a number of issues that can facilitate mutual understanding, such as dress, manners, titles, space usage, sex roles, image enhancers, and taboos. The existing 14 volumes in this series are well researched, readable, and cover a representative number of countries. Although not without its limitations, this series provides the best model for developing a comprehensive series of descriptions of foreign business cultures. It is hoped that in the not too distant future a private publisher (or perhaps more likely, a public agency such as the U.S. Department of Commerce) will be willing to develop a business culture series that will (1) be comprehensive, (2) cover a wide range of countries, (3) employ consistent units of analysis, and (4) be updated periodically.

## HUMAN RESOURCES FOR CULTURE-SPECIFIC INFORMATION

Given the generally inaccessible nature of much culture-specific information, the successful international businessperson must be creative in his or her search for relevant information. This search, of course, requires the use of human resources as well as published ones. Every businessperson bound for a foreign assignment has a vast variety of experts to draw on, but it requires knowing where to look. Unfortunately most businesspeople do not take advantage of the resources at hand, many of which are free. Here are some major sources of expertise that should be utilized.

### One's Own Company

Frequently expertise on the cultural environment of a particular country can be found in one's own corporation. Depending on the size of the corporation, there may be people working right down the hall with experience in living and working in a specific part of the world. Frequently, Western multinational corporations are so large and decentralized, with divisions operating independently of one another, that most divisions do not know what types of international expertise exist in other divisions. If this is the case, the wise international businessperson will do well to contact the one division within the corporation that might have that type of information—the personnel department. Once the appropriate person or persons have been identified, it is more than likely that they will be willing to share all sorts of culturally relevant information, if for no other reason than because they have just become instant experts on a subject of mutual concern.

### Other Companies

Perhaps the greatest source of culture-specific information resides with the thousands of repatriated international businesspeople who have worked and lived abroad. Even those who have not been particularly successful can be valuable resources, provided they have learned something about the local culture despite their own negative experience. Again, most international businesspersons would not think of contacting another firm in the same or nearby city to inquire about personnel with experience in a particular country. However, such a request would be quite appropriate, provided that the firm contacted is not in direct competition with one's own. There is, in other words, no reason for a clothing exporter headquartered in New York City to withhold culture-specific information on Kuwait from an employee of an office furniture company headquartered in Newark, New Jersey. In fact, great gains will be made in the procurement of culture-specific information if and when noncompeting U.S. industries begin to cooperate by pooling their culture-specific expertise in a consortium arrangement, in which all participating corporations can draw on a common pool of experts with experience in different parts of the world.

### Academia

Local colleges and universities are excellent sources of culture-specific information. Interestingly, U.S. businesses have turned to universities for technical assistance but have not, by and large, utilized the cultural, social, or political expertise that is also part of the academic world. Many mid- to large-sized universities and community colleges have well-established area studies programs made up of faculty, and usually graduate students, who have had considerable experience in various parts of the world. For many of these faculty members the prime purpose for living abroad was to study first-hand the sociocultural realities of the area. Perhaps the most relevant are the small but growing number of academic programs in the United States that are designed to integrate international business studies with area studies (that is, language and culture). Although it would be impossible to list them all, this type of program is exemplified by the Masters of International Management offered at the American Graduate School of International Business in Glendale, Arizona; the Masters in International Business Studies (MIBS) offered at the University of South Carolina at Columbia; and the MBA/MA in International Management and International Studies at the Wharton School, University of Pennsylvania. Yet even those institutions that do not offer programs in international business employ faculty from a wide variety of disciplines with extensive knowledge of different parts of the world. For example, a political science professor who had taught several years earlier as a Fulbright professor at the University of Cairo will no doubt be a valuable resource on the general cultural, social, political, and economic environments of Egypt. Such academic experts can be identified with a few well-placed phone calls to the office of the director of the International Studies Program, the dean of the Business School, or the dean of Arts and Sciences.

### International Trade Administration (ITA)

With an unfavorable balance of trade growing at alarming rates since the mid-1970s, the federal government has attempted to stimulate U.S. exports by expanding the services provided by the International Trade Administration of the Department of Commerce, the major federal agency for U.S. firms seeking advice on conducting business abroad. Operating as a service agency for U.S. business, ITA encourages new firms to expand their productivity through exports and suggests new foreign market opportunities to those firms already exporting. The agency is made up of a cadre of foreign commercial officers who provide direct and professional counseling in Washington, D.C., at 47 district offices in the United States, and in over 120 cities throughout the world. Advice is offered in a wide variety of areas, including shipping, documentation requirements, trade exhibitions, tax advantages, and even free legal counseling, to mention only a few. And in addition, these ITA specialists can give excellent advice on local culture and business practices. Unfortunately, ITA remains one of the best kept secrets in U.S. business circles. Despite the fact that many of ITA's extensive resources and services are provided free, it has been estimated (Chesanow, 1985:30) that the overwhelming majority of U.S. businesses have not turned to ITA for assistance. Free literature describing the services of ITA can be obtained by calling ITA headquarters in Washington, D.C., or any of the 47 U.S. and Foreign Commercial Service District Offices throughout the United States.

### Foreign Trade Offices

Many foreign governments maintain foreign trade offices (FTOs) in the United States whose very raison d'etre is to assist U.S. importers and exporters. Although most FTOs are located in Washington or New York, some of the larger foreign governments may have branches in other major cities throughout the country. These offices usually publish excellent (and usually free) brochures, booklets, and so forth on both the technical and the cultural aspects of doing business in their countries. The extent of the services provided by any foreign trade office will vary according to the country's relative affluence and its commitment to stimulating trade with the United States. The Japan External Trade Organization (JETRO) maintains the most elaborate services. To illustrate, JETRO makes available over 100 complimentary publications and films on doing business in Japan and employs Japanese trade experts in New York, Houston, Los Angeles, and San Francisco to answer personal questions. Not all foreign governments provide such extensive services, but frequently helpful culture-specific information can be obtained from the appropriate embassy in Washington or consulate in other cities in the United States.

### Private Sector Consultants and Trainers

Before the 1950s there were virtually no cross-cultural consultants specializing in business. Then with the appearance of Lederer and Burdick's *The Ugly American* (1958) and the "discovery" of culture shock by Oberg (1960), there was an increasing awareness of the hazards involved in conducting business in an unfamiliar cultural environment. In the past several decades an entire specialized consulting and training industry has developed. The problem today is not a shortage of qualified cross-cultural consultants and trainers but rather sorting through all their credentials to find someone with the particular knowledge and skills needed to address a firm's particular, and frequently unique, situation. For a listing of some of the major private cross-cultural consultants, see Hoopes (1984:151–59).

It is critical that a consultant and trainer be able to address the firm's special needs and problems. Does the consultant have the proper culture-specific experience and training? Are the proposed training and/or services designed to meet the specific needs and objectives of the corporation? Are the learning objectives clearly stated? Are the methods of training realistic and compatible with company policies and procedures? How will the program be evaluated to determine if it has accomplished what it promised? Once these questions have been answered to the firm's satisfaction a program can be designed and executed. These may include predeparture briefings for the international businesspersons and their families on such topics as customs, history, political structure, and a host of practical matters necessary for living and working in the assigned country.

In recent years there has been a relatively dramatic increase in the number of people claiming to be cross-cultural trainers or consultants. Many are well trained and effective, but others may be considerably less effective or just plain charlatans. Before hiring such a cross-cultural trainer, one should insist on their demonstrating a number of important qualifications. First, they should possess considerable knowledge of the target area gained through both formal academic study and firsthand living experience. Second, they should understand a number of important anthropological principles and concepts that they can apply to their country-specific area of expertise. Third, they should have personal experience with culture shock and should have made a successful adjustment to living in another culture. Fourth, they should have a sound understanding of their own culture and how their own values and attitudes influence them. Fifth, they should be experienced trainers who feel comfortable using a wide variety of educational strategies, including experiential learning techniques. And finally, they should have a "presentation of self" that corporate personnel would not find offensive.

## THE SEARCH FOR CULTURAL INFORMATION UPON ARRIVAL

So far we have considered a number of possible sources of cultural information that should be consulted before one's departure for a foreign business assignment. This constitutes the predeparture aspect of one's preparation, which should provide a solid background for the most important learning that is yet to come. Regardless of how much predeparture preparation has taken place, the new arrival will be a stranger in a very different, and perhaps frightening, cultural environment. Despite occasional claims to the contrary, this is no different from the position most cultural anthropologists find themselves in when first arriving at the site of a field research project. It is now time for the newly arrived Western businessperson to become his or her own "ethnographer" by becoming an active learner while immersed in the culture. If the businessperson is serious and purposeful about mastering the new cultural environment, there should be no shortage of sources of cultural information, both documentary and human. Moreover, the quality of one's cultural learning during this "on-site" phase should be significant because it will be acquired *experientially*. In short, if the newly arrived businessperson realizes that the culture *is* the classroom, there can be virtually no end to the amount of cultural learning that can occur.

### In-Country Documentary Resources

Since tourism represents a welcome source of foreign exchange, most countries make considerable efforts to attract tourists and make certain that they see the sights, spend their money, and leave with a desire to return. Consequently, most foreign countries, even small third world countries, maintain tourist information centers (at least in the major cities), where the new arrivals can obtain printed information (brochures, booklets, maps, and so on) on things to do and see while in the country. Thus, one of the first stopping places in one's continuing search for cultural information is the local tourist center. However, having in one's possession information on national monuments, historic sites, scenic areas, and museums is just the beginning of the learning process. One's understanding of the culture will be greatly enhanced by actually exploring these places and learning about them first hand. According to Kohls, "there is a high correlation between those foreigners who function at their best overseas and those with the keenest interest in exploring the country to which they are assigned" (1979:45).

It is hard to imagine any country without a public or university library with books on national history, culture, and contemporary issues. Shortly after arrival one should seek permission to use the local library and get to know the most valuable person there, the reference librarian.

Private sector bookstores can also be valuable sources of local cultural data. Not only is one likely to find a number of valuable written sources, but it is also possible to learn a good deal about a culture by noticing how the bookstores are organized. Are some topics or categories of books not sold? Are some topics or categories unusually large? Frequently it is possible to get a feel for what a particular culture emphasizes by looking at how much space is devoted to certain topics in local bookstores. For example, several years ago I was struck by the unusually large section of books in an all-white bookstore in Johannesburg, South Africa, dealing with self-defense, martial arts, fortifying your home, and how to use handguns.

One of the best entries into a culture, and by far the most accessible type of documentary source, are local or national newspapers, some of which will be printed in English. Not only are local newspapers the best source of contemporary happenings but also they reflect a wide range of cultural values. To illustrate, what does it say about a society if there are no letters to the editor? If there is an editorial page, are certain topics restricted or limited? What clues might one get about a culture if male suitors advertise for "brides wanted" in the classified section? Can information be gleaned from the jobs section of the classifieds about the degree of labor specialization within the society? What can you learn about the family structure by reading the obituary pages? And what insights into the culture can one pick up by reading the "comics"? These are only some of the questions that the culturally sensitive businessperson should raise when reading local newspapers in a foreign country.

In addition to reading in-country newspapers daily, many have found it helpful to clip and file some of the more interesting articles. Clipping articles is more convenient than taking notes and can provide a sizable amount of data that can be referred to and studied for years to come.

### In-Country Human Resources

Clearly it would be unwise to spend all or most of one's time in a new country reading various printed materials. There is no substitute for people, for most of the important insights into a culture will come from interacting with local people. After all, they are the real experts in the local culture. Although cultural anthropologists do, in fact, draw on whatever reliable documentary materials are available, the lion's share of their data comes from a combination of being a participant observer and asking questions of knowledgeable local people. These are the two best sources of cultural data for the international businessperson as well.

The stock-in-trade of the field anthropologist is participant observation—that is, immersing oneself in the culture to as great an extent as possible while at the same time making systematic observations and recording what is taking place. Although much has been written in recent years about some of the methodological fine points of participant observation, the primary prerequisite for being a successful participant observer is the desire to do so. Unfortunately, many Western businesspeople when living and working abroad all too often make no attempt to involve themselves personally with the local culture, preferring instead to spend their leisure time with their families, friends, and colleagues in a Western ghetto.

Of course, most international businesspeople operate under certain work and time constraints not usually facing the field anthropologist, thereby making a total immersion into the local culture impractical if not impossible. Yet there are a number of opportunities for expatriate businesspersons to become involved in the local culture. The critical question is whether they choose to take advantage of these opportunities. If they do, they will increase their cultural learning geometrically, and they will most likely enjoy themselves in the process.

Being a participant observer in the local culture involves making a conscious decision, and it also involves taking some personal risks. The newly arrived participant observer, particularly at first, will feel very much out of control of the situation. Much of what will be observed will not be understood, and there will be opportunities at every turn to contract "foot-in-mouth" disease. Yet to succeed as a field anthropologist or international businessperson, one must be patient and able to live with ambiguity. Gradually, more and more of what is observed begins to make sense until eventually an increasingly logical and coherent picture of the culture emerges.

Once the international businessperson decides to become a participant observer in the new culture, the question of how best to record the cultural data arises. The best advice is to always carry a pocket notebook. As new bits of cultural information are experienced it is important to jot down as soon as possible some key words that can be transformed into more elaborate notes at the end of the day. Periodically, perhaps every month or two, one's daily notes should be reviewed to discover both recurring themes and possible inconsistencies, which may require additional focused research to resolve.

When one is acting as one's own ethnographer, participant observation alone is not enough. Bound by one's own cultural perspective, the participant observer can possibly misinterpret what is observed. Thus, as a check the international businessperson turned ethnographer should use the interview method, or put in more mundane terminology, ask questions of local people. Key informants should be chosen carefully, and the sample of interviews should be as large and representative of the total society as possible. Lists of questions useful for developing well-rounded cultural profiles have been suggested by Kohls (1979:46–49) and Darrow and Palquist (1977).

## CONCLUSION

This chapter has explored a number of sources of information available to the international businessperson when attempting to construct a cultural profile of another country. These sources of cultural data include both written materials and human resources. And they include resources that should be consulted in the United States before entering the international business arena as well as those likely to be found abroad. This discussion of sources certainly does not pretend to be definitive but is rather meant to be suggestive. Many valuable data sources have not been mentioned specifically.

The international businessperson should keep several major points in mind when constructing foreign cultural profiles. First, there is a direct correlation between the amount of culture-specific information a person has and the success of his or her personal and professional overseas experience. Second, it is important to be constantly on the lookout for new sources of cultural information *and* to be sufficiently creative and openminded to see how they can be integrated with other sources. And finally, the cultural learning process does not end with an orientation program or the completion of a reading list, but rather is an ongoing process that starts before leaving home and continues throughout one's assignment abroad.

The aim of this chapter has been to explore some sources of information that can help the international businessperson acquire a measure of "cultural literacy" when entering a foreign business setting. According to Hirsch (1987) literacy requires more than knowing how to read; it also requires a certain level of comprehension of background information about the culture. Just as a U.S. high school graduate cannot be considered culturally literate if he or she identifies Karl Marx as one of the Marx Brothers or the Great Gatsby as a magician, the international businessperson attempting to conduct business in Germany cannot be considered culturally literate without knowing something about Nietzsche, Wagner, and the Schwarzwald. The sources discussed in this chapter are intended to provide the Western international businessperson with a starting point in the quest for "literacy" in another culture.

### CROSS-CULTURAL SCENARIOS

Read the following cross-cultural scenarios. In each mini-case study there is a basic cultural conflict between the actors involved. Try to identify the source of the conflict and suggest how it could have been avoided or minimized. Then see how well your analyses compare to the explanations in the Appendix.

**6–1.** Jeff Walters, owner and manager of a highly successful bookstore in Philadelphia during the 1960s and 1970s, had gone on a three-week safari to East Africa. He and his wife had been so struck by the beauty of the area that they had decided soon after returning to the United States to sell the bookstore and start a book distribution company based in Nairobi that would supply books from all over the world to eastern and southern African countries. Although the new business was only four years old, Jeff's enthusiasm for combining his love of books with his newfound love of East Africa was largely responsible for the great success of the new enterprise. In only four years Jeff, as president of the company, had put together a professional and administrative staff of 18 local Kenyans.

Jeff found that he was behind schedule in preparing a lengthy proposal for a possible government contract due in the U.S.A.I.D. office in Nairobi the next day. The deadline was so critical that he had to work very closely with some of his staff to make sure that it was met. In the final hours Jeff found himself helping the secretaries make copies, collate, and assemble the multiple copies of the proposal. But minutes after pitching in to help he began to notice that his staff became very noncommunicative and he seemed to be getting a lot of cold stares. Jeff couldn't understand why his attempts to be helpful were so unappreciated.

HOW COULD YOU HELP JEFF BETTER UNDERSTAND THIS CROSS-CULTURAL PROBLEM?

**6–2.** Bill Nugent, an international real estate developer from Dallas, had made a 2:30 P.M. appointment with Mr. Abdullah, a high-ranking government official in Riyadh, Saudi Arabia. From the beginning things did not go well for Bill. First, he was kept waiting until nearly 3:45 before he was ushered into Mr. Abdullah's office. And when he finally did get in, several other men were also in the room. Even though Bill felt that he wanted to get down to business with Mr. Abdullah, he was reluctant to get too specific because he considered much of what they needed to discuss sensitive and private. To add to Bill's sense of frustration Mr. Abdullah seemed more interested in engaging in meaningless small talk rather than dealing with the substantive issues concerning their business.

HOW MIGHT YOU HELP BILL DEAL WITH HIS FRUSTRATION?

**6–3.** Jim Ellis, vice president of a North Carolina knitwear manufacturer, was sent by his company to observe firsthand how operations were proceeding in their Korean plant and to help institute some new managerial procedures. Before any changes could be made, however, Jim wanted to learn as much as possible about the problems that existed at the plant. During his first week he was met with bows, polite smiles, and the continual denial of any significant problems. But Jim was enough of a realist to know that he had never heard of any manufacturing operation that didn't have some problems. So after some creative research, he uncovered a number of problems that the local manager and staff were not acknowledging. None of the problems were particularly unusual or difficult to solve. But Jim was frustrated that no one would admit that any problems existed. "If you don't acknowledge the problems," he complained to one of the managers, "how do you expect to be able to solve them?" And then to further exasperate him, just today when a problem was finally brought to his attention, it was not mentioned until the end of the workday when there was no time left to solve it.

HOW COULD YOU HELP JIM BETTER UNDERSTAND THE DYNAMICS OF THIS SITUATION?

**6–4.** Bill Higgins had served as the manager of a large U.S. timber company located in a rather remote rain forest in a South American country. Since it began its logging operations in the 1950s a major problem facing the company has been the recruitment of labor. The only nearby source of labor is the sparsely populated local Indian groups in the area. Bill's company has been in direct competition for laborers with a German company operating in the same region. In an attempt to attract the required number of laborers, Bill's company has invested heavily in new housing and offered considerably higher wages than the German company as well as a guaranteed 40-hour work week. Yet the majority of the available workers continued to work for the German company, despite its substandard housing and a minimum hourly wage. Bill finally brought in several U.S. anthropologists who had worked among the local Indians. The answer to Bill's labor recruitment problem was quite simple, but it required looking at the values of the Indian labor force rather than simply building facilities that would appeal to the typical U.S. laborer.

WHAT DID THE ANTHROPOLOGISTS TELL BILL?

**6–5.** Directly after completing a master's degree in international business Dick Sutton decided to accept a job with a firm in Tokyo. He had studied Japanese for a year and was most interested in immersing himself in Japanese culture. Within the first month of his arrival he was invited to an office party. As was the custom, most of the employees were expected to entertain the group with a song, poem, or joke. Knowing the keen interest the Japanese have in baseball, Dick recited the poem "Casey at the Bat," which seemed to be well received. Dick was having a good time at the party and was secretly congratulating himself on his decision to come to Japan. In fact, he couldn't help thinking how informal and playful all his colleagues were, including the upper-level executives, a far cry from all the descriptions he had read of the Japanese as austere and humorless businesspeople. Later in the evening Dick found himself talking with two of his immediate superiors. Wanting to draw on the informality and good humor of the moment, Dick casually brought up some plans he had for a new marketing strategy, only to be met with near total indifference. For the remainder of the evening Dick felt as though he was not being included in the party.

WHAT ADVICE COULD YOU GIVE DICK?

# 7

# NEGOTIATING
# ACROSS CULTURES

In a very general sense, the process of negotiating is absolutely fundamental to human communication and interaction. If we stop to consider it, we are negotiating all the time. We negotiate with our spouses, children, co-workers, friends, bosses, landlords, customers, bankers, neighbors, and clients. Because negotiating is such an integral part of our everyday lives, it becomes largely an unconscious process, for we do not spend a lot of time thinking about how we do it. As with so many other aspects of our behavior, the way we negotiate is colored by our cultural assumptions. Whether we are effective negotiators or not, our culturally conditioned negotiating styles are largely operating at an unconscious level.

When negotiating within our own culture, it is possible to operate effectively at the intuitive or unconscious level. However, when we leave our familiar cultural context and enter into international negotiations, the scene changes dramatically. There are no longer shared values, interests, goals, ethical principles, or cultural assumptions between the negotiating parties. As we demonstrated in previous chapters, different cultures have different values, attitudes, morals, behaviors, and linguistic styles, all of which can greatly affect the process and outcome of our negotiations. Thus, we cannot negotiate across cultural lines without being conscious of the negotiation process. This chapter is aimed at analyzing the cross-cultural negotiation process, for by heightening our awareness of some of the potential pitfalls, we may become more effective international negotiators.

## THE NATURE OF CROSS-CULTURAL NEGOTIATION

Because the act of negotiating is so central to our lives, we frequently fail to define it. Those who write about the process of negotiation, on the other hand, do define it—sometimes in excruciating detail—but fail to agree on a common definition. But, as Moran and Stripp (1991:71–72) remind us, the common theme running through all of the definitions is that two or more parties, who have both common and conflicting interests, interact with one another for the purpose of reaching a mutually beneficial agreement.

Effective negotiation does not involve bludgeoning the other side into submission. Rather, it involves the more subtle art of *persuasion,* whereby all parties feel as though they have benefited. There is no simple formula for success. Each situation must be assessed within its own unique set of circumstances. The successful negotiator must choose the appropriate strategy, project the correct personal and organizational images, do the right type of homework, ask the most relevant questions, and offer and request the appropriate types of concession at the right time. Negotiating within one's own culture is sufficiently difficult, but the pitfalls increase geometrically when one enters the international/intercultural arena.

Being a skilled negotiator in any context entails being an intelligent, well-prepared, creative, flexible, and patient problem solver. International negotiators, however, face an additional set of problems/obstacles not ordinarily encountered by domestic negotiators. As we have tried to establish from the outset of this book, one very important obstacle to international negotiations is culture. Because culture involves everything that a people have, think, and do, it goes without saying that it will influence or color the negotiation process. The very fact that usually one party in a negotiation will travel to the country of the other party establishes a foreign negotiating setting for at least one party, and this "strangeness" can be a formidable barrier to communication, understanding, and agreement.

There are other barriers as well. For example, international negotiation entails working within the confines of two different, and sometimes conflicting, legal structures. Unless the negotiating parties are able to both understand and cope with the differing legal requirements, a joint international contract may be governed by two or more legal systems. Another barrier may be the extent to which government bureaucracies in other countries exert their influence on the negotiation process, a problem not always understood by Westerners whose governments are relatively unobtrusive in business negotiations.

And, finally, an additional obstacle that goes beyond cultural differences is the sometimes volatile, or at least unpredictable, geopolitical realities of the two countries of the negotiating parties. Sudden changes in governments, the enactment of new legislation, or even natural disasters can disrupt international business negotiations either temporarily or permanently. For example, the disintegration of the Soviet Union, Iraq's invasion of Kuwait, or an earthquake in Mexico could all have far-reaching implications for Western businesspersons who were in the process of negotiating business deals in those parts of the world.

While we recognize the importance to international negotiations of these noncultural obstacles (different legal structures, interference by government bureaucracies, and geopolitical instability), our discussion of international business negotiation will focus on the cultural dimension.

It should be apparent by now that success in negotiating international business contracts requires a deep understanding of the culture of those on the other side of the table. The reason for this cultural awareness, however, is not for the purpose of bringing the other side to its knees—to make them do what we want them to do. Nor is it to accommodate them by giving up some of our own strongly adhered-to principles. Rather, an appreciation of the important cultural elements of the other side is essential if one is to get on with the business at hand so that all parties concerned can feel as though they are better off after the negotiations than before. Moreover, it is equally the responsibility of both sides in the negotiating process to understand the cultural realities of their negotiation partners. Intercultural communication, in other words, is a two-way street, with both sides sharing the burden and responsibility of cultural awareness.

## WHERE TO NEGOTIATE

Earlier we defined negotiation as a process between people who share some common interests, people who stand to benefit from bringing the process to a successful conclusion. Both sides have a stake in the outcome, so it stands to reason that the place of negotiations could be on the home turf of either party or in a neutral environment. The selection of a site for the negotiations is of critical importance because there are a number of advantages of negotiating in your own backyard. In the world of international diplomatic negotiations, the question of where a summit meeting will occur is taken very seriously because it is assumed that the location will very likely affect the nature and the outcome of the negotiations. The business negotiator who travels abroad is confronted with an appreciable number of problems and challenges not faced by those who negotiate at home. Let us consider some of the difficulties encountered when negotiating abroad.

First, and perhaps most important, the negotiator abroad must adjust to an unfamiliar environment during the days, weeks, or even months of the negotiations. This involves getting used to differences in language, foods, pace of life, and other aspects of culture. The negotiator who is well prepared will make a relatively smooth and quick adjustment, yet not without moments of discomfort, awkwardness, and general psychological disorientation. Time and effort must be spent learning about the new environment, such as how to make a telephone call, where to find a fax machine, or simply how to locate the rest room. For those who are less well prepared, the adjustment process may be so difficult that there is little energy left for the important work of negotiating.

Second, the business negotiator cannot avoid the deleterious effects of jet lag. Even for those international travelers who heed all of the conventional wisdom concerning minimizing jet lag (avoid alcohol and eat certain foods), an intercontinental flight will nevertheless take its toll on one's physical condition. Thus, the traveling negotiator is likely not to be as rested or alert as his or her counterpart who doesn't have to cope with jet lag.

Third, the negotiator has little or no control over the setting in which the discussions take place. The size of the conference room, the seating arrangements, and the scheduling of times for both negotiating and socializing are decisions made by the host negotiating team. The side that controls these various details of the process can use them to their own advantage.

Fourth, the negotiator working in a foreign country is further hampered by being physically separated from his or her business organization and its various support personnel. Frequently, before negotiators can agree to certain conditions of a contract, they must obtain additional information from the manufacturing, shipping, or financial department of their home office. Those negotiating at home have a marked advantage over the traveling negotiator because it is always easier to get a question answered by a colleague down the hall than by relying on transcontinental telephones or fax messages.

Finally, negotiators working on foreign soil are under pressure to conclude the negotiations as soon as possible, a type of pressure not experienced by those negotiating at home. The longer negotiations drag on, the longer the negotiator will be away from the other operations of the office that need attention, the longer his or her family and social life will be disrupted, and the more it will cost the firm in terms of travel-related expenses. Given these very real pressures, negotiators working abroad are more likely to make certain concessions than they might if they were negotiating at home.

It would appear that negotiating abroad has a number of distinct disadvantages as compared to negotiating at home, including the hassle of an unfamiliar cultural setting, uncertain lines of communication with the home office, lack of control over the negotiating setting, and considerable expenditure of both time and travel funds. There is little doubt that, given the choice, most Western businesspeople would opt to conduct their negotiations at home. Yet, more often than not, Westerners are attempting to sell their products and ideas abroad. And if the potential international customers are to learn about the products or services, it is essential that the Westerners go to them. Moreover, in many parts of the world, particularly in developing areas, potential customers from both the private and public sectors have very limited resources for traveling. Thus, in many cases, if Westerners desire to remain competitive in the international marketplace, they will have no other choice than to do their negotiating on foreign soil.

## EFFECTIVE STRATEGIES FOR INTERNATIONAL NEGOTIATORS

In keeping with the conceptual nature of this book, this chapter does not attempt to list all of the do's and don't's of negotiating in all of the cultures of the world. Such an approach—given the vast number of features found in each culture—would be well beyond the scope of the present book and certainly beyond any single individual's capacity to comprehend. Whereas some works have taken a country-by-country approach to international negotiating (Kennedy, 1985; Moran & Stripp, 1991), here we will focus on certain general principles of cross-cultural negotiating that can be applied to most, if not all, international situations. This chapter will not provide a cookbook-style guide for avoiding negotiating faux pas in all of the major cultures of the world, but it will draw upon some of the most positive experiences of successful intercultural negotiators.

### Concentrate on Long-term Relationships, Not Short-term Contracts

If there is one central theme running through the literature on international business negotiations it is that the single most important consideration is building relationships over the long run rather than focusing on a single contract. At times U.S. businesspersons have been criticized for their short-term view of doing business. Some feel that they should not waste time; they should get in there and get the contract signed and get on other business. If the other side fails to meet their contractual obligations, the lawyers can sue. Frequently this approach carries with it the implicit analogy of a sports contest. Negotiating across cultures is like a football game, the purpose of which is to outmaneuver, outmanipulate, outsmart, and generally overpower the other side, which is seen as the opponent. And the wider the margin of victory, the better. But conventional wisdom, coupled with the experience of successful negotiators, strongly suggests that international business negotiating is not about winning big, humiliating the opposition, making a killing, and gaining all of the advantages. Rather, successful international business negotiating is conducted in a cooperative climate in which the needs of both sides are met and in which both sides can emerge as winners.

To be certain, there exists considerable variation throughout the world in terms of why people enter into business negotiation in the first place. In some societies, such as our own, businesspeople may enter into negotiations for the sake of obtaining the signed contract; other societies, however, view the negotiations as primarily aimed at creating a long-standing relationship and only secondarily for the purpose of signing a short-term contract. As Salacuse (1991:60) reminds us, for many Americans a signed contract represents *closing* a deal, whereas to a Japanese, signing a contract is seen as *opening* a relationship. With those cultures that tend to emphasize the relationship over the contract, it is likely that there will be no contract unless a relationship of trust and mutual respect has been established. And even though relationship building may not conform to the typical American's time frame, the inescapable truth is that, because relationships

*If you are to build long-lasting relationships with international business associates, it helps to get to know them informally as people.*

are so important in the international arena, negotiations are unlikely to succeed without them.

Building relationships requires that negotiators take the time to get to know one another. Frequently this involves activities—eating, drinking, visiting national monuments, playing golf—that strike the typical North American as being outside the realm of business and consequently a waste of time. But this type of ritual socializing is vital because it represents an honest effort to understand, as fully as possible, the needs, goals, values, interests, and opinions of the negotiators on the other side. It is not necessary for the two sides to have similar needs, goals, and values in order to have a good relationship, for it is possible to disagree in a number of areas and still have a good working relationship. However, both parties need to be willing to identify their shared interests while at the same time work at reconciling their conflicting interests in a spirit of cooperation and mutual respect. And this twofold task, which is never easy to accomplish, has the very best chance of succeeding if a relationship built on trust and mutual respect has been established between the negotiating parties.

### Focus on the Interests Behind the Positions

After the parties in a negotiation have developed a relationship, the discussion of positions can begin. This stage of negotiating involves both sides setting forth what they want to achieve from the negotiations. From a seller's perspective, it may involve selling a certain number of sewing machines at $X$ dollars per unit. From the perspective of the purchaser, it may involve receiving a certain number of sewing machines within a month's time at $X$ minus $30 per unit. Once the positions have been clearly stated, the effective international negotiator will then look behind those positions for the underlying needs of the other party. The stated position is usually one way of satisfying needs. But often the position of one side is in direct opposition to the position of the other side. If the negotiators focus just on the positions, it is unlikely that they will resolve or reconcile their differences. But by looking beyond the position to the basic needs that gave rise to those positions in the first place, it is likely that creative solutions can be found that will satisfy both parties.

The need to distinguish between a *position* and the *needs underlying the position* has been effectively illustrated by Foster (1992:286–87). The representative of a U.S. telecommunications firm had been negotiating with the communications representative from the Chinese government. After months of relationship building and discussing terms, the finalization of the agreement appeared to be in sight. But at the eleventh hour the Chinese representative raised an additional condition that took the American by surprise. The Chinese representative argued that since they were about to embark on a long-term business relationship between friends, the U.S. firm should give its Chinese friends a special reduced price that it would not give to other customers. The problem with this request was that the U.S. firm had a strict policy of uniform pricing for all countries with which it did business.

If we look at this situation solely in terms of the positions of the two parties, it would appear to be an impasse. For anything to be resolved, one party would have to get what it wanted while the other would have to abandon its position. But, by understanding the basic needs behind the positions, both sides have more room to maneuver so that a win-win situation can result. Let us consider the needs behind the positions. The Chinese position was based on two essential needs: to get a lower price, thus saving money, and to receive a special favor as a sign of the American's friendship and commitment to the relationship. The position of the U.S. firm was based on its need to adhere to the principle of uniform pricing. By looking at the situation from the perspective of underlying needs rather than positions, it now became possible to suggest some alternative solutions. In fact, the U.S. negotiator offered another proposal: to sell the Chinese some new additional equipment at a very favorable price in exchange for sticking with the original pricing agreement. Such an arrangement met all of the needs of both parties. The Chinese were saving money on the new equipment *and* they were receiving a special favor of friendship from the U.S. firm. At the same time, the U.S. company did not have to violate its own policy of uniform pricing. In this example, a win-win solution was possible because the negotiators were able to concentrate on the needs behind the positions rather than on the positions themselves. Once the negotiators were willing to look beyond a prepackaged, non-negotiable, unilateral position for having their own needs met, they were able to set out to explore new and creative ways of satisfying each other's needs.

### Avoid Overreliance on Cultural Generalizations

The central theme of this book has been that success in any aspect of international business is directly related to one's knowledge of the cultural environment in which one is operating. Simply put, the more knowledge a person has of the culture of his or her international business partners, the less likely he or she will be to misinterpret what is being said or done, and the more likely one's business objectives will be met. Communication patterns—both linguistic and nonverbal—need to be mastered as well as the myriad of other culture-specific details that can get in the way of effective intercultural business communication. But just as it would be imprudent to place too little emphasis on cultural information, it is equally inadvisable to be overly dependent on such knowledge.

As was pointed out in Chapter 2, cultural "facts" are generalizations based on a sample of human behavior, and as such can only point out *tendencies* at the negotiating table. Not all Middle Easterners engage in verbal overkill, and not all Japanese are reluctant to give a direct answer. If we tend to interpret cultural generalizations too rigidly, we run the risk of turning the generalizations into cultural stereotypes. We may chuckle when we hear heaven defined as the place where the police are British, the cooks French, the mechanics German, the lovers Italian, and it's all organized by the Swiss; and, conversely, hell is defined as the place where the cooks are British, the mechanics French, the lovers Swiss, the police German, and it's all organized by Italians. Such cultural stereotypes can be offensive to those being lumped together uncritically, but they can be particularly harmful in the process of international business negotiations because they can be wrong. Sometimes negotiators on the other side of the table do not act the way the generalization would predict.

To be certain, people's negotiating behavior is influenced by their culture, but there may be some other factors at work as well. How a person behaves also may be conditioned by such variables as education, biology, or experience. To illustrate, a Mexican business negotiator who has an MBA from the Wharton School may not object to discussing business at lunch, as most other Mexicans might. We should not automatically assume that all Mexicans will act in a stereotypical way. Owing to this particular Mexican's education and experience, he has learned how to behave within the U.S. frame of reference. It is, therefore, important that we move beyond cultural stereotyping and get to know the negotiators on the other side not only as members of a particular cultural group, but also as individuals with their own unique set of personality traits and experiences.

### Be Sensitive to Timing

Timing may not be everything, but in international negotiations it certainly can make a difference between success and failure. As pointed out in Chapter 5, different cultures have different rhythms and different concepts of time. In cultures like our own, with tight schedules and a precise reckoning of time, it is anticipated that business will be conducted without wasting time. But in many parts of the world it is not realistic to expect to arrive one day and consummate a deal the next before jetting off to another client in another country. The more likely scenario involves spending what may seem like inordinately long periods on insignificant details, frustrating delays, and unanticipated postponements. Bringing the U.S. notion of time into an international negotiation will invariably result in either frustration or the eventual alienation of those with whom one is negotiating.

As a general rule, international negotiations, for a number of reasons, take longer than domestic negotiations. We should keep in mind that McDonald's engaged in negotiations for nearly a decade before it began selling hamburgers in Moscow. In another situation, a high-level salesperson for a U.S. modular office furniture company spent months negotiating a deal in Saudi Arabia. He made frequent courtesy calls, engaged in long discussions on a large number of topics other than office furniture, and drank enough coffee to float a small ship. But the months of patience paid off. His personal commission (not his company's profit) was in excess of $2 million dollars! The lesson here is clear. An international negotiator must first understand the local rhythm of time, and if it is slower than at home, exercise the good sense to be patient.

Another important dimension of time that must be understood is that some times of the year are better than others for negotiating internationally. All cultures have certain times of the year when people are preoccupied with social or religious concerns or when everything having to do with business simply shuts down. Before negotiating abroad, one should become familiar with the national calendar. To illustrate, one should not plan to do any global deal making with the Taiwanese on October 10, their national day of independence; or with the Japanese during "Golden Week," when most people take a vacation; or anywhere in the Islamic world during Ramadan, when Muslin businessmen are more concerned with fasting than with negotiating. Any attempt to conduct negotiations on these holidays, traditional vacation times, or times of religious observance will generally meet with as much success as a non-American might have trying to conduct business negotiations in the United States during the week between Christmas and New Year's.

Still another consideration of time has to do with the different time zones between one's home office and the country in which the negotiations are taking place. Owing to these different time zones, an American negotiating in Manila cannot fax the home office in New York and expect an answer within minutes, as might be expected if the negotiations were taking place in Boston. If at 4:00 P.M. (Manila time) a question is raised in the negotiations that requires clearance or clarification from the home office, it is not likely that an answer will be received until the next day because in New York it is 3:00 in the morning. Thus, attempting to operate between two distant time zones can be frustrating for most Americans because it tends to slow down the pace of the negotiations.

### Remain Flexible

Whenever entering an international negotiating situation, the Western negotiator, despite the best preparation, will always have an imperfect command of how things work. In such an environment some of the best laid plans frequently go unexecuted: schedules change unexpectedly; government bureaucrats become more recalcitrant than predicted; people don't follow through with what they promise. When things don't go as expected, it is important to be able to readjust quickly and efficiently. To be flexible does not mean to be weak; rather, it means being capable of responding to changing situations. Flexibility, in other words, means avoiding the all too common malady known as "hardening of the categories."

The need for remaining open and flexible has been well illustrated by Foster (1992:254–55), who tells of a U.S. businessman trying to sell data processing equipment to a high-level government official in India. After preparing himself thoroughly, the American was escorted into the official's office for their initial meeting. But much to the American's surprise, seated on a nearby sofa was another gentleman who was never introduced. For the entire meeting the host government official acted as if the third man were not there. The American became increasingly uncomfortable with the presence of this mystery man who was sitting in on the negotiations, particularly as they discussed specific details. After a while the American began having paranoid delusions. Who was this man listening in on these private discussions? He even imagined that the man might be one of his competitors. The American negotiator became so uncomfortable with this situation that he lost his capacity to concentrate on the negotiations and eventually lost the potential contract. Here was a perfect example of a negotiator who was unsuccessful because he could not adjust to an unfamiliar situation. In India, as in some other parts of the world as well, it is not unusual for a third party to be present at negotiations. They may be friends, relatives, or advisors of the host negotiator invited to listen in to provide advice—and perhaps a different perspective. Unaware of this customary practice in India, this U.S. negotiator began to imagine the worst until it had irreparably destroyed his capacity to focus on the negotiations at hand.

We can see how flexibility is important in order to most effectively adapt to unfamiliar cultural situations that are bound to emerge when negotiating internationally. But remaining flexible has another advantage as well. Flexibility creates an environment in which creative solutions to negotiating problems can emerge. We have said earlier that negotiations should be a win-win situation, whereby both sides can communicate their basic needs and interests, rather than just their positions, and then proceed to brainstorm on how best to meet the needs of both sides. A win-win type of negotiation is most likely to occur when both sides remain flexible and open to exploring nontraditional solutions.

### Prepare Carefully

It is hard to imagine any undertaking—be it in business, government, education, or athletics—where advanced preparation would not be an asset. Nowhere is this more true than in the arena of international negotiating where the variables are so complex. There is a straightforward and direct relationship between the amount of preparation and the chances for success when engaging in global deal making. Those who take the rather cavalier attitude of "Let's go over and see what the Japanese have to say" are bound to be disappointed. Rather, what is needed is a substantial amount of advanced preparation, starting, of course, with as full an understanding as possible of the local cultural realities. But in addition, the would-be negotiator needs to seek answers to important questions concerning his or her own objectives, the bottom line position, the types of information needed as the negotiations progress, an agenda, and the accessibility of support services, to mention a few. These and many other questions need to be answered *prior* to getting on the plane. Failure to prepare adequately will have at least two negative consequences. First, it will communicate to the other side that you don't consider the negotiations sufficiently important to have done your homework. And second, ill-prepared negotiators frequently are forced into making certain concessions that they may later regret.

We often hear the old adage "knowledge is power." Although most North Americans would agree, we are a society that tends to downplay, at least in principle, status distinctions based on power. Our democratic philosophy, coupled with our insistence on universal education, encourages people from all parts of the society to get as much education (and information) as possible. Even the recent computer revolution in the United States now puts vast quantities of information into virtually anyone's hands. Consequently, Americans usually do not equate high status or power with the possession of information. In some other cultures, however, there is a very close association between knowledge and power. Unless Americans negotiating in such cultures have as much information as possible, they are likely to be seen as weak and, by implication, ineffectual negotiators.

A basic part of preparing for negotiations is self-knowledge. How well do you understand yourself, the assumptions of your own culture, and your own goals and objectives for this particular negotiation? If you are part of a negotiating team, a number of questions must be answered: Who are the team members? How have they been selected? Is there general consensus on what the team hopes to accomplish? Is there a proper balance between functional skills, cross-cultural experience, and negotiating expertise? Has a rational division of labor been agreed upon in terms of such tasks as note taking, serving as a spokesperson, or making local arrangements? Has there been sufficient time for team building, including discussions of strategies and counterstrategies?

A particularly important area of preparation has to do with getting to know the negotiators on the other side of the table. At the outset, it must be determined if the organization is the appropriate one to be negotiating with in the first place. Once that has been decided, it is important to know whether their negotiators have the authority and responsibility to make decisions. Having this information *prior* to the negotiations can eliminate the possibility of long delays stemming from the last-minute disclosure that the negotiators on the other side really cannot make final contractual decisions. But once involved in the negotiating process, it is important, as a general rule, to get to know the other team's negotiators as people rather than simply as members of a particular culture.

### Learn to Listen, Not Just Speak

The style of oral discourse in the United States is essentially a very assertive one. Imbued with a high sense of competition, most North Americans want to make certain that their views and positions are presented as clearly and as powerfully as possible. As a consequence, they tend to concentrate far more on sending messages than on receiving them. Many Westerners treat a discussion as a debate, the objective of which is to win by convincing the other party of the superiority of their position. Operating under such an assumption, many North Americans are concentrating more on their own response than what the other party is actually saying. They seem to have a stronger desire to be heard than to hear. Although public speaking courses are quite common in our high schools and colleges, courses on how to listen are virtually nonexistent. Because effective listening is a vital component of the negotiating process, Westerners in general, and North Americans in particular, are at a marked disadvantage when they appear at the negotiating table.

If, as we have tried to suggest throughout this chapter, the best negotiator is the well-informed negotiator, then active listening is absolutely essential for understanding the other side's positions and interests. The understanding that comes from your active listening can have a positive persuasive effect on your negotiating partners in at least two important ways. First, the knowledge gleaned through listening can convince your negotiating partners that you are knowledgeable and, thus, worthy of entering into a long-term relationship. And second, the very fact that you made the effort to really hear what they were saying will, in almost every case, enhance the rapport and trust between the two parties.

Developing good listening skills may be easier said than done. Nevertheless, there are some general guidelines that, if followed, can help us receive oral messages more effectively.

1. Be aware of the phenomenon that psychologists call *cognitive dissonance,* the tendency to discount, or simply not hear, any message that is inconsistent with what we already believe or want to believe. In other words, if the message does not conform to our preconceived way of thinking, we subconsciously tend to dismiss its importance. It is important to give yourself permission to actively hear all messages—those that you agree with and those that you don't. It is not necessary that you agree with everything that is being said, but it is important to hear the message so that you will then be in a position to seek creative ways of resolving whatever differences may exist.

2. Listen to the whole message before offering a response. Focus on understanding rather than interrupting the message so that you can give a rebuttal/response. Because no one likes to be cut off before he or she is finished speaking, it is vital for the effective negotiator to practice allowing other people to finish their ideas and sentences.

3. Concentrate on the message rather than the style of the presentation. It is easy to get distracted from what is being said by focusing instead on how it is presented. No matter how inarticulate, disorganized, or inept the speaker might be, try to look beyond those stylistic features and concentrate on the content of the message.

4. Learn to ask open-ended questions which are designed to allow the speaker to elaborate on a particular point.

5. Be conscious of staying in the present. All people bring into a negotiation session a wide variety of baggage from the past. It is tempting to start thinking about yesterday's racquetball game with a friend, this morning's intense conversation with your boss, or the argument you had with your spouse at breakfast, but to do so will distract you from actively hearing what is being said.

6. Consider the possibility of having a friend or close associate serve as an official listener whose job it is to listen to the other side with another set of ears. Such a person can provide a valuable new perspective on what is being said and can also serve as a check on your own perceptions.

7. In almost all situations, taking notes will help you become a more effective listener. Provided you don't attempt to record every word, selective note taking can help to highlight what is being said. Not only will note taking help to document the messages, but when the speaker notices that you are taking notes, he or she will, in all likelihood, make a special effort to be clear and accurate.

## THE USE OF INTERPRETERS

Throughout this book we have stressed the importance of knowing as much as possible about the language and culture of the people with whom one is doing business. To speak the language of your business partner gives you an enormous advantage, in that it enhances rapport and allows you to understand more fully the thought patterns of your business partners. However, when deciding on which language to use in the negotiation, you should not be guided by the principle that a little knowledge is better than none at all. In other words, unless you are extremely well versed in a foreign language, you should not try to negotiate in that language directly, but rather rely on the services of a competent interpreter. But even if the negotiator has a relatively good command of the language, it may be helpful to work through an interpreter because it allows you more time to formulate your response. On the other hand, use of an interpreter has certain disadvantages, such as increasing the number of people involved, increasing the costs of the negotiations, and serving as a barrier to the two sides really getting to know one another.

When considering the use of a linguistic intermediary in cross-cultural negotiations, it is important to make the distinction between a translator and an interpreter. Although both roles are aimed at turning the words of one language into the words of another language, the translator usually works with documents, whereas the interpreter works with the spoken word in a face-to-face situation. Translators have the luxury of using dictionaries and generally are not under any great time constraints. Interpreters, on the other hand, must listen to what is being said and then instantaneously translate those words into the other language. Interpreting is a demanding job, for it requires constant translating, evaluating, and weighing the meaning of specific words within the specific social context. A good interpreter not only will need to be aware of the usual meaning of the words in the two languages but must also consider the intent of the words and the meanings of the nonverbal gestures as well. Because of these special demands, language interpretation is more exhausting—and consequently, less accurate—than language translation.

When selecting an interpreter, it is important for that person to be both intimately knowledgeable of the two languages and have a technical expertise in the area being negotiated. For example, while a U.S. university professor of Spanish literature may have an excellent command of the language, he or she may not be particularly effective at translating scientific terms or highly technical data on weaving equipment. It is this type of shortcoming that could lead an interpreter to translate the term "hydraulic ram" into the term "wet sheep."

Because the use of an interpreter involves placing an additional person between the two primary negotiators, one should take a number of precautions to ensure that the interpreter clarifies communication rather than obscures it. First, the negotiator and the interpreter should allow sufficient time before the negotiations begin to get to know one another. Only when the interpreter understands your goals and expectations can he or she represent your interests to the other side and be on the lookout for the type of information that you need. Second, help the interpreter by speaking slowly and in discreet sentences. By pausing momentarily between sentences, you are actually providing a little more time for the interpreter to do his or her job. Third, because interpreting is an exhausting job that requires intense concentration, interpreters should be given breaks periodically to recharge their intellectual batteries. Fourth, plan your words carefully so as to avoid ambiguities, slang, or other forms that do not translate well. And finally, it is imperative that interpreters be treated with respect and acknowledged as the highly qualified professionals that they are. The purposeful development of cordial relations with your interpreter can only help to facilitate the process of communication at the negotiating table.

## THE GLOBAL NEGOTIATOR

We have examined, in a very general way, some of the problems and challenges of negotiating abroad. This chapter is not intended to be a cookbook for the would-be international negotiator. Rather, it is offered as a set of general guidelines for those who find themselves negotiating across cultures. We should bear in mind that there are never any two negotiating situations that are exactly alike. But most of the strategies suggested here are applicable to whatever type of cross-cultural negotiating session one can imagine. We have suggested that international negotiators should: (a) concentrate on building long-term relationships rather than short-term contracts, (b) focus on the interests that lay behind the positions, (c) avoid overdependence on cultural generalizations, (d) develop a sensitivity to timing, (e) remain flexible, (f) prepare carefully ahead of time, (g) learn to listen effectively, and (h) know when to use interpreters.

A major theme running through the contemporary literature is that because negotiating across cultures involves mutual interdependence between the parties, it must be conducted in an atmosphere of mutual trust and cooperation. Quite apart from your position on the issues that are being negotiated, it is important to maintain a high degree of personal respect for those on the other side of the table. Even though it is very likely that the negotiators on the other side of the table view the world very differently than you do, they should always be approached with respect and with a willingness to learn. You should not try to reform the other culture at the negotiating table in hopes that they will eventually be more like yourself, for the simple reason that it will not work. On the other hand, you should not go overboard in the other direction by "going native." Most people tend to be suspicious of anyone imitating their gestures or behaviors. The soundest advice is to learn to understand and respect cultural differences while retaining one's own. This spirit of mutual respect and cooperation has been cogently expressed by Salacuse (1991:164):

> At times the two sides at the negotiating table are like two persons in a canoe who must combine their skills and strength if they are to make headway against powerful currents, through dangerous rapids, around hidden rocks, and over rough portages. Alone they can make no progress and will probably lose control. Unless they cooperate, they risk wrecking or overturning the canoe on the obstacles in the river. Similarly, unless global deal makers find ways of working together, their negotiations will founder on the many barriers encountered in putting together an international business transaction.

### CROSS-CULTURAL SCENARIOS

Read the following cross-cultural scenarios. In each mini-case study there is a basic cultural conflict between the actors involved. Try to identify the source of the conflict and suggest how it could have been avoided or minimized. Then see how well your analyses compare to the explanations in the Appendix.

**7–1.** Bob Mitchell, a retired military attaché with considerable experience in the Middle East, was hired by a large U.S. computer software company to represent it in a number of Persian Gulf countries. Having received an introduction from a mutual acquaintance, Bob arranged to meet with Mr. Saade, a wealthy Lebanese industrialist, to discuss the prospects of a joint venture between their companies. Having spent many years in the Middle East, Bob knew that they would have to engage in considerable small talk before they would be able to get down to business. They talked about the weather, Bob's flight from New York, and their golf games. Then Mr. Saade inquired about the health of Bob's elderly father. Without missing a beat Bob responded that his father was doing fine, but that the last time he saw his father at the nursing home several months ago he had lost a little weight. From that point on Mr. Saade's demeanor changed abruptly from warm and gracious to cool and aloof. Though the rest of the meeting was cordial enough, the meeting only lasted another two hours and Bob was never invited back for further discussions on the joint venture.

WHAT WENT WRONG?

**7–2.** Margaret Errington, a corporate attorney for a San Francisco department store chain, was responsible for negotiating leases for their outlets abroad. Because she had been particularly successful in similar negotiations in Europe, she was looking forward to securing attractive leasing agreements from a shopping mall developer in Osaka, Japan. She was especially optimistic because of her successful telephone communications with her counterparts in Japan. But when she arrived with her two assistants, John Gresham and Mel Watt, she was told by her Japanese hosts how surprised they were that she should come to negotiate in person. Margaret was usually not included in the after-hours socializing, and frequently the Japanese negotiators would direct their questions to John or Mel rather than to Margaret.

CAN YOU EXPLAIN WHY MARGARET WAS TREATED AS SHE WAS?

**7–3.** Steve Lee, an executive with a Hartford insurance company, was sent to Kuwait immediately after the 1990 Gulf War to investigate damage claims to several hotels his company had insured. Back in the States, Steve had the reputation of being extremely affable and sociable. The day after Steve arrived in Kuwait City, he met with Mr. Said, the manager of one of the insured tourist hotels. His previous telephone conversations with Mr. Said were upbeat and had led him to expect that Mr. Said was interested in getting the claims settled quickly and efficiently. His initial meeting with Mr. Said went extremely well, with both men agreeing on most of the issues discussed. At the end of that first meeting they shook hands, and to emphasize the depth and sincerity of his goodwill, Steve grasped Mr. Said's hand with two hands and shook vigorously. For reasons that Steve never understood, the subsequent meetings with Mr. Said were never as cordial and friendly as that first meeting.

WHAT EXPLANATION MIGHT YOU GIVE TO STEVE?

**7–4.** Bob Tunis, marketing vice president for a Seattle-based lumber company, was making a sales presentation to a plywood wholesaler in Tokyo. Bob had just proposed what he considered to be a fair price for a large shipment of first quality plywood. Much to his amazement, the three Japanese executives did not respond immediately, but rather sat across the table with their hands folded and their eyes cast downward, saying nothing. Fifteen seconds passed, then 30, and still no response. Finally, Bob became so exasperated that he said with a good deal of irritation in his voice. "Would you like for me to repeat the offer?" From that point onward the talks were stalled and Bob never did successfully negotiate a contract for plywood.

WHAT ADVICE WOULD YOU GIVE BOB FOR FURTHER NEGOTIATIONS?

**7–5.** Tom Putnam, the president of a Boston publishing company, had been working for several months with a French architectural firm that was designing the company's new printing facility in Fontainbleau, France. However, Tom was becoming increasingly frustrated with the many delays caused by the French architects. When the preliminary plans for the building—which the architects had promised by a certain date—had not arrived, Tom called them to inquire when he would be receiving the plans. The architects, somewhat indignant that he called, felt that Tom doubted their integrity to deliver the plans. Tom was equally annoyed because they had missed the deadline, and what was worse, they didn't seem to be the least bit apologetic about it. By the end of the phone call, Tom was convinced that his company's relationship with the French architectural firm had suffered a major setback.

HOW MIGHT YOU EXPLAIN THE CONFLICT IN THIS CASE?

# COPING
# WITH CULTURE SHOCK

Preparing for a two-year overseas assignment in Lagos, Nigeria, a U.S. businessperson during the 1970s submitted to no fewer than 27 shots as a protective measure against everything from yellow fever to hepatitis. Although he managed to avoid any dreaded tropical disease during his assignment, he contracted one malady for which there was no known vaccination. The disease was culture shock, that psychological stress resulting from trying to adjust to major differences in life-styles, living conditions, and business practices in another cultural setting.

## THE NATURE OF CULTURE SHOCK

*Culture shock,* a term first popularized by the anthropologist Kalvero Oberg, refers to the psychological disorientation experienced by people who suddenly find themselves living and working in radically different cultural environments. Oberg describes culture shock as that anxiety that results when all of the familiar cultural props have been knocked out from under a person who is entering a new culture:

> Culture shock is precipitated by the anxiety that results from losing all our familiar signs and symbols of social intercourse. These signs or cues include the thousand and one ways in which we orient ourselves to the situations of daily life: when to shake hands and what to say when we meet people, when and how to give tips, how to give orders to servants, how to make purchases, when to accept and when to refuse invitations, when to take statements seriously and when not. Now these cues which may be words, gestures, facial expressions, customs, or norms are acquired by all of us in the course of growing up and are as much a part of our culture as the language we speak or the beliefs we accept. All of us depend for our peace of mind and our efficiency on hundreds of these cues, most of which we do not carry on the level of conscious awareness. (1960:177)

Culture shock ranges from mild irritation to a deep-seated psychological panic or crisis. Culture shock occurs when U.S businesspeople abroad, all of a sudden, try to play a game in which they have little or no understanding of the basic rules. They must struggle to uncover what is meaningful in this new cultural environment, being cognizant of the fact that many of their own familiar cultural cues may be irrelevant. And they are forced to try out new and unfamiliar modes of behavior, all the while never really knowing when they might be unwittingly committing a gross social indiscretion. Culture shock usually carries with it feelings of helplessness and irritability, at the same time producing fears of being cheated, injured, contaminated, or discounted. Even though everyone, to some extent, suffers the anxiety of culture shock when first having to struggle in an unfamiliar cultural setting, the very success or failure of an overseas living assignment depends largely on how well one can make the psychological adjustment and get beyond the frequently debilitating effects.

The term *culture shock* is used by social scientists and laypeople alike to define in very broad terms the unpleasant consequences of experiencing a foreign culture. Since the 1960s a number of writers in the field have attempted to elaborate on Oberg's (1960) original formulation by using such terms as *role shock* (Byrnes, 1966), *culture fatigue* (Guthrie, 1975), and *pervasive ambiguity* (Ball-Rokeach, 1973). Yet despite these variations on Oberg's original theme, there is general agreement that culture shock involves the following dimensions:

- A sense of confusion over expected role behavior
- A sense of surprise, even disgust, after realizing some of the features of the new culture
- A sense of loss of the old familiar surroundings (friends, possessions, and so on) and cultural patterns
- A sense of being rejected (or at least not accepted) by members of the new culture
- A sense of loss of self-esteem because the inability to function in the new culture results in an imperfect meeting of professional objectives
- A feeling of impotence at having little or no control over the environment
- A strong sense of doubt when old values (which had always been held as absolute) are brought into question

Despite the use of the word *shock,* which implies a sudden jolt, culture shock does not occur quickly nor is it the result of a single event. Rather it results from a series of cumulative experiences. When first arriving in a new culture, usually flying into a major city, the cultural contrasts do not seem too obvious. There are usually traffic lights, taxis, tall buildings with elevators, banks, and modern hotels with English-speaking desk clerks. But before long the very real cultural differences become painfully apparent. People push in front of you in line rather than lining up in an orderly fashion; when people say yes, they don't always mean yes; you try to be thoughtful by asking about the health of your business partner's wife and he acts insulted; you cannot buy things that you are accustomed to having every day at home; people promise to have something done by tomorrow, but it doesn't get done; you try to be friendly, but people don't respond. As those first days and weeks pass, the differences become more apparent and the anxiety and sense of frustration build slowly. Eventually, the cultural differences become the focus of attention. The foreign ways of thinking and acting are no longer quaint and fascinating alternative ways of living but rather are pathological, clearly inferior to your own. When this occurs, culture shock has set in.

Robert Kohls (1984:65) suggests a fairly comprehensive list of the major symptoms that have been observed in relatively severe cases of culture shock:

- Homesickness
- Boredom
- Withdrawal (for example, spending excessive amounts of time reading; seeing only other Americans; avoiding contact with host nationals)
- Need for excessive amounts of sleep
- Compulsive eating
- Compulsive drinking
- Irritability
- Exaggerated cleanliness
- Marital stress
- Family tension and conflict
- Chauvinistic excesses
- Stereotyping of host nationals
- Hostility toward host nationals
- Loss of ability to work effectively
- Unexplainable fits of weeping
- Physical ailments (psychosomatic illnesses)

Since culture shock is characterized by a large and diverse set of symptoms, the malady is frequently difficult to predict and control. It is important to point out, however, that not everyone will experience all the symptoms, but almost all people will experience some. Moreover, some symptoms, or combination of symptoms, will vary in severity from one case to another. Yet whenever any of the symptoms manifest themselves while one is living and working abroad, one can be sure that culture shock has set in.

Individual international businesspeople vary greatly in the extent to which they suffer from culture shock. A few people are so ill suited to working in culturally different environments that they become repatriots shortly after arriving in the host country. Others manage to get by with a minimum of psychological discomfort. But for most Westerners, operating aboard involves a fairly severe bout with culture shock. According to Oberg (1960), culture shock usually occurs in the following four stages:

1. *The honeymoon stage:* As most people begin their foreign assignment with a positive attitude, this initial stage is usually characterized by euphoria. At this point, all that is new is exotic and exciting. Attitudes about the host country, and one's capacity to operate in it successfully, are unrealistically positive. During this initial stage, which may last from several days to several weeks, the recent arrival is probably staying temporarily at a Western-style hotel or staff guesthouse where food, conditions of cleanliness, and language are not appreciably different from those at home. The sojourner's time is devoted to getting established—finding a house, a maid, and perhaps schools for the children. It is possible that the

family's standard of living in this foreign land will be more opulent than they were accustomed to while living in the United States. And by and large, it is the similarities between this new country and the United States that stand out—which leads one to the erroneous conclusion that people are really all alike under the skin.

2. *Irritation and hostility:* But as with marriages, honeymoons do not last forever. Within several weeks or perhaps months problems arise at work, at home, and at the marketplace. Things taken for granted at home simply don't occur. A number of small problems become insurmountable obstacles. Now, all of a sudden, it is the cultural differences, not the similarities, that loom so large. And for the first time it becomes clear that, unlike a two-week vacation, one will be in this situation for the next 12 to 18 months. The second stage of culture shock has set in.

This second stage represents the crisis stage of the disease. Small problems are blown out of proportion. It is during this stage that one or more of the symptoms mentioned are manifested to some degree. A commonly used mode for dealing with this crisis stage is to band together with other expatriates to disparage the local people. "How can they be so lazy?" "So dirty?" "So stupid?" "So slow?" Now is when ethnic jokes proliferate. The speed with which one passes through this crisis stage of culture shock will vary directly with the ultimate success of the international assignment. Unfortunately, some never get past stage 2, and they become premature return statistics or somehow manage to stick it out but at a high cost to themselves, their families, and their companies.

3. *Gradual adjustment:* Stage 3 marks the passing of the crisis and a gradual recovery. This stage may begin so gradually that the "patient" is unaware that it is even happening. Slowly an understanding emerges of how to operate within the new culture. Some cultural cues now begin to make sense; *patterns* of behavior begin to emerge, which enable a certain level of predictability; some of the language is becoming comprehensible; and some of the problems of everyday living—which seemed so overwhelming in stage 2—are beginning to be resolved. The culture, in short, seems more natural and more manageable. A capacity to laugh at one's situation is a sure sign that adjustment—and ultimate recovery—is well under way.

4. *Biculturalism:* The fourth and final stage, representing full, or near full, recovery, involves the ability to function effectively in two different cultures. The local customs that were so unsettling months earlier are now both understood and appreciated. Without having to "go native," the international businessperson now accepts many of the new cultural ways for what they are. This is not to imply that all strains in intercultural relationships have disappeared, but the high levels of anxiety caused by living and working in a different cultural environment are gone. Moreover, in a number of situations those making a full recovery from culture shock find that there are many local customs to which they have become accustomed and which will be missed upon returning home. Again, many people never reach stage 4. It is possible to "get by" with a modicum of success by never going beyond stage 3. But for those who do become bicultural, the international assignment can be a truly positive, growth-producing experience.

The description of culture shock presented here so far paints a rather bleak picture of the helpless victim suffering from the debilitating psychological effects of a serious illness. Although not glossing over the very real deleterious consequences of culture shock, we can view it more positively as a potentially profound experience leading to cultural learning, self-awareness, and personal growth. For example, Adler (1975) contends that the conflicts, problems, and frustrations associated with culture shock can result in "transitional experiences" for the international businessperson, which "can be the source of higher levels of personality development." Cultural learning is most likely to occur under situations of high anxiety, such as is common in moderate to severe cases of culture shock. At lower levels of anxiety the motivation to learn about the host culture is absent. But when anxiety, frustration, and pain are high, the motivation will be powerful to acquire new knowledge and skills, which can be used to reduce the anxiety. Moreover, culture shock encourages the sufferers to confront their own cultural heritage and develop a new awareness of the degree to which they are products of it. Although we are indebted to Adler for reminding us of the more positive consequences of culture shock, the suggestion that it can be growth producing does have its limitations. As Brislin has suggested, if the anxiety of culture shock is too high, "people may be so upset that they are unable to focus on new learning possibilities" (1981:158).

As has been too often the case, many Western businesspeople fail to meet their overseas objectives because they are ill prepared to cope with culture shock. Yet even for those who are successful at managing culture shock during their foreign assignment (that is, by reaching stage 3 or 4), the phenomenon has an additional surprise in store—reverse culture shock, or what has come to be known as "reentry" shock. Most Westerners are not prepared for the enormous letdown they feel when returning home after an overseas assignment. An in some cases, reentry shock—the disorientation faced when trying to reorient oneself to life and work in the United States—can be more anxiety producing than the original culture shock.

Although most international businesspeople will anticipate a certain number of problems and discomfort when entering a new cultural environment, they are frequently unprepared for the myriad of problems they will face when returning home. First, many U.S. businesspeople, after returning from a long assignment abroad, soon realize that one problem is finding a new niche in the corporate structure at home. Those who originally decided to send them abroad may no longer be on the scene, and consequently the corporation's plan for how it would use them now may no longer exist.

Second, while trying to overcome the original dose of culture shock, many U.S. businesspeople tend to embellish (in some cases grossly exaggerate) their fond memories of life in the United States. They remember that things are better made, cheaper, and cleaner, and people are more efficient, polite, and competent. But upon reentry to the United States many of these myths are shattered. One of the byproducts of a successful adjustment to the host culture is that our old notions of our culture will never again be the same. After one lives for a while in Switzerland or Germany, the United States no longer seems to be the epitome of cleanliness; when compared to the Japanese, the typical American seems loud and boisterous; after a stint in a developing nation, people in the United States seem rushed and impersonal. Somehow home isn't what one had remembered.

Third, one's standard of living may actually decrease when returning to the United States. Such luxuries as servants, large company houses, chauffers, live-in babysitters, and other perks used to entice people into an international assignment are likely to disappear. One is now faced with cutting one's own lawn and spending several hours a day on a commuter train.

Fourth, in those cases in which the U.S. businessperson has made a successful adaptation to a third world cultural environment, there can be additional problems of adjustment. The returnee has seen, on a daily basis, the economic standards of people living in the host country. Per capita income may be no more than several hundred dollars per year; infant mortality may be 15 times as high as it is in the United States; disease and lack of medical facilities keep the average life expectancy to less than 40 years of age; government attention to human rights might be nonexistent; and the prospects of changing these conditions in any meaningful way are highly unlikely. And then, upon return, they encounter friends, colleagues, neighbors, and relatives complaining bitterly that they are unable to find at the grocery store the correct color of toilet tissue for the downstairs bathroom. Such complaints stir up (1) considerable anger at how unaware and unappreciative most North Americans are of their own material well-being, and (2) guilt for having mouthed many of these same inane complaints at an earlier time.

And, fifth, and perhaps the most unsettling aspect of reentry shock, there is an almost total dearth of psychological support for the returnee. When encountering the initial stage 2 culture shock during the foreign assignment there were (it is hoped) some preparation, an understanding (however inadequately developed) that there would be rough times, and other expatriates (who were experiencing many of the same frustrations) who could provide reassurance and support. But when returning home, U.S. businesspeople and their families feel alone and unable to express their feelings with someone who has been through the same type of experience. Friends and relatives whom they have not seen for months or even years will say, "Oh, I can't wait to hear about your stint in Singapore." But after listening half-heartedly for about five minutes they will change the subject to a new TV show they have just seen. In short, returnees have a great need to share their overseas experiences (some of which may have been life altering) with others, but frequently no one seems to be interested. Since they have had the unusual experience of living and working abroad, many of their friends and acquaintances, whose lives may have gone on uninterrupted or changed in other ways, have no way of relating to these experiences. The result is a feeling of alienation from the returnees' own culture because they feel that they are not being understood.

## MINIMIZING CULTURE SHOCK

Just about everyone living and working abroad for extended periods of time can expect to experience culture shock to some degree. Tourists and occasional (short-term) business travelers are, by and large, shielded from some of the more debilitating effects of culture shock because their experiences are limited to hotels and restaurants geared to Americans. Yet those who must live and work in a foreign culture for a year or two are faced with new ways of behaving, thinking, and communicating. Even U.S. businesspeople who have lived and worked in a number of different countries claim that they have experienced culture shock in each country. For some, each subsequent assignment becomes a little easier, but for many culture shock must be confronted for each new situation. Although there are no bottled remedies to be found in the medicine cabinet, simply knowing that culture shock exists, that it happens to everyone to some extent, and that it is not permanent is likely to reduce the severity of the symptoms and speed the recovery. In addition, a number of purposeful steps can be taken to minimize the negative impact of culture shock.

One very effective way of totally avoiding culture shock is to choose (or have your employer choose) to stay at home rather than enter the international business arena. Some people simply do not have the desire, inclination, or temperament for international business. There may be others who are suited for some foreign cultures but not others. The old Greek adage "Know thyself" could not be more appropriate than in the process of self-selection for an international assignment. Before deciding to live abroad it is imperative to have a realistic grasp of one's motives and feelings. If people decide to move into the international arena solely on the basis of the lure of more money or possible promotion, they will probably do themselves (and their organizations) a favor by staying home. The international businessperson who is most likely to do well abroad is the person who (1) has a realistic understanding of the problems and promises of international business, (2) possesses a number of important cross-cultural coping skills, and (3) sees the world marketplace as providing vast opportunities for professional and personal growth. Those who cannot meet these criteria may be so ill suited to working in an international business setting that they would be virtually unable to overcome the more deleterious side effects of culture shock.

For those who do select the international business arena, the best single piece of advice for minimizing culture shock is to be prepared. The more thorough the preparation for an overseas assignment, the fewer surprises there will be, and consequently, the smaller will be the accumulated negative effect. A major factor in adjusting to a foreign cultural environment is the degree of familiarity with the host culture, or as Gudykunst (1984:217) has suggested, knowledge about the host culture adds to the individual's capacity to adjust. It is important to recognize that culture shock will never be totally avoided, but it can be minimized through careful preparation. To prepare for an international business encounter, we should refer to the major substantive chapters of this book (Chapters 2 through 6), which really suggest a fourfold approach.

First, as suggested in Chapter 2, a general understanding of the *concept* of culture can provide a fuller appreciation of other cultures, regardless of where one might be conducting business. For example, that cultures are learned (as opposed to being acquired genetically) should remind the international businessperson that although culturally different people have learned different things, they are no less capable of learning efficiently. The concept of an integrated culture—where many or most of the parts of the culture are interconnected—should serve to convince us that all cultures, no matter how incomprehensible they may appear at first, do in fact have a consistently logical structure and should not be given such disparaging epithets as "primitive," "savage," "crazy," "stupid," and so on. And we should realize that our culture is so thoroughly internalized that it can have very real effects on our physiological functioning. These and other general concepts—which hold equally true for Indonesians, the French, Bolivians, or Japanese—can be helpful in gaining a greater understanding of the foreign cultural environment.

A second way of preparing for culture shock (see Chapters 3 and 4) is to become familiar with local patterns of communication, both verbal and nonverbal. Since any type of business depends on communication to such a significant degree, learning to communicate in a foreign business context is absolutely essential. It enhances rapport with native colleagues who have bothered to learn English; it enables the international businessperson to understand the full context of the negotiations and transactions; it frequently gives access to otherwise exclusive realms of local business; and it opens a window onto the rest of the culture. But proficiency in communications can also play a major role in adjusting to culture shock. Since living in a foreign culture involves doing hundreds of things a day—from taking taxis, to making appointments, to having a watch repaired—knowing how to communicate efficiently can both minimize the frustrations, misunderstandings, and aggravations that always face the linguistic outsider *and* provide a sense of safety, mastery, and self-assurance. In addition to the mastery of the local language, a vital part of communicating in an international business situation involves being able to send and receive nonverbal messages accurately. As mentioned in Chapter 4, any communication event is incomplete without a consideration of the additional layers of meaning conveyed by nonverbal behavior.

The third segment of the fourfold approach, as spelled out in Chapter 5, involves a healthy dose of cultural self-awareness. Before it is possible to understand the internal structure and logic of another culture, it is essential to first understand our own culture and how it influences who we are and what we do. We are as much products of our culture as the Japanese, French, and Cubans are products of theirs. All people face a number of universal societal problems, from how to make decisions to how to help young people make the transition to responsible adulthood, from how to gain a livelihood to how to explain the unexplainable. How any particular culture solves these problems varies widely. Middle-class North Americans have worked out one set of cultural patterns, whereas the Indonesians may have developed a radically different solution. In most cases, one solution is probably not more inherently rational than another. They simply represent different answers to similar societal problems. Only after we understand why we do the things we do can we appreciate the internal logic of why other, culturally different people do what they do.

And finally, before entering the international business scene, it is important to become familiar with as much specific cultural information as possible about the country or countries with which one is conducting business (see Chapter 6). There is no shortcut to the acquisition of culture-specific data. It will take time, effort, and no small amount of creativity, but the effort will be worth it. It is important not to be limiting when learning about a new culture. The number of sources of culture-specific information are nearly endless. There are, for example, many scholarly sources (books, journal articles, and so on) from such disciplines as anthropology, religious studies, intercultural communication, cross-cultural psychology, and comparative sociology. In addition to the scholarly literature (which is not always easily accessible or comprehensible) there are many other sources of excellent information, including commercially published sources for the business traveler, State Department publications, newspapers, and information published and distributed by the various foreign embassies. In addition to publications, people are also valid sources of information. In short, it is advisable to draw on as wide a range of culture-specific sources as possible. The more cultural information at hand, the fewer surprises there are likely to be, and consequently, the more likely it will be that serious culture shock can be avoided.

This fourfold approach to understanding the cultural environment constitutes the cornerstone of the *cognitive* approach. By conscientiously pursuing these four content areas—general cultural concepts, local communication patterns, cultural self-awareness, and culture-specific information—the international businessperson will have touched on the major areas of cultural knowledge, thereby avoiding total alienation and some of the more debilitating consequences of culture shock. But one's preparation for coping with, and eventually adjusting to, radically different cultural environments involves more than the mere acquisition of information. Also required are developing certain skills, acquiring new attitudes, and modifying old ways of doing things. What follows are some additional suggestions for enhancing the international business experience by reducing clashes with the local culture.

1. *Develop cross-cultural skills.* Based on our accumulated knowledge of a wide range of people who work and live abroad, a number of attributes associated with effectiveness in cross-cultural business settings consistently emerge. These include the following:

   a. *Tolerating ambiguity:* This attribute refers to the capacity to react to new and unpredictable situations without irritation. Trying to operate in a new cultural environment is, by definition, a highly ambiguous situation. In fact, it is hard to imagine a situation that could be more ambiguous, particularly at the initial stages. In such a situation, the person who insists on having clearcut answers for everything is likely to be very frustrated. To (1) preserve one's own mental health and (2) give oneself time to learn and adjust, it is important to realize that it is normal for there to be a great number of unanswered questions. By exercising patience and learning to live with ambiguity, the international businessperson is "buying the time" that is absolutely necessary for learning more answers, reducing some of the ambiguity, and thus eventually adjusting to the new cultural environment.

   b. *Displaying empathy:* It has been suggested by people in a number of disciplines that the ability to put oneself in someone else's shoes enhances positive human relations. Some people are genuinely able to feel and reflect the thoughts, feelings, and experiences of another person, whereas others are not. It is only natural for people to be attracted to those individuals who can understand things from the other's point of view. Although there are limits to empathy, it is possible to achieve an appreciable level through focused listening and a diligent effort to understand the other person's point of view.

   c. *Being resourceful:* Success in the international arena requires resourcefulness, that is, the capacity to draw on a wide range of resources to solve problems. This attribute involves both a grasp of what material resources exist in the host country as well as a willingness and ability to call on others for help. Resourceful people are usually quite adept at working with other people and taking advantage of available opportunities.

   d. *Personalizing observations:* There is a wide range of differences in terms of how people view their knowledge and perceptions. Some assume that what they know and perceive is valid information for all people; others believe that their knowledge and perceptions are valid only for themselves. According to Ruben, "the more a person recognizes the extent to which knowledge is individual in nature, the more easily he or she will be able to adjust to other people in other countries, whose views of what is 'true' or 'right' are likely to be quite different" (1977:476).

   e. *Showing respect:* The ability to display respect for others is an important ingredient in effective human relations in every culture. How respect is shown may vary from culture to culture, but there are no known cultures in which people do not want others to respect them, their ideas, or their accomplishments. To show respect does not mean to "go native." As Chesanow (1985:52) reminds us, "If . . . you wear a 'Mao Suit' when dealing in Beijing, you'll seem as clownish as a Chinese visiting your U.S. office wearing an Apache war bonnet."

   f. *Being nonjudgmental:* An effective administrator has the ability to make decisions quickly and effectively and to bring successful closure to the problem-solving task. In a cross-cultural situation, however, that quality of being able to "get the show on the road" or to "wrap things up" can be a liability rather than an asset. Since in an unfamiliar cultural environment rules, procedures, and meanings are not well understood, the international businessperson may very well not have all the data needed to make a decision. It therefore makes sense to postpone making the judgment or decision until more of the facts are at hand. Moreover, it is particularly advisable not to be judgmental concerning the "appropriateness" or the "inappropriateness" of certain cultural practices until one has the chance to see how they fit into the total cultural framework of which they are a part.

**g.** *Having a sense of humor:* People in any situation, either at home or abroad, are likely to get into trouble if they take themselves too seriously. When trying to cope with a new cultural environment the international businessperson is bound to make a number of mistakes that may well be discouraging, annoying, embarrassing, or downright stupid. The ability to laugh at one's own mistakes (or at least not lose sight of the humorous side) may be the ultimate defense against despair.

2. *Avoid U.S. ghettos abroad.* Perhaps the single best way to reinforce culture shock and ensure an unsuccessful international experience is to limit oneself to an isolated and insulated U.S. enclave, where one will be able to get a hamburger and ice in one's Coke but little else. Here is where all too many Americans, petrified of having any social contact with "those people," spend their time while overseas. It is here that U.S. expatriates attempt to recreate their former lifestyle, complaining about the lack of amenities, the pace of life, and the inconveniences of the host culture. The two major pastimes seem to be (a) counting the days before returning home and (b) thinking up the latest and most disparaging ethnic joke about the local people. Although it is important to have a support system of other Americans, particularly for the first several months abroad, life in a ghetto can be a serious mistake. By remaining isolated in a U.S. ghetto, expatriates are sending the local population the message that they feel superior and reinforcing their own negative attitudes.

3. *Be adventurous.* All too often U.S. businesspeople assigned abroad for a year or two view it as a "hardship" experience that will eventually pass, particularly if they become immersed in work. But an overseas business assignment can be much more than a job simply to be endured. Provided there is willingness to experiment, the new culture and environment can provide an exciting new world. There are new places to explore, people to meet, customs to learn, food to eat, all of which are available if the expatriate is willing to take the risk and experiment. This spirit of adventure is exemplified by the Bank of America's Laurie Dorman:

> My fondest memories of Tokyo are bike riding with another American. We would get on our bikes and put 13 miles on our bikes in a day, just riding anywhere. It was a lot less threatening than driving a car. We would stop and look at shops; we would find neighborhood parades going on; we would eat lunch. . . . You can have a tremendous time there if you just jump in. Do it. (Quoted in Copeland & Griggs, 1985:203)

4. *Involve the whole family.* Researchers (Harvey, 1985; Harris & Moran, 1989; Black & Gregersen, 1991) have found that spouse adjustment is a major factor in the success or failure of expatriates. Gaylord (1979) has suggested that relocating to another culture is hardest on the unemployed spouse, who in all but a handful of cases is the wife. Whereas the international employee has the support of the familiar corporate structure and work routine, the spouse—oftentimes the wife—is frequently operating in a vacuum. The unemployed spouse is the one who is home alone taking care of the children and all the routines connected with running a house. She may spend hours cashing a check or getting a package from home through customs. If there is a problem at school, she will have to handle it. When the telephone goes dead (assuming she has one at all) she is isolated at home alone.

A career may have been suspended when leaving home, and employment opportunities for spouses in other countries are nearly nonexistent. Moreover, in some countries the role of women is severely restricted, so that in Saudi Arabia, for example, a woman is not allowed to drive a car. Given the fact that the wife is under the greatest stress (and deserves the most credit for a successful adjustment), it becomes vital that she be involved intimately in the decision to accept the position and in the preparation for making the relocation. If the unemployed spouse is unable to adjust to the new cultural environment, it will have a serious effect on the employee and may even result in the premature termination of the assignment.

5. *Manage the stress.* Culture shock results from the anxiety brought about by (a) the loss of familiar cultural props and (b) the exposure to a new and possibly incomprehensible culture. How an individual responds to such anxiety varies considerably, as do the techniques for coping with stress. What works for one person may be meaningless for another. Some manage stress through physical exercise such as jogging, tennis, or racquetball. Others use such techniques as biofeedback, acupressure, progressive relaxation, massage, yoga, and meditation. Also prayer and communal worship have been helpful for generations for reducing the stress associated with living in a different cultural environment. Whatever method or methods one chooses it is important that the international businessperson develop some comfortable ways of managing stress as a means of reducing the consequences of culture shock.

6. *Take appropriate health precautions.* There is nothing that can spoil an international business assignment quicker than illness or death. Although one can hardly prevent illness or death, there are a number of available preventive measures that will severely reduce their occurrence. Before leaving home be certain that all required and recommended shots are current. If traveling to a malaria-infested country, be sure to take the required malarial suppressants before, during, and after the assignment. While abroad follow the same good health habits recommended generally—that is, eat well-balanced meals; get sufficient rest; exercise regularly; and avoid excessive amounts of alcohol, tobacco, and drugs. And obtain accurate information about which local foods can be eaten safely and which should be avoided. In the event that illness occurs, know where to obtain the best medical care. Lists

One way of minimizing the negative effects of culture shock is to take care of yourself physically.

of Western-trained physicians practicing throughout the world can be obtained through either the International Association for Medical Assistance to Travelers (IAMIT) in Lewiston, New York, or Intermedic, Inc., in New York City.

7. *Be realistic.* Just as one should not overreact to problems encountered when doing business abroad, one should not minimize them or discount one's feelings. There are a myriad of very real problems while living abroad not normally encountered at home. Most problems, stemming from an imperfect grasp of the culture and language, range from trouble with local office staff to problems with schooling for the children. There will be some people who will not become close friends for reasons that will not be clear. There will be others whom you simply don't like and vice versa. There will be some things that will never be understood. It is important to face these problems and frustrations realistically. Once it is understood that these problems, though real and frustrating, are perfectly normal reactions faced by virtually all Western businesspeople abroad, then one can begin to search for solutions.

8. *Let go of home (for now).* Before an overseas assignment it is important to say the proper goodbyes to friends, family, and the way of life in general that is being left behind, if only temporarily. Arranging to say goodbye provides the sojourner with a symbolic separation from home, which is necessary before one can begin to step inside of and understand another culture. This does not, of course, mean cutting oneself off totally from home. In fact, part of the farewell process should involve determining ways of maintaining contact with people at home. If, indeed, one does maintain contact through letters, telephone calls, and photographs, some of the problems of reentry will be lessened. Nevertheless, before leaving, saying goodbye, however one chooses to do it, is important; while at the same time one must fully understand that both the sojourner and those left behind will have changed upon return to the United States.

9. *Realize there are no absolutes.* As with any social or behavioral science, we must realize that when studying culture there are no absolutes. Every culture is, to some extent, unique, as is every situation within a culture. Moreover, each individual brings into the foreign business setting his or her own unique perceptions based on past experience. There is, in other words, no way of predicting with absolute certainty how people will behave in any given social situation. The generalizations made throughout this book should not be viewed as ironclad rules but rather as general statements valid most of the time for most cases. The advice herein should serve as a general guide to those engaged in international business, not as a step-by-step set of prescriptions to be used like a cookbook.

10. *Keep the faith.* Finally, after having prepared as thoroughly as possible for an international assignment, it is important to have self-confidence and confidence in the local people. The U.S. businessperson abroad will experience frustrations and will make mistakes. But eventually his or her basic good will and humanity will come across to the local people, provided, of course, an honest effort to participate in the local culture is being made. At the same time, it is important to have faith in the inherent goodwill of the local population. People the world over, by and large, are tolerant of our indiscretions if they result from a sincere attempt to learn about the local culture. If the international businessperson is able to communicate to the local people in a genuine way that he or she is the *student* wanting to learn about their culture, and they are the *teachers and experts,* very few people in the world would refuse to share their expertise. And, in fact, they *are* the experts, and the visiting U.S. businesspeople are the uneducated, at least in terms of local cultural knowledge. If the American businessperson abroad is able to acknowledge openly his or her own "subordinate" position when dealing with local people, many doors of learning and friendship will be open.

# APPENDIX

## CHAPTER 2

**2-1.** Public humiliation is one of a number of techniques that can be used quite effectively in the United States to change people's behavior. In the world of Islam, however, where the preservation of dignity and self-respect is absolutely essential, public reprimand will be totally counterproductive. If Arabs feel that they have suffered a loss of personal dignity because they have been criticized in public, they take it as a dishonor to both themselves and their families. And when Sam insisted on using this "motivational" technique, he was alienating not only the individual to whom the reprimand was directed but also all of his fellow workers, who felt hurt on his behalf. When this happens the person giving the reprimand loses the respect of those witnessing it.

**2-2.** The key to understanding this apparently innocent exchange which left LeBec offended and Wayne confused revolves around the use of personal questions. People in the United States think it perfectly natural to ask a number of personal questions early on in one's initial conversation. In the United States this is considered a normal way of finding a common ground on which to build a relationship quickly. Given the highly mobile nature of U.S. society, it is imperative to build relationships quickly because next week our new friends may be transferred across the country. In less mobile societies like France people move to establish social relationships at a slower pace. The personal life of the French, and that of their families, is considered private. They will be quite reluctant to make any moves toward intimacy until there has been sufficient time to assess the newcomer. Thus Wayne's questions appeared overly personal to LeBec, whose culture handles such introductory amenities much more slowly.

**2-3.** This scenario illustrates the high value Americans place on science, logic, and rational thought. Since there were no logical links between any of these unfortunate happenings at the plant, Ned and his fellow Americans concluded that they were just an unfortunate, yet unrelated, series of accidents. The local work force, on the other hand, believed that there were some sinister forces at work that required the services of a religious specialist. And it was these beliefs that were the direct cause of Ned's two managerial problems—morale and absenteeism. Unfortunately, Ned and his colleagues got caught up in their own value system and missed the major point: It makes little difference whether or not the belief in evil spirits is true or false. Ned was no more capable of proving that evil spirits did not in fact cause this series of events than the local workers could prove that they did. What Ned and his American staff failed to understand was that (1) the workers did believe that evil spirits were at work and (2) this belief, whether true or false, was causing a major problem for the company. The only reasonable way to solve that problem is take an action that will enable the workers to perceive that the power of evil spirits has been neutralized and that their safe work environment has been restored.

**2–4.** Despite Ray's Hispanic heritage, his dramatic rise in his company's organization required him to adopt the mainstream U.S. cultural interpretation of time. That is, Ray was operating under the assumption that since time is money, there is no reason to waste it. Such a definition of time assumes that the end product of negotiations between two companies is more important than the process that brings it about. But in Argentina, and in many South American cultures, the *process* is also very important. It is not enough just to make a decision on the merits of the product, but to many South Americans it is important that those entering into a business relationship enjoy one another's company and build a strong foundation of mutual trust. To the Argentines, Ray's insistence on getting down to business as quickly as possible was bypassing some very important components of the negotiation process.

**2–5.** Although this fertilizer company did a good deal of research in developing its product, it was woefully lacking in cultural information that would have enabled the company to market it. First, the company tried to convince the village men to accept an agricultural innovation when in fact it was the women who were the farmers. That they failed to understand this basic ethnographic fact did little for their general credibility. Second, many East Africans have two important beliefs that can help to explain their reaction: (1) the theory of *limited good,* which assumes that there is a finite amount of good in the world (such as fertility), and (2) witchcraft, the notion that evil forces embodied in people can harm members of the community. Given these two beliefs, any individual East African farmer would never participate in any scheme that promises to produce considerably more per acre than her neighbor, for to do so would open her up to charges of having bewitched the fertility from the neighbor's soil. In short, to continue to grow the same amount as one had in the past is a far preferable alternative to being killed for witchcraft.

# CHAPTER 3

**3–1.** The unwillingness of these four Korean accountants to leave their current employer stems from a sense of loyalty felt by many Korean workers that is not shared by their U.S. counterparts. The vast literature on Japanese business practices suggests that Japanese workers have a strong loyalty to their employers because their lives revolve around the company and, in fact, they gain a sense of their own importance primarily through the prestige of the company. However, Koreans, unlike the Japanese, have relatively little loyalty to their companies, per se. There is a good deal of job mobility in Korea, for employees are always on the lookout for better job opportunities. Koreans, however, have a strong sense of loyalty to their *bosses* within the company. When Korean employees do change companies, they frequently are following bosses who take them along when they move. Even though it may be every bit as difficult for foreign firms to recruit Koreans away from their current jobs as it would be to recruit Japanese, the nature of the workers' loyalty is different in these two countries. Whereas Japanese workers have a strong sense of loyalty to the company (that is, the group), Koreans express loyalty to their bosses to whom they have strong personal ties.

**3–2.** The demise of these joint venture negotiations cannot be explained by the fact that contemporary Japanese firms are inextricably wedded to traditional practices. Present-day Japanese firms have shown an enormous willingness to adopt innovative policies and strategies, which has contributed to their rapid rise in the world economy. Yet, equally high on the Japanese list of cultural priorities is the value placed on respect for elders and saving face. Even though Hayakawa may have disagreed with his grandfather's position, it would have been totally inappropriate for him to have disagreed with his grandfather in a *public* meeting. The Japanese way would have involved private discussions between Hayakawa and his grandfather to try gently to convince the former president of the need for these innovative policies. Tom's impassioned attempt to change the old man's mind in the public meeting was seen as a serious breech of etiquette, which caused the old man to lose face.

**3–3.** Having graduated near the top of his class, Eric had always met with academic success and high levels of achievement. Unlike many of the courses that he had taken in the past (for example, mathematics, sciences, and engineering), this language course produced few concrete results in the early stages. Anyone ever taking a foreign language for the first time will feel incompetent and "lost" for the first several months. Eric's dissatisfaction with the language course and the project resulted from his strong need to achieve, which, he felt, was not being satisfied.

**3–4.** Even though Fred and his company thought they had been well prepared for the presentation, they made two tactical errors. First, despite Fred's knowledge of the product and his proficiency in German, he had one important factor working against him, namely, his age. By and large, managers in German corporations as a whole tend to be older than their U.S. counterparts. A young U.S. executive, however bright and charming, making a presentation before a group of older German executives may not be taken seriously because he is seen as relatively inexperienced. And second, Fred did not win any points by trying to set an informal, relaxed atmosphere by telling a few jokes. Although this may be an acceptable approach for an after-lunch speech at the Rotary Club, it was viewed as quite inappropriate in a German business setting.

**3–5.** France is one of the few nations in the world where an *attempt* to speak the language is not appreciated. There are many nuances in the French language that are difficult to grasp by anyone not very accomplished in the language. Clearly Betty's three years of college French, although perhaps adequate to give directions to the cab driver, fell far short of being sufficient for conducting business. As a general rule, if you do not speak French well, it is best to use English (if possible) or work through an interpreter.

## CHAPTER 4

**4–1.** In any society gifts are given as a way of symbolizing certain thoughts. Yet like other aspects of culture, certain gifts symbolize different thoughts in different cultures. In the United States chrysanthemums are given for a number of general purposes. But in Italy, and in some other European countries, chrysanthemums are used traditionally as funeral flowers. Also Don's flowers sent another unintended message. Although it is appropriate to take flowers as a gift when invited to someone's home for dinner, to present flowers at other times to the mother of an unmarried woman is seen as an expression of a man's serious intentions toward the daughter.

**4–2.** This is an excellent example of what can happen if one assumes that banks in Bogota operate under the same system as they do in Manhattan. In the United States we expect to line up in an orderly fashion and wait our turn. In most banking transactions in the United States the teller handles the entire transaction. But in Bogota, in the absence of a sophisticated electronic system, most checks must be verified to ensure sufficient funds to cover them. That process may take five or ten minutes under normal circumstances. Thus, it is expected in Colombia that a person will walk up to the teller directly, hand over the check, and then step aside until the check has cleared, thereby allowing others to hand their checks to the teller. When the check has cleared, the person's name will be called and he or she will be given the money. Clearly this is a very different system of customer service than would be found in the United States. Had Tom understood this very logical system he could have avoided an unpleasant situation.

**4–3.** In a sincere but misguided attempt to convey to their Japanese counterparts their interest in the project, the U.S. businesspersons made two serious cultural blunders. First, by taking off their jackets and rolling up their sleeves, they were trying to communicate sincerely, in a nonverbal way, that they were interested in working hard to arrive at a satisfactory agreement between the two corporations. The Japanese, however, who tend to be much more formal in dress, interpreted this symbolic gesture as most unbusinesslike and inappropriate, a breech in professional protocol. The second faux pas resulted from Harry's invitation to start their discussions off on a first-name basis. Although by making such a suggestion, Harry was genuinely interested in facilitating their work relationship, he failed to realize that Japanese business relationships tend to be based on quite rigid status differences. In the eyes of the Japanese being on a first-name basis involved an unacceptable level of informality and egalitarianism.

**4–4.** Here is another example of how certain nonverbal actions—in this case the pounding of one's fist into one's palm—have a very different meaning in a foreign country than in the United States. In Singapore, as well as in several other Southeast Asian countries, such a gesture is a sexual insult, comparable in the United States to extending the middle finger.

**4–5.** The meaning of time and punctuality varies not only from culture to culture but also within any culture, depending on the *social context.* In Portugal a person of high status should never be kept waiting by a person of lesser status; a woman may keep a man waiting but it would be considered very bad form for a man to keep a woman waiting; an older person can be late for an appointment with a younger person, but the reverse is not true. Although punctuality for its own sake is not valued in the same absolute sense as it is in the United States, there are some social situations that demand punctuality and others that do not. This example should remind us that when in Portugal, and most other cultures as well, it is important to understand the nuances of values, attitudes, and behaviors.

## CHAPTER 5

**5–1.** Although cameras can be valuable for documenting a foreign culture, they must be used with care. There is the simple matter of violating one's privacy, a notion that most North Americans can relate to. How would a typical middle-class American, for example, feel if someone dressed in foreign clothing started taking his picture while he was cutting his front lawn? At the very least such behavior would be met with suspicion. But for a number of other cultural reasons many East Africans would be reluctant to have their picture taken. First a sizable number of people living along the Kenya coast are Muslims, and as such resist being photographed because of the Koranic prohibition of depicting the human form. Second, whereas the Westerner looks for "picturesque" scenes of people doing traditional things, the local people themselves may feel that the foreign photographer is documenting their "backwardness" or lack of modernization. And third, some East Africans who do not understand the technology of the camera believe that having their pictures taken is tantamount to having their soul entrapped in the camera. In a society where witchcraft is widely believed, the thought of anyone, particularly a witch, capturing one's soul can be terrifying.

**5–2.** The employee-employer relationship in Japan is very different than in the United States. When a Japanese firm hires an employee, he or she becomes part of the corporate family. Whereas labor and management in the United States operate largely from an adversarial perspective, the relationship between the Japanese worker and the company is based on loyalty and a long-term commitment to one another. Not only do most employees expect to stay with the firm for the duration of their careers, but also the firm takes an active role in the personal lives of its employees and their families. Housing, recreation, and schooling for the children are just some of the areas arranged by the employers for their workers. Moreover, there is far less separation of business and personal matters between Japanese employees and their supervisors. Thus, it is little wonder that the Japanese mechanics thought that George Burgess was not acting like a responsible supervisor because he was unwilling to become involved in their personal lives.

**5–3.** Australians take a great deal of pride in their sense of hospitality, their conviviality, and their ability to throw and enjoy a good party. And no good Australian party is without a generous supply of things to drink. Native Australians take their drinking seriously and expect others to do so as well. In fact, "spirited drink" is such an integral part of the social process that most Australians do not know how to cope with a nondrinker. Frequently they interpret a refusal of a drink as a rejection of their friendship and hospitality. Martha, being a Mormon and a nondrinker, would have been better off to have accepted the drink, simply carrying it around with her rather than actually drinking it. And even though women are frequently included in such business affairs, they are often segregated and don't offer their own opinions. Martha, being a strong proponent of the ERA, had difficulty accepting this secondary role.

**5–4.** Life in rural Turkey is quite different from life in Istanbul. Located in two different continents (Europe and Asia), Istanbul reflects a good deal of its past European influence. The further one gets from Istanbul, the more traditional, non-Western, and Islamic the people become. The arrival of a foreigner in a small Turkish town is not a common event. Andy and his wife received stares not out of hostility but rather out of curiosity. But in addition to the general interest in foreigners, there was another source of confusion, which many of the local people no doubt felt. The presence of a woman in the generally all-male domain of the coffeehouse was an unusual sight. Rural Turkish women (who frequently wear dark clothing, cover their faces, and have little contact with the general public) do not enjoy the same liberties as their urban counterparts.

**5–5.** The scenario can best be understood by first appreciating the very different views in U.S. culture and Saudi culture concerning "locus of control." In the United States it is believed that ultimately people are responsible for their own destiny. If something goes wrong, it is believed, it is frequently possible for the individual to *do* something (that is, to change certain behavior) to bring about the desired outcome. In Saudi Arabia, and indeed throughout the Arab world, people are taught from an early age that all things are subject to the direct will of Allah. All plans for the future (including, of course, business plans) are viewed with a sense of inevitability and will be realized only if God wills it. This is not to say that people in the Arab world would not work hard to help bring about the desired results. Rather, they believe that despite the effort, the desired ends will not happen unless God is willing. Perhaps Stefan would have been less frustrated if he had translated *inshallah* to mean "if possible" or "God willing" rather than as a knee-jerk response used to absolve oneself of all responsibility for one's actions.

## CHAPTER 6

**6–1.** In Nairobi, as in many other parts of the world, status and rank are important elements of social and business relationships. In the United States, where people have a tendency to play down status differences, it is not unusual for the boss to roll up his or her sleeves and start working alongside those of lower rank and position. In fact, the boss in the United States is likely to become more popular by engaging in manual labor alongside the workers, for its shows a true spirit of empathy and democracy. In Kenya, however, a boss doing manual labor is seen as a deliberate rejection of self-respect. And if those in high positions are not willing to maintain their high status and self-respect, it is unlikely that they will continue to receive the respect of their employees. To the African employees it would have been far preferable to have missed the deadline than to have their boss lose his self-respect by engaging in manual labor.

**6–2.** Saudis do not budget their time in the same way that North Americans do. Time is considered to be a much more flexible commodity. The best piece of advice we might give Bill is to be patient and allow more time when conducting business affairs in Saudi Arabia than would be normal in the United States. Moreover, what Bill considered to be "small talk" is a very important part of the process of doing business in Saudi Arabia. Trust is an important ingredient in business affairs. Before engaging in meaningful business relations most Saudis need time to get to know those with whom they are about to do business. They feel that there is no better way to do this than to discuss a wide variety of nonbusiness topics while drinking coffee. And finally, Saudis define private and public space somewhat differently than they do in Dallas, Texas. Although Saudis are extremely private in their personal lives, they are quite open in those things they consider to be public, and business is thought to fall into the public domain. Thus, even though the Western businessperson may want to discuss confidential business matters, it is not at all uncommon for a "personal" appointment to be conducted with other people in the room.

**6–3.** Asians in general, and Koreans in particular, place a high value on harmonious personal relationships. Conflicts are avoided at all costs and every effort is made to be polite and nonconfrontational. Also, Koreans have great difficulty in admitting failure, for to do so is to be humiliated or shamed, that is, to lose face. It is therefore important to maintain a high degree of *kibun,* translated as "morale" or "self-esteem." The reporting or acknowledging of a problem is far more serious than the problem itself, for it causes a loss of face for the teller and a loss of morale for the hearer. Thus, when the Korean employees withheld knowledge about plant problems from Jim, they did so to (1) preserve his *kibun* and (2) not lose face themselves. If anything negative has to be reported it should be done, according to the Korean way, at the end of the day so the parties involved will at least have the evening to restore their damaged *kibun.*

**6–4.** For the local Indian labor pool, flexibility of time was of greater significance than housing or high wages. Under the German system, which paid an hourly wage (rather than a 40-hour per week salary, as with Bill's company), local laborers were able to take time off for their festivals and ceremonies without fear of losing their jobs. The solution to Bill's labor recruitment problem required the relatively simple task of changing to a more flexible hourly wage system rather than a weekly salary system.

**6–5.** Dick's problem stemmed from making the unwarranted assumption that informality at the party could carry over into a business context. In fact, Japanese make a very real distinction between these two social situations. Japanese senior executives can be informal and playful at parties, but his is not the environment in which to discuss business matters. The two realms are kept quite distinct in Japan.

## CHAPTER 7

**7–1.** Although Bob Mitchell thought he was giving a straightforward answer to a rather mundane question about his father's health, his response, from Mr. Saade's perspective, made Bob appear to be a very undesirable business partner. Coming from a society that places a very high value on family relationships, Mr. Saade thought it quite inhumane to leave one's aging father at a nursing home in the care of total strangers. If Bob Mitchell couldn't meet his primary obligations to his own family members, Saade reasoned, how could he be trusted to meet his obligations to his business partners?

**7–2.** Even though Japanese women receive considerable education, they have not been accepted into the higher echelons of the corporate world. The Japanese negotiators simply were not very subtle in their efforts to disguise their displeasure with having to negotiate with a woman.

**7–3.** Among middle-class men in the United States, it is customary to shake hands as a gesture of friendship, as it is also among men in Kuwait. When communicating extreme friendliness, a U.S. male may grasp his friend's right hand with both of his hands. If, however, a U.S. male gives such an emphatic handshake to a Kuwaiti male, he will be sending an extremely offensive message. In Kuwait, and generally throughout the Muslin world, where the right hand is sacred and the left hand is profane, touching someone with the left hand is highly offensive.

**7–4.** The Japanese have great difficulty saying "no." Instead of saying "no" in a direct, unequivocal way, the Japanese are more likely to give a conditional response, an irrelevant tangential response, ask a counterquestion, change the subject, leave the room, or say nothing at all. Of all the indirect ways that the Japanese say "no," silence is the most difficult for North Americans to handle gracefully. North Americans place such importance on words that the absence of words becomes very disorienting. Because most North Americans feel that silence is inherently unnatural, they frequently say things that get them into trouble in their haste to fill the silence. Bob would have been better off to have waited out the silence and then come back with another proposal or a question that would have kept the discussions on track.

**7–5.** Although both U.S. and French culture are what Hall would call monochronic (emphasizing promptness and schedules), they differ in terms of the degree to which each emphasizes the primacy of meeting deadlines. For North Americans, keeping to an agreed-upon schedule takes priority, even when confronted with unanticipated contingencies. If need be, personal pleasure or even quality will take second place to meeting the deadline. The French, too, are interested in efficiency and meeting schedules, but they don't give deadlines the same top priority as in the United States. For the French, the emphasis is on quality. In the event that time runs short, the French will choose to take additional time to ensure high quality, whereas North Americans are more willing to sacrifice a number of things—including quality—in order to meet the deadline.

# REFERENCES

ADLER, PETER. "The Transitional Experience: An Alternative View of Culture Shock." *Journal of Humanistic Psychology,* 15(4) (Fall 1975), 13–23.

ALLPORT, F. H. *Social Psychology.* Boston: Houghton Mifflin, 1924.

ALSTON, JON P. *The Intelligent Businessman's Guide to Japan.* Boston: Charlie E. Tuttle, 1990.

ANDERSON, DAVID C. "How to Offend a Mexican Businessman." *Across the Board,* June 1985, pp. 53–56.

ARGYLE, MICHAEL. *Bodily Communication.* New York: International University Press, 1975.

ARGYLE, M., and M. COOK. *Gaze and Mutual Gaze.* Cambridge: Cambridge University Press, 1976.

BABA, MARIETTA L. *Business and Industrial Anthropology: An Overview,* Bulletin 2. Washington, D.C.: National Association for the Practice of Anthropology, 1986.

BAKER, EDWIN. "Managing Organizational Culture." *Management Review,* July 1980, pp. 8–13.

BAKER, JAMES C. "Foreign Language and Predeparture Training in U.S. Multinational Firms." *Personnel Administrator,* July 1984, pp. 63–72.

BALL-ROKEACH, S. J. "From Pervasive Ambiguity to a Definition of the Situation." *Sociometry,* 36 (1973), 3–13.

BARNUM, C., and N. WOLNIANSKY. "Talk Isn't Cheap if You Can't Speak the Language." *Management Review* July 1989, pp. 52–56.

BARRETT, RICHARD A. *Culture and Conduct: An Excursion in Anthropology.* Belmont, Calif.: Wadsworth, 1984.

BARRY, DAVE. "Europe on Five Vowels a Day." *Miami Herald Tropic Magazine,* February 1, 1987, p. 7.

BAXTER, J. C. "Interpersonal Spacing in Natural Settings." *Sociometry,* 33 (1970), 444–56.

BEALS, RALPH L., HARRY HOIJER, and ALAN R. BEALS. *An Introduction to Anthropology,* 5th ed. New York: Macmillan, 1977.

BEFU, H. "Konnichiwa" Essay read at the April 1975 meetings of the Japan Society, San Francisco. Quoted in Sheila J. Ramsey, "Nonverbal Behavior: An Intercultural Perspective." In *Handbook of Intercultural Communication,* pp. 105–43, M. K. Asante, E. Newmark, and C. Blake, Eds. Beverly Hills, Calif.: Sage Publications, 1979.

BERNSTEIN, BASIL. "Elaborated and Restricted Codes: Their Social Origins and Some Consequences." In *The Ethnography of Communication,* J. J. Gumpers and Dell Himes, Eds. *American Anthropologist,* 66(6) (Part II) (1964), 55–69.

BESNER, PATRICIA. "Watch Your Language." *Pace,* 9(2) (March/April 1982), 53f.

BIRDWHISTELL, R. L. "The Kinesis Level in the Investigation of the Emotions." In *Expressions of the Emotions in Man,* P. H. Knapp, Ed. New York: International University Press, 1963.

BLACK, J. STEWART, and H. B. GREGERSEN. "The Other Half of the Picture: Antecedents of Spouse Cross-Cultural Adjustment." *Journal of International Business Studies* 22 (3) (1991), 461–77.

BONHAM, GEORGE W. "The Future Forsaken." *Change Magazine,* 10(9) (October 1978), 12–13.

BRISLIN, RICHARD W. *Cross-Cultural Encounters: Face-to-Face Interaction.* New York: Pergamon Press, 1981.

BROWN, ROGER, and MARGUERITE FORD. "Address in American English." *Journal of Abnormal and Social Psychology,* 62 (1961), 375–85.

BUREK, DEBORAH, Ed. *Encyclopedia of Associations 1993,* 27th ed. Detroit: Gale Research, 1992.

BURGOON, JUDEE K., DAVID B. BULLER, and W. GIL WOODALL. *Nonverbal Communication: The Unspoken Dialogue.* New York: Harper and Row, 1989.

BYRNES, F. C. "Role Shock: An Occupational Hazard of American Technical Assistants Abroad." *Annals of the American Academy of Political and Social Science,* 368 (1966), 95–108.

CANNON, W. "Voodoo Death." *American Anthropologist,* 44 (1942), 169–81.

CASAGRANDE, JOSEPH B. "The Southwest Project in Comparative Psycholinguistics: A Preliminary Report." In *Men and Cultures: Selected Papers of the Fifth International Congress of Anthropological and Ethnological Sciences,* Anthony F. C. Wallace, Ed. pp. 777–82, Philadelphia: University of Pennsylvania Press, 1960.

————. "Comanche Baby Language." *International Journal of American Linguistics,* 14 (1948), 11–14.

CAUDRON, SHARI. "Training Ensures Success Overseas." *Personnel Journal,* December 1991, pp. 27–30.

CHAMBERS, ERVE. *Applied Anthropology: A Practical Guide.* Englewood Cliffs, N.J.: Prentice Hall, 1985.

CHAMPNESS, B. G. "Mutual Glance and the Significance of the Look." *Advancement of Science,* 26 (1970), 309–12.

CHESANOW, NEIL. *The World Class Executive: How to Do Business Like a Pro Around the World.* New York: Rawson Associates, 1985.

COLLETT, P. "Training Englishmen in the Nonverbal Behavior of Arabs." *International Journal of Psychology,* 6 (1971), 209–15.

CONDON, JOHN, and FATHI YOUSEF. *Introduction to Intercultural Communication.* Indianapolis: Bobbs-Merrill, 1975.

COPELAND, LENNIE, and L. GRIGGS. *Going International.* New York: Random House, 1985.

COUNCIL OF ECONOMIC ADVISORS. *Economic Indicators.* Washington, D. C.: U.S. Government Printing Office, 1985.

COUNCIL ON INTERNATIONAL EDUCATION EXCHANGE. *Educating for Global Competence: The Report of the Advisory Council for International Educational Exchange.* New York: Council on International Educational Exchange, August 1988.

*Countries of the World and Their Leaders Yearbook 1987.* Detroit: Gale Research, 1987.

CUMMINGS, JACK. *Business Travel Survival Guide.* New York: Wiley, 1991.

DARROW, KEN, and BRAD PALMQUIST, Eds. *Transcultural Study Guide.* Stanford, Calif.: Volunteers in Asia, 1977.

DARWIN, CHARLES R. *The Expression of Emotions in Man and Animals.* London: John Murray, 1872.

DAVIS, FLORA. *Inside Intuition: What We Know About Nonverbal Communication.* New York: McGraw-Hill, 1971.

DAVIS, KINGSLEY. "Final Notes on a Case of Extreme Isolation." *American Journal of Sociology,* March 1947, pp. 432–37.

DAVIS, STANLEY. *Managing Corporate Culture.* Cambridge, Mass.: Ballinger, 1984.

DEAL, TERRENCE E., and ALLEN KENNEDY. *Corporate Cultures: The Rites and Rituals of Corporate Life.* Reading, Mass.: Addison-Wesley, 1982.

DE MENTE, BOYE. *Business Guide to Japan: Opening Doors and Closing Deals.* Boston: Charles E. Tuttle, 1989.

DENISON, DANIEL R. *Corporate Culture and Organizational Effectiveness.* New York: Wiley, 1990.

DEUTSCH, MICHAEL F. *Doing Business with the Japanese.* New York: New American Library, 1984.

DICKSON, PAUL. "Striking Out on Your Own." *Washington Monthly,* 3(6) (August 1971), 46–53.

DOWNS, JAMES F. *Cultures in Crisis.* Beverly Hills, Calif.: Glencoe Press, 1971.

DRIVER, HAROLD E. *Indians of North America.* Chicago: University of Chicago Press, 1961.

EDWARDS, LINDA. "Present Shock, and How to Avoid It Abroad." *Across the Board,* February 1978, pp. 36–43.

EFRON, DAVID. *Gesture and Environment.* New York: King's Crown, 1941.

EIBEL-EIBESFELDT, I. "Similarities and Differences Between Cultures in Expressive Movement." In *Non-Verbal Communications,* Robert E. Hinde, Ed. London: Cambridge University Press, 1972.

———. "Transcultural Patterns of Ritualized Contact Behavior." In *Behavior and Environment: The Use of Space by Animals and Men,* pp. 297–312. A. H. Esser, Ed. New York: Plenum Press, 1971.

EISENBERG, A. M. and R. R. SMITH. *Nonverbal Communication.* Indianapolis: Bobbs-Merrill, 1971.

EKMAN, P., W. V. FRIESEN, and P. ELLSWORTH. *Emotions in the Human Face: Guidelines for Research and an Integration of the Findings.* New York: Pergamon Press, 1972.

ELLSWORTH, P. C. "Direct Gaze as a Social Stimulus: The Example of Aggression." In *Nonverbal Communication of Aggression,* P. Pliner, L. Kramer, and T. Alloway, Eds. New York: Plenum Press, 1975.

EMBER, CAROL R., and MELVIN EMBER. *Anthropology,* 7th ed. Englewood Cliffs, N.J.: Prentice Hall, 1993.

*The Encyclopedia of the Third World.* New York: Facts on File, 1982.

ENGHOLM, CHRISTOPHER. *When Business East Meets Business West: The Guide to Practice and Protocol in the Pacific Rim.* New York: Wiley, 1991.

*The Europa Year Book, 1987: A World Survey.* London: Europa Publications, 1987.

"Even the British Find It Pays to Learn Languages." *The Economist,* May 16, 1987, pp. 67–68.

FARB, PETER. "How Do I Know You Mean What You Mean?" *Horizon,* 10(4) (Autumn 1968), 52–57.

———. *Word Play: What Happens When People Talk.* New York: Knopf, 1974.

FISCHER, DAVID H. *Growing Old in America.* New York: Oxford University Press, 1977.

FODOR, EUGENE. *Wall Street Journal Guide to Business Travel—International Cities.* New York: McKay, 1991.

FOSTER, DEAN ALLEN. *Bargaining Across Borders: How to Negotiate Business Anywhere in the World.* New York: McGraw-Hill, 1992.

FRANK, SERGEY, "Avoiding the Pitfalls of Business Abroad." *Sales and Marketing Management,* March 1992, pp. 48–52.

FROST, PETER J., ET AL. *Reframing Organizational Culture.* Newbury Park, Calif.: Sage Publications, 1991.

GARDNER, BURLEIGH. *Human Relations in Industry.* Homewood, Ill.: Irwin, 1945.

GARZA, CHRISTINA E. "Studying the Natives on the Shop Floor." *Business Week,* September 30, 1991, pp. 74–78.

GAYLORD, MAXINE. "Relocation and the Corporate Family." *Social Work,* May 1979, pp. 186–91.

GEERTZ, CLIFFORD. "Distinguished Lecture: Anti Anti-Relativism." *American Anthropologist,* 86 (June 1984), 263–78.

GOFFMAN, ERVING. *Behavior in Public Places.* Glencoe, Ill.: Free Press, 1963.

GORER, GEOFFREY. *Africa Dances: A Book About West African Negroes.* New York: Knopf, 1935.

GRAHAM, JOHN L., and YOSHIHIRO SANO. *Smart Bargaining: Doing Business with the Japanese.* New York: Harper Business, 1989.

GUDYKUNST, WILLIAM B., and Y. Y. KIM. *Communicating with Strangers: An Approach to Intercultural Communication.* Reading, Mass.: Addison-Wesley, 1984.

GUTHRIE, G. M. "A Behavioral Analysis of Culture Learning." In *Cross-Cultural Perspectives on Learning,* R. W. Brislin, S. Bochner, and W. J. Lonner, Eds. New York: John Wiley, 1975.

HAAS, MARY. "Men's and Women's Speech in Koasati." *Language in Culture and Society,* pp. 228–33, Dell Hymes, Ed. New York: Harper & Row, 1964.

HALL, EDWARD T. *Beyond Culture.* Garden City, N.Y.: Doubleday, 1976.

———. *The Hidden Dimension.* Garden City, N.Y.: Doubleday, 1966.

———. *The Silent Language.* Garden City, N.Y.: Doubleday, 1959.

HALL, EDWARD T., and M. R. HALL. *Hidden Differences: Doing Business with the Japanese.* Garden City, N.Y.: Anchor Press-Doubleday, 1987.

HALL, J. A. "Gender Effects in Decoding Nonverbal Cues." *Psychological Bulletin,* 85(4) (1978), 845–57.

HARRIS, DIANA, and WILLIAM E. COLE. *Sociology of Aging.* Boston: Houghton Mifflin, 1980.

HARRIS, PHILIP. "The Unhappy World of the Expatriate." *International Management,* July 1979, pp. 49–50.

HARRIS, PHILIP R., and ROBERT T. MORAN. *Managing Cultural Differences.* Houston, Tex.: Gulf Publishing, 1989.

HARRISON, RANDALL P. *Beyond Words: An Introduction to Nonverbal Communication.* Englewood Cliffs, N.J.: Prentice Hall, 1974.

HARVEY, MICHAEL G. "The Executive Family: An Overlooked Variable in International Assignments." *Columbia Journal of World Business* (Spring 1985), 84–92.

HAYS, R. D. "Expatriate Selection: Insuring Success and Avoiding Failure." *Journal of International Business Studies,* 5 (1974), 25–37.

HERON, J. "The Phenomenology of Social Encounter: The Gaze." *Philosophy and Phenomenological Research,* 31 (1970), 243–64.

HERSKOVITS, M. J. *Cultural Anthropology.* New York: Knopf, 1955.

HEWES, GORDON. "World Distribution of Certain Postural Habits." *American Anthropologist,* 57 (1955), 231–44.

HICKERSON, NANCY P. *Linguistic Anthropology.* New York: Holt, Rinehart & Winston, 1980.

HIRSCH, E. D. *Cultural Literacy: What Every American Needs to Know.* Boston: Houghton Mifflin, 1987.

HOFSTEDE, GEERT. *Culture's Consequences: International Differences in Work-Related Values.* Beverly Hills, Calif.: Sage Publications, 1980.

HOLMES, LOWELL D. *Anthropology: An Introduction.* New York: Ronald Press, 1971.

HOOPES, DAVID S., Ed. *Global Guide to International Business.* New York: Facts on File, 1984.

HORTON, ROBIN. "African Traditional Thought and Western Science (Part II)." *Africa,* 37(2) (April 1967), 155–87.

HUEBENER, THEODORE. *Why Johnny Should Learn Foreign Languages.* Radnor, Pa.: Chilton, 1961.

*International Business Travel and Relocation Directory,* 4th ed. Detroit: Gale Research, 1985.

JAPAN AIRLINES. *A Businessman's Guide to Japan,* 1982.

JENSEN, J. V. "Perspective on Nonverbal Intercultural Communication." In *Intercultural Communication: A Reader,* pp. 260–76, L. A. Samovar and Richard E. Porter, Eds. Belmont, Calif.: Wadsworth, 1982.

JETRO (JAPAN EXTERNAL TRADE ORGANIZATION). *Doing Business in Japan.* Tokyo: Gakuseisha, 1984.

KAMAU, LUCY. "Semipublic, Private and Hidden Rooms: Symbolic Aspects of Domestic Space in Urban Kenya." *African Urban Studies,* NS 3 (Winter 1978–79), 105–15.

KAPP, ROBERT A. *Communicating with China.* Chicago: Intercultural Press, 1983.

KATZNER, KENNETH. *The Languages of the World.* New York: Funk & Wagnalls, 1975.

KENNEDY, GAVIN. *Doing Business Abroad.* New York: Simon & Schuster, 1985.

KENYATTA, JOMO. *Facing Mount Kenya: The Tribal Life of the Gikuyu.* London: Secker & Warburg, 1953.

KLINEBERG, OTTO, Ed., *Characteristics of the American Negro.* New York: Harper & Row, 1969.

KLUCKHOHN, CLYDE. *Mirror for Man.* New York: Fawcett, 1968.

KLUCKHOHN, C., and W. H. KELLY. "The Concept of Culture." In *The Science of Man in the World Crisis,* pp. 78–106, Ralph Linton, Ed. New York: Columbia University Press, 1945.

KLUCKHOHN, FLORENCE, and F. L. STRODTBECK. *Variations in Value Orientations.* New York: Harper & Row, 1961.

KNAPP, M. L. "The Field of Nonverbal Communication: An Overview." In *On Speech Communication: An Anthology of Contemporary Writings and Messages,* pp. 57–72, C. J. Steward and B. Kendall, Eds. New York: Holt, Rinehart & Winston, 1972.

KOBRIN, STEPHEN J. *International Expertise in American Business.* New York: Institute for International Education, 1984.

KOHLS, L. R. "Basic Concepts and Models of Intercultural Communication." In *USIA Intercultural Communication Course: 1977 Proceedings,* Michael Prosser, Ed. Washington, D.C.: U.S. Information Agency, 1978.

———. *Survival Kit for Overseas Living.* Chicago: Intercultural Press. 1984.

KOTTAK, CONRAD P. *Anthropology: The Exploration of Human Diversity,* 4th ed. New York: Random House, 1987.

KOTTER, JOHN P. *Corporate Culture and Performance.* New York: Free Press, 1992.

KRAMER, CHERIS. "Folk-Linguistics: Wishy-Washy Mommy Talk." *Psychology Today,* 8(1) (1974), 82–85.

KROEBER, A. L., and C. KLUCKHOHN. "Culture: A Critical Review of Concepts and Definitions." *Papers of the Peabody Museum of American Archaeology and Ethnology,* 47(1) (1952).

KUETHE, J. L. "Social Schemas." *Journal of Abnormal and Social Psychology,* 64 (1962), 31–38.

KUPFER, ANDREW. "How to Be a Global Manager." *Fortune,* March 14, 1988, pp. 52–58.

LABARRE, WESTON. "The Cultural Basis of Emotions and Gestures." *Journal of Personality,* No. 16 (1947), 49–68.

LANIER, ALISON R. *The Rising Sun on Main Street: Working with the Japanese.* Morrisville, Pa.: International Information Associates, 1990.

———. "Selecting and Preparing Personnel for Overseas Transfers." *Personnel Journal,* March 1979, pp. 160–63.

LEDERER, WILLIAM J., and EUGENE BURDICK. *The Ugly American.* New York: Norton, 1958.

LEVINE, ROBERT, and E. WOLFE. "Social Time: The Heartbeat of Culture." *Psychology Today,* March 1985, pp. 29–35.

LINTON, RALPH. *The Study of Man.* New York: Appleton-Century-Crofts, 1936.

LITTLE, K. B. "Cultural Variations in Social Schemata." *Journal of Personality and Social Psychology,* 10 (1968), 1–7.

———. "Personal Space." *Journal of Experimental Social Psychology,* No. 1 (1965), 237–47.

LYSTAD, ROBERT A. "Basic African Values." In *New Forces in Africa,* pp. 10–24, William H. Lewis, Ed. Washington, D.C.: Public Affairs Press, 1962.

MACHAN, DYAN. "Ici on Parle Bottom Line Responsibility." *Forbes,* February 8, 1988, pp. 138–40.

MAGRATH, C. PETER. "What We Don't Know Can Hurt Us: The Shortfall in International Competence." A report of the Division of International Education of the American Council on Education, Washington, D.C., 1983.

MAYO, ELTON. *The Human Problems of an Industrial Civilization.* New York: Macmillan, 1933.

MBITI, JOHN S. *African Religions and Philosophy.* New York: Praeger, 1969.

MEHRABIAN, ALBERT. *Silent Messages,* 2nd ed. Belmont, Calif.: Wadsworth, 1981.

MONTAGU, ASHLEY. *Touching: The Human Significance of the Skin.* New York: Harper & Row, 1972.

MORAN, ROBERT T, and WILLIAM G. STRIPP. *Dynamics of Successful International Business Negotiations.* Houston: Gulf Publishing, 1991.

MORRIS, DESMOND. *Manwatching: A Field Guide to Human Behavior.* New York: Abrams, 1977.

MORRIS, DESMOND, PETER COLLETT, PETER MARSH, and MARIE O'SHAUGHNESSY. *Gestures: Their Origins and Distribution.* New York: Stein & Day, 1979.

MORSBACH, HELMUT. "Aspects of Nonverbal Communication in Japan." In *Intercultural Communication: A Reader,* 3rd ed., pp. 300–16, Larry Samovar and R. E. Porter, Eds. Belmont, Calif.: Wadsworth, 1982.

MURDOCK, GEORGE P. *The Outline of Cultural Materials,* 4th ed. New Haven, Conn.: Human Relations Area Files, 1971.

―――. *The Outline of World Cultures,* 4th ed. New Haven, Conn.: Human Relations Area Files, 1972.

NAISBITT, JOHN. *Megatrends: Ten New Directions Transforming Our Lives.* New York: Warner Books, 1982.

NATIONAL GOVERNORS' ASSOCIATION. *America in Transition: The International Frontier.* Washington, D.C. 1989.

NEHRT, LEE C. *Business and International Education.* A Report Submitted by the Task Force on Business and International Education. Washington, D.C.: American Council on Education, May 1977.

OBERG, KALERVO. "Culture Shock: Adjustments to New Cultural Environments." *Practical Anthropology,* July–August 1960, pp. 177–82.

OUCHI, WILLIAM. *Theory Z.* Reading, Mass.: Addison-Wesley, 1981.

PALMORE, ERDMAN. *The Honorable Elders.* Durham, N.C.: Duke University Press, 1975.

PARKIN, DAVID. *The Cultural Definition of Political Response: Lineal Destiny Among the Luo.* London: Academic Press, 1978.

PASCALE, R. T., and A. G. ATHOS. *The Art of Japanese Management.* New York: Simon & Schuster, 1981.

PERRY, RALPH. *Characteristically American.* New York: Knopf, 1949.

PIKE, E. ROYSTON. *The Strange Ways of Man.* New York: Hart, 1967.

PLOG, FRED, and DANIEL BATES. *Cultural Anthropology.* New York: Knopf, 1980.

POTTER, DAVID. *People of Plenty.* Chicago: Chicago University Press, 1954.

PRESIDENT'S EXPORT COUNCIL. "The Export Imperative: A Report Submitted by the President's Export Council." Washington, D.C., December 1980.

PROTHRO, E. T. "Arab-American Differences in the Judgement of Written Messages." *Journal of Social Psychology,* 42 (1955), 3–11.

REYNOLDS, J. I., and G. H. RICE. "American Education for International Business." *Management International Review,* 28 (3) (1988), 48–57.

RICHARDSON, FRIEDRICH, and C. WALKER. *Human Relations in an Expanding Company.* New Haven, Conn.: Yale University Labor Management Center, 1948.

RICKS, D. A. *Big Business Blunders: Mistakes in Multinational Marketing.* Homewood, Ill.: Dow Jones-Irwin, 1983.

RICKS, D. A., M. Y. C. FU, and J. S. ARPAN. *International Business Blunders.* Columbus, Ohio: Grid, 1974.

ROBINSON, RICHARD D. *Internationalization of Business: An Introduction.* New York: Dryden Press, 1983.

ROETHLISBERGER, F. J., and W. J. DICKSON. *Management and the Worker: An Account of a Research Program Conducted by a Western Electric Company, Hawthorne Works, Chicago.* Cambridge, Mass.: Harvard University Press, 1939.

ROGERS, EVERETT. *Communication of Innovations: A Cross-Cultural Approach.* New York: Free Press, 1971.

ROSENTHAL, ROBERT, DANE ARCHER, JUDITH A. HALL, M. ROBIN DIMATTEO, and PETER L. ROGERS. "Measuring Sensitivity to Nonverbal Communication: The PONS Test." In *Nonverbal Behavior: Applications and Cultural Implications,* pp. 67–98, A. Wolfgang, Ed. New York: Academic Press, 1979.

ROSS, MARC H. *Grass Roots in an African City: Political Behavior in Nairobi.* Cambridge, Mass.: MIT Press, 1975.

RUBEN, BRENT D. "Guidelines for Cross-Cultural Communication Effectiveness." *Group and Organization Studies,* 2(4) (December 1977), 470–79.

RUHLY, SHARON. *Intercultural Communication,* 2nd ed. Chicago: Science Research Association, 1982.

SALACUSE, JESWALD W. *Making Global Deals: Negotiating in the International Marketplace.* Boston: Houghton Mifflin, 1991.

SALMANS, SANDRA. "Industry Learns to Speak the Same Language." *International Management,* April 1979, pp. 45–47.

SAMOVAR, LARRY A., and R. PORTER. *Communication Between Cultures.* Belmont, Calif.: Wadsworth, 1991.

SAPIR, EDWARD. "The Status of Linguistics as a Science." *Language,* 5 (1929), 207–14.

SCHEINFELD, AMRAM. *The New You and Heredity.* Philadelphia: Lippincott, 1950.

SCHLESINGER, ARTHUR M. "What Then Is the American, This New Man?" In *The Character of Americans: A Book of Readings,* pp. 102–17, Michael McGiffert, Ed. Homewood, Ill.: Dorsey Press, 1970.

SCHWARTZ, HOWARD, and STANLEY DAVIS. "Matching Corporate Culture to Business Strategy." *Organizational Dynamics,* Summer 1981, pp. 30–48.

SERRIE, HENDRICK. "Anthropological Contributions to Business in Multicultural Contexts." In *Anthropology and International Business,* pp. ix–xxx, Hendrick Serrie, Ed. Williamsburg, Va.: Department of Anthropology, College of William and Mary, 1986.

SHARP, LAURISTON. "Steel Axes for Stone Age Australians." *Human Organization,* 11(2) (Summer 1952), 17–22.

SHEFLEN, ALBERT E. *Body Language and the Social Order.* Englewood Cliffs, N.J.: Prentice Hall, 1972.

SHIMODA, K., M. ARGYLE, and R. BITTI. "The Intercultural Recognition of Emotional Expressions by Three National Groups—English, Italian and Japanese." *European Journal of Social Psychology,* 8 (1978), 169–79.

SHUTER, ROBERT. "A Field Study of Nonverbal Communication in German, Italy, and the United States." *Communication Monographs,* 44 (1977), 298–305.

SIMON, PAUL. *The Tongue Tied American.* New York: Continuum Press, 1980.

SIVAROL, R. L. *World Military and Social Expenditures 1983.* Washington, D.C.: World Priorities, 1983.

SLATER, JONATHAN R. "The Hazards of Cross-Cultural Advertising." *Business America,* April 2, 1984, pp. 20–23.

SNOWDEN, SONDRA. *The Global Edge.* New York: Simon & Schuster, 1986.

SOMMER, R. "Studies in Personal Space." *Sociometry,* 22 (1959), 247–60.

STEIN, JESS, Ed. *The Random House College Dictionary.* New York: Random House, 1979.

STESSIN, LAWRENCE. "Culture Shock and the American Businessman Overseas." In *Toward Internationalism: Readings in Cross Cultural Communication,* pp. 214–25, E. C. Smith and L. F. Luce, Eds., Rowley, Mass.: Newbury House, 1979.

STEVENSON, BURTON. *The Home Book of Proverbs, Maxims and Familiar Phrases.* New York: Macmillan, 1948.

STEWART, EDWARD C. *American Cultural Patterns: A Cross Cultural Perspective.* Chicago: Intercultural Press, 1971.

"Strength Through Wisdom: A Critique of U.S. Capability." A Report to the President from the President's Commission on Foreign Language and International Studies. Washington, D.C., November 1979.

TELBERG, INA. "They Don't Do It Our Way." *Courier* (UNESCO), 3(4) (1950), 6–7.

TERPSTRA, VERN. *The Cultural Environment of International Business.* Cincinnati, Ohio: Southwestern, 1978.

THADANI, V. N. "The Forgotten Factor in Social Change: The Case of Women in Nairobi, Kenya." Doctoral dissertation, Bryn Mawr College, Bryn Mawr, Pa., 1976.

TOFFLER, ALVIN. *The Third Wave.* Toronto: Bantam Books, 1981.

TOMKINS, S. S. *Affect, Imagery Consciousness, Vol. 1: The Positive Affects.* New York: Springer-Verlag, 1962.

TUNG, ROSALIE L. "Selection and Training of Personnel for Overseas Assignments." *Columbia Journal of World Business,* Spring 1981, pp. 68–78.

TYLOR, EDWARD. *Origins of Culture.* New York: Harper & Row, 1871.

U.S. DEPARTMENT OF COMMERCE. *1990 Census of Population and Housing: Summary Population and Housing Characteristics (Florida)*. Washington, D.C.: U.S. Government Printing Office, August 1991a.

———. *Statistical Abstract of the United States, 1991*. Washington: D.C.: U.S. Government Printing Office, 1991b.

U.S. DEPARTMENT OF TREASURY. *Treasury Bulletin*. Washington, D.C.: U.S. Government Printing Office, March 1992.

VAN PELT, PETER, and NATALIA WOLNIANSKY. "The High Cost of Expatriation." *Management Review*, July 1990, pp. 40–41.

WARNER, W. L., and J. LOW. *The Social System of the Modern Factory: The Strike, A Social Analysis*. New Haven, Conn.: Yale University Press, 1947.

WATSON, O. M. *Proxemic Behavior: A Cross-Cultural Study*. The Hague: Mouton, 1970.

WATSON, O. M., and T. D. GRAVES. "Quantitative Research in Proxemic Behavior." *American Anthropologist* 68 (1966), 971–85.

WHORF, BENJAMIN LEE. *Language, Thought, and Reality*. Cambridge, Mass.: MIT Press, 1956.

WILLIAMS, ROBIN M. "Changing Value Orientations and Beliefs on the American Scene." In *The Character of Americans*, pp. 212–30, Michael McGiffert, Ed. Homewood, Ill.: Dorsey Press, 1970.

WILSON, G. M. "Homicide and Suicide Among the Joluo of Kenya." In *African Homicide and Suicide*, Paul Bohannan, Ed. Princeton, N.J.: Princeton University Press, 1960.

*The World Almanac and Book of Facts*. New York: World Almanac, 1991.

YA'ARI, EHUD, and IRA FRIEDMAN. "Curses in Verses." *Atlantic* 267 (2) (1991), 22–26.

YOUNG, MARGARET W., Ed. *Cities of the World: A Compilation of Current Information on Cultural, Geographical, and Political Conditions in the Countries and Cities of Six Continents, Based on the Department of State's "Post Reports."* Detroit: Gale Research, 1982.

ZIMMERMAN, MARK. *How to Do Business with the Japanese: A Strategy for Success*. New York: Random House, 1985.

# PHOTO CREDITS

# INDEX